Spirituality

**Edited by
Sharon Reed**

THE WORLD OF
Don Bosco
MULTIMEDIA

New Rochelle, NY

Access Guides to Youth Ministry: Spirituality is published as a service for adults who love the young and want to share the Gospel with them.

It is a guide to understanding the young and a resource book for helping them. As such, it is addressed to parents, parish youth ministers, clergy who work with the young, and teachers.

Forthcoming *Access Guides*:
Leadership

Prepared in conjunction with
The Center for Youth Ministry Development

Access Guides to Youth Ministry: Spirituality
©1991 Salesian Society, Inc. / Don Bosco Multimedia
475 North Ave., P. O. Box T, New Rochelle, NY 10802
All rights reserved

Library of Congress Cataloging-in-Publication Data
Spirituality / edited by Sharon Reed.
p. cm. — (Access guides to youth ministry)
Includes bibliographical references.
    1. Adolescent Spirituality   2. Youth—Religious life.
       I. Reed, Sharon.   II. Title: Spirituality.   III. Series.

ISBN 0-89944-210-2 $14.95

Printed in the United States of America

09/91   9 8 7 6 5 4 3 2 1

Table of Contents

PART ONE
FOUNDATIONAL UNDERSTANDINGS

PART TWO
PRACTICAL APPROACHES

Typist: Alicia Carcy

PREFACE TO THE ACCESS GUIDES

A NEW CONCEPT

Welcome to the *Access Guides to Youth Ministry* series. The Center for Youth Ministry Development and Don Bosco Multimedia have created the *Access Guides* series to provide leaders in ministry with youth with both the foundational understandings and the practical tools they need to create youth ministry programming for each component outlined in *A Vision of Youth Ministry*. *Access Guides* have been developed for pop culture, evangelization, liturgy & worship, justice, retreats, and ministry with early adolescents. Upcoming *Access Guides* will address leadership, family life, prayer, and spirituality. Each of the *Access Guides* provides foundational essays, processes for developing that particular component of youth ministry, and approaches and program models to use in your setting. The blend of theory and practice makes each of the *Access Guides* a unique resource in youth ministry. To help you understand the context of the *Access Guides* series, we would like to provide you with a brief overview of the goals and components of a comprehensive approach to ministry with youth.

A RENEWED MINISTRY

Over a decade ago, Catholic youth ministry engaged in a process of self-reflection and analysis that resulted in a re-visioning of youth ministry — establishing the goals, principles, and components of a comprehensive, contemporary ministry with youth. *A Vision of Youth Ministry* outlined this comprehensive approach to ministry with youth and became the foundation for a national vision of Catholic youth ministry. In the years since the publishing of *A Vision of Youth Ministry*, Catholic youth ministry across the United States has experienced tremendous growth.

From the outset, the *Vision* paper made clear its ecclesial focus: "As one among many ministries of the Church, youth ministry must be understood in terms of the mission and ministry of the whole Church" (*Vision* 3). The focus is clearly ministerial. "The Church's mission is threefold: to proclaim the good news of salvation; to offer itself as a group of people transformed by the Spirit into a community of faith, hope, and love; and to bring God's justice and love to others through service in its individual, social, and political dimensions" (*Vision* 3). This threefold mission formed the basis of the framework or components of youth ministry: Word (evangelization and catechesis), worship, community, justice and service, guidance and healing, enablement, and advocacy.

This threefold mission also gives youth ministry a dual focus. Youth ministry is a ministry within the community of faith — ministering to believing youth *and* to the wider society — reaching out to serve youth in our society. While the experience of the past decade has emphasized ministry *within* the community, youth ministry must also address the social situation and needs of all youth in society. A comprehensive approach demands a balance between ministry *within* the Christian community and ministry *by* the Christian community *to* young people within our society and world.

The *Vision* paper described a broad concept of ministry with youth using four dimensions. Youth ministry is...

To youth — responding to youth's varied needs;

With youth — working with adults to fulfill their common responsibility for the Church's mission;

By youth — exercising their own ministry to others: peers, community, world;

For youth — interpreting the needs of youth, especially in areas of injustice and acting on behalf of or with youth for a change in the systems which create injustice.

Two goals were initially developed for the Church's ministry with youth:

Goal #1: Youth ministry works to the total personal and spiritual growth of each young person.

Goal #2: Youth ministry seeks to draw young people to responsible participation in the life, mission, and work of the faith community. (*Vision* 7)

The first goal emphasizes *becoming* — focusing on the *personal* dimension of human existence. Our understanding of the unique life tasks and social-cultural context of adolescence provides directions for fostering their growth in discipleship and Catholic identity. The second goal emphasizes *belonging* — focusing on the *interpersonal* or *communal* dimension of human existence. Active engagement of youth in the Christian community's life and mission provides an important context for growth and overcomes the danger of marginalizing youth in the Church, segregating them from the real centers of power, responsibility, and commitment in community life.

In light of the Church's priority upon justice and peace, the mission of the Church to transform society (*The Challenge of Peace* and *Economic Justice for All*), and the need to engage in a critical assessment of our culture and society, it is necessary to add a third goal to the two goals from 1976. This third goal emphasizes *transforming* — focusing on the public or *social structural* dimension of human existence. This third goal could be framed in the following manner:

Goal #3: Youth ministry empowers young people to transform the world as disciples of Jesus Christ by living and working for justice and peace.

This third goal seeks to help young people realize that living and working for justice and peace is grounded in the Gospel and Catholic social vision and is essential for being a Christian. Youth ministry needs to empower young people with the knowledge and skills to transform the unjust structures of society (locally and globally) so that these structures promote justice, respect human dignity, promote human rights, and build peace.

An underdeveloped, but increasingly important section of the *Vision* paper is the context of youth ministry. "In all places, youth ministry occurs within a given social, cultural, and religious context which shapes the specific form of the ministry" (*Vision* 10). This contextual approach seeks to view young people as part of a number of social systems which impact on their growth, values, and faith, rather than as isolated individuals. Among these systems are the family, society, the dominant culture, youth culture, ethnic culture, school, and local church community. In the last several years, youth ministry has become much more aware of the impact of these systems.

A COMPREHENSIVE APPROACH

The framework (or components) describes distinct aspects for developing a comprehensive, integrated ministry with youth. Briefly, these components include:

Evangelization — reaching out to young people who are uninvolved in the life of the community and inviting them into a relationship with Jesus and the Christian community. Evangelization involves proclaiming the Good News of Jesus through programs and relationships.

Catechesis — promoting a young person's growth in Christian faith through the kind of teaching and learning that emphasizes understanding, reflection, and transformation. This is accomplished through systematic, planned, and intentional programming (curriculum). (See *The Challenge of Adolescent Catechesis*).

Prayer and Worship — assisting young people in deepening their relationship with Jesus through the development of a personal prayer life; and providing a variety of prayer and worship experiences with youth to deepen and celebrate their relationship with Jesus in a caring Christian community; involving young people in the sacramental life of the Church.

Community Life — building Christian community with youth through programs and relationships which promote openness, trust, valuing the person, cooperation, honesty, taking responsibility, and willingness to serve; creating a climate where young people can grow and share their struggles, questions, and joys with other youth and adults; helping young people feel like a valued part of the Church.

Guidance and Healing — providing youth with sources of support and counsel as they face personal problems and pressures (for example, family problems, peer pressure, substance abuse, suicide) and decide on careers and important life decisions; providing appropriate support and guidance for youth during times of stress and crisis; helping young people deal with the problems they face and the pressures people place on them; developing a better understanding of their parents and learning how to communicate with them.

Justice, Peace, and Service — guiding young people in developing a Christian social consciousness and a commitment to a life of justice and peace through educational programs and service/action involvement; infusing the concepts of justice and peace into all youth ministry relationships and programming.

Enablement — developing, supporting, and utilizing the leadership abilities and personal gifts of youth and adults in youth ministry, empowering youth for ministry with their peers; developing a leadership team to organize and coordinate the ministry with youth.

Advocacy — interpreting the needs of youth: personal, family, and social especially in areas of injustices towards or oppression of youth, and acting with or on behalf of youth for a change in the systems which create injustice; giving young people a voice and empowering them to address the social problems that they face.

This is the vision and scope that the *Access Guides* series seeks to promote through foundational understandings and practical, pastoral approaches. We, at the Center, hope that this series will empower you with the knowledge and skills to become more effective in your ministry with youth.

WORKS CITED

The Challenge of Adolescent Catechesis. Washington DC: NFCYM Publications, 1986.

A Vision of Youth Ministry. Washington DC: USCC, Department of Education, 1976.

ABOUT THE AUTHORS

Jacquelin Bergan and **S. Marie Schwan** are the co-authors of *Take and Receive: A Guide for Prayer*, a five-book series. They founded the Center for Christian Renewal through which they have been extensively involved in the direction of retreats, parish days of prayer, and workshops on spirituality.

Thomas Bright is Justice Ministries Coordinator on the staff of the Center for Youth Ministry Development. He is editor of *Poverty : Do It Justice!* and co-editor of *Access Guides to Youth Ministry: Justice* (DBM).

Joan Chittister, O.S.B. is the Executive Director of the Alliance for International Monasticism (AIM), and a widely published author and lecturer. She concentrates on the renewal of religious life, on the promotion of justice and peace, and on Christian feminism. She is the author of *WomanStrength: Modern Church, Modern Women.*

Corita Clarke, R.D.C. holds a doctorate in ministry from Immaculate Conception Seminary, Huntington, New York. She is Director of the Divine Compassion Center for Spiritual Renewal in White Plains, NY where she is involved in retreats, workshops, and spiritual direction. She currently serves on the General Council of her congregation.

Leonard Doohan is Professor of Religious Studies at Gonzaga University in Spokane, WA, and a well-known writer and lecturer. He has authored 12 books including, *Leisure: A Spiritual Need* and *The Lay-Centered Church.*

Kathleen Fischer holds a Ph.D. from The Graduate Theological Union and an M.S.W. from The University of Washington. She teaches theology at Seattle University, counsels older adults and their families, and does spiritual direction. She is the author of *Women at the Well* and *Reclaiming the Connections*, as well as numerous articles on spirituality.

Austin Fleming, a priest of the Archdiocese of Boston, is Parochial Vicar and Campus Minister at St. Ann Parish and Student Center in Boston. He is the author of *Preparing for Liturgy.*

Donald P. Gray is Professor of Religious Studies at Manhattan College in the Bronx. He is considered one the foremost Teilhardian scholars in the United States and has written *Jesus: The Way to Freedom.*

Thomas H. Groome is Associate Professor of Theology and Religious Education at Boston College. He is the author of *Christian Religious Education: Sharing Our Story and Vision* and dozens of published articles on religious education. He is the senior author of *God With Us* religion series.

Maria Harris is Visiting Professor of Religious Education at Fordham University and New York University. Her publications include *Portrait of Youth Ministry, Fashion Me a People*, and *Teaching and Religious Imagination.*

Thomas N. Hart teaches Theology at Seattle University and is a marriage and family counselor at the Catholic Counseling Center of Seattle. He is the author of *Living Happily Ever After: Toward a Theology of Christian Marriage* and *The Art of Christian Listening.*

James McGinnis is founder and staff member of the Institute for Peace and Justice in St. Louis. He is a well-known lecturer and workshop leader and author of numerous books and articles, including *Bread and Justice, Solidarity With the People of Nicaragua, A Spirituality of Compassion, Helping Kids Care*, and *Helping Families Care.*

Sharon Reed is Associate Staff member of The Center for Youth Ministry Development and a licensed professional counselor in Columbus, OH. She is a member of the Spirituality Ministry Network in Columbus, where she is involved in retreats, workshops, and spiritual direction. Sharon also coordinates the supervised ministry component of the diocesan Lay Ministry Formation Program.

Greg Rohde is the Coordinator of the CYC's Office of Youth Ministry in the Archdiocese of St. Louis. He has a Masters Degree in Religious Studies, focusing on Christian Spirituality, from Mundelein. Greg's specialization is resourcing and support of youth ministers and is also involved in training of lay ministers in his diocesan formation program.

Thomas N. Tomaszek is Coordinator of Youth Ministry for the Archdiocese of Milwaukee. He holds a Masters of Education and a Masters in Theological Studies. He has contributed to a variety of publications, including the *Access Guides to Youth Ministry: Liturgy and Worship* from Don Bosco Multimedia.

ACKNOWLEDGMENTS

"Gospel Spirituality" by Donald P. Gray first appeared as "Love and Compassion" by Donald P. Gray and is reprinted courtesy of *Church* magazine (Spring 1986).

"Growth in the Christian Life" by Thomas Hart is reprinted from *The Art of Christian Listening* by Thomas Hart (1980). Used by permission of Paulist Press.

"Growth in the Spiritual Life" and "Prayer and Spirituality" by Kathleen Fischer are reprinted from *Reclaiming the Connections* by Kathleen Fischer (1990). Used by permission of Sheed & Ward.

"Spirituality and Contemporary Culture" by Joan Chittister, O.S.B. is reprinted from *WomanStrength: Modern Church, Modern Women* by Joan Chittister (1990). Used by permission of Sheed & Ward.

"Spirituality for the Future" by Leonard Doohan is reprinted courtesy of *Praying* No 22 (January-February 1988). Used by permission of National Catholic Reporter Publishing Company.

"The Spirituality of the Minister" by Thomas Groome is reprinted from *The Journal of Religious Education*, Volume 83, Number 1, by permission from the publisher: The Religious Education Association, 409 Prospect Street, New Haven CT 06511-2177. Membership, $35 per year; full-time student, $17.50.

"An Integrated Spirituality" by Corita Clarke, R.D.C. is reprinted from *A Spirituality For Active Ministry* by Corita Clarke, R.D.C. (1991). Used by permission of Sheed & Ward.

"Education, Imagination, and Spirituality" by Maria Harris is reprinted from *Teaching & Religious Imagination* by Maria Harris (1987). Used by permission of Harper and Row.

"Spirituality and Liturgy" by Austin Fleming is reprinted from *Preparing for Liturgy* by Austin Fleming (1985). Used by permission of The Pastoral Press.

"Justice, Solidarity, and Spirituality" by James McGinnis is reprinted from *Journey into Compassion* by James McGinnis (1989). Used by permission of The Institute for Peace and Justice.

"Approaches to Prayer" by Jacquelin Bergan and S. Marie Schwan is reprinted from *Take and Receive: Surrender* by Jacquelin Bergan and S. Marie Schwan (1985). Used by permission of St. Mary's Press.

Part One
Overview

UNDERSTANDING SPIRITUALITY

Part One begins with foundational writings critical to our understanding of spirituality and its application to the life of the adolescent. It focuses on a variety of perspectives which nourish spiritual growth, while also highlighting the demands and challenges involved in attending to the presence of God in our daily lives.

Chapter 1 deals with "A Spiritually Challenging Vision for Youth" as a priority for today's church. Adolescents need a framework that is worthy of their time, attention, and commitment. **Sharon Reed** explores a challenging vision of God, self, church, and world and the implications of each for our ministry with young people. A balanced, integrated spirituality will be difficult unless we begin by articulating a vision of what that might entail.

Chapter 2 offers a Gospel perspective of spirituality. **Donald Gray** examines the life and message of Jesus, as well as Jesus' relationship with his Father, as the basis of the power and presence we share with young people. "We have perhaps for too long associated the divine with stability and order, certainty and security. When purchased at the price of human suffering, these concerns are to be rejected in favor of a new order with all the insecurity and uncertainty that may entail." The Good News to be shared is one of conversion and compassion — a challenging invitation for all of us!

Thomas Hart believes that "we reach the fullness of our human potential in the measure we are conformed to Jesus." In Chapter 3, he examines Jesus' way of life and teaching as the foundation of Christian growth. His vision is that of one basic Christian spirituality, uniquely lived out by each person. Christian holiness is not ensured within any particular lifestyle but by modeling our lives after Christ's.

Kathleen Fischer agrees with Hart's vision and expands on the meaning of spiritual growth, understanding the will of God in our lives, and the role of systems in our spirituality. In Chapter 4, she asserts that growing spiritually is not a matter of discovering some predetermined plan but making the best choices we can given our circumstances. Thus, not only personal decisions but the dynamics of systems are urgent concerns for contemporary spirituality.

In Chapter 5 **Joan Chittister** examines the cultural realities challenging the Gospel and how the Gospel can best challenge the culture. She presents a spirituality of "contemplative co-creation" where we become aware of the spiritual link between the personal and the political. Through examining the seven capital sins, she calls us to reevaluate our role in the liberation of culture.

Corita Clarke's essay on "An Integrated Spirituality" speaks of the search to become holy and whole and the need for conversion through the Paschal Mystery. She addresses Christian tradition, contemporary culture, and ministry as sources of community in need of redemption and integration. She also offers several concrete practices and reflections to encourage this on-going conversion.

Thomas Groome's look at the "heart" of the minister in Chapter 7 is crucial for our own self-reflection. He addresses passion for the people, the gift of hospitality, love for the tradition, and commitment to the reign of God as essential elements for a spirituality of ministers. "The level to which these are reflected in our ministry will be both the measure and source of our own holiness."

Leonard Doohan offers ten characteristics of a Christian spirituality for the future in Chapter 8. He believes "spiritual growth will integrate work, community-building, the joys of life and the celebrational elements of prayer and worship. Christians will be intensely conscious that they are a church that serves and prophetically challenges each generation."

Chapter 9 concludes Part One with a sampler of insights and challenges necessary for the formulation of an holistic spirituality. Drawing from experts in global, ecological, cultural, women's, and family concerns, a wide variety of perspectives are offered to broaden our view of the scope of our spirituality and the structures in need of transformation.

Thus, through some remarkably different windows, we get a wide-angle view of the problems and possibilities for nourishing spirituality in today's world. Young people depend on the vision, the direction, the balance, and the challenge presented here and call us to attend and respond to the God-presence in our lives creatively and compassionately.

Chapter 1

A Spiritually Challenging Vision for Youth

Sharon Reed

Spirituality has become one of the focal words of our vocabulary these days, just as "ministry" and "collaboration" and "grace" and even "sin" seem to have had their heyday. All are rather vague words in some respect; they can be defined and interpreted to the point that they mean everything or absolutely nothing. So what do we mean by spirituality, by Christian spirituality, and how can we help our young people develop such a spirituality? Rather than telling teenagers how to live, can we look at the ways they are already living the life of the Spirit? And can we offer them a spiritually challenging vision that is exciting and worthy of their time, attention, and commitment? I believe we can, and must, if we expect young people to pay attention to the presence of God in their lives and respond to that presence. If this spiritual vision is not nourished, our lives become unbalanced and out of perspective. Richard Osmer attests to this when he cites that:

> An important part of youth's dissatisfaction with the church stems from the absence of a spiritually challenging and world-shaping vision that meets their hunger for the chance to participate in a worthy adventure… As long as the churches continue to present the issues of discipleship in a context they find relatively manageable and unthreatening, youth will fail to find sufficient scope there for their very considerable zeal. We should not be surprised then, if they look elsewhere. (Osmer 6)

Therefore, spirituality is both a deeply personal and dynamically interpersonal thing. Gerard Broccolo refers to it as "a way of viewing life and a way of experiencing life" (Broccolo 11). Thus, spirituality involves our worldview — our way of seeing and hearing, attending to, being aware of the call of God in every aspect of our lives. But it also means experiencing that call, living it out, being responsive and responsible, being a person of action and involvement.

From a personal point of view, my spirituality is that which from within me and beyond me calls me to be more authentically human, more freely all that God has destined me to be… This joint call of the Holy Spirit and of the deepest part of my own spirit is an invitation to me to respond. And, if I choose to answer authentically, my response will have two distinct moments:

> - A contemplative moment; for instance, being moved by the beauty of nature, or by the mystery of another person, or the experience of God's providence, or by the experience of solidarity with people who are poor or powerless.
> - An active moment; for instance, helping the poor or working to promote peace, or to care for our planet.
> (Dorr 270)

I believe that the vision presented to adolescents today must advocate these two dimensions of a dynamic relationship with God through a variety of "faces," and an active living out of that relationship through action committed to justice. There must be an awareness of who and what I am called to be as well as an awareness that demands response. One nourishes the other. Adolescents may realize that on a head level, but it must be recognized and lived at the heart and gut level as well — a way of viewing and experiencing the world. Obviously, this is easily said and not so easily done. "It is hard to get a sense of God's promise of fulfillment unless we experience that promise being fulfilled in the lives of people around us" (Rohr and Martos 17). Our challenge is to not only present the vision clearly, but to live the vision in our ordinary lives. For adolescents, walking the talk is absolutely essential!

And so our task remains: to name the vision. To say for what we stand, in what we believe, for what we are willing to die. We grasp for the ideal and wander through the real, and discover ourselves in the spaces in-between.

> I would like to learn, or remember, how to live. I come to Hollins Pond not so much to learn how to live as, frankly, to forget about it… I might learn something of mindlessness, something of the purity of living in the physical senses and the dignity of living without bias or motive. The weasel lives in necessity and we live in choice. I would like to live as I should, as the weasel lives as he should. And I suspect for me the way is like the weasel's: open to time and death painlessly, noticing everything, remembering nothing, choosing the given with a fierce and pointed will. (Dillard 15)

What is the "given" (the vision) that we invite others, especially adolescents, to choose? And is it worthy enough that they might choose with "fierce and pointed will?" We need a vision because it "gives life predictability and consistency. A vision enables us to know how to act" (Powell 53). And that is exactly where we are; unsure of where we're headed. And our adolescents call us to task: "Tell me where you stand and I'll tell you if I stand with you."

OUR VISION OF GOD

If our spirituality depends on attending to the God moments in our day-to-day lives, then much depends on how and where we recognize God. Who is God for today's adolescent? How is God imaged? How is their childhood image of God changing? Where do I find God and how is God revealed to me in my ordinary life? Why do I need God? Adolescents need to know about a God who is unconditionally loving, a God who never stops believing in them, a God of faithfulness, who keeps promises and is actively involved in their lives. This God actually wants a relationship and once we commit ourselves to this relationship, we are responsible for nourishing it. James DiGiacomo also believes we need to talk about a God "who is transcendent as well as immanent; whose ways are not always our ways; who makes demands" (DiGiacomo 7). In this relationship, as in any relationship, there are struggles as well as joys, accountability, expectations, misunderstandings that must be dealt with to fully come to grips with the meaning of "unconditional love." It is not soft, manipulative, and controlling but freely responsive to all we experience. Adolescents need a vision of what God is like and what God wants for and from them.

Have young people ever been introduced to the real Jesus? Not just the best friends version who is kind, honest, and trustworthy, but the Jesus of the Gospels — the one who confronts comfortableness, who challenges the status quo, who affirms women, the poor, the accused, the infirm, and every other social outcast? Do we really know what Jesus asks of us? Our lives — total surrender — nothing more, nothing less. Do we teach what Jesus taught? William O'Malley believes that "we've had too much of the meek and gentle Jesus and too little of the Galilean firebrand who said he'd come to bring not peace but a sword." (O'Malley 78) Jesus was so much more than "safe." He was radical in every sense of the word and called for a radical conversion in every arena of life. This Jesus proclaimed a radical vision of the Kingdom of God and how we are called to build that Kingdom — no one was untouched by his challenge. This is a Jesus who is "good news"! This is the person young people must meet in liturgy, retreats, Scripture study, religious education, youth groups, parish, school, job, and family. This is a God worth believing in!

And what about the Spirit? Is there such a thing other than class or school spirit? At least twice in our lifetimes the impact of the Spirit is considered — baptism and confirmation. Unfortunately, the Spirit is rarely considered in between or after those two sacraments. And yet, what a powerful God image! Spirit — RUAH — breath of life. The One who fashions meaning out of chaos, anoints, encourages, empowers, sustains our actions. Teenagers certainly need a vision of the Spirit — the one promised by Jesus to dwell with us forever. Young people need to know and experience this God of wholeness and integrity and to be able to discover the presence of the Spirit in all aspects of their lives. This Spirit transforms and brings peace to all creation. Unfortunately, there is no consistent vision of the role of the Spirit in our world and consequently, no awareness of the Spirit's continual touch.

If we are to return to the basics, we might begin by allowing young people to come to grips with who God is for them. Their images have changed many times over, and they need to integrate new images into their worldview. We must be willing to challenge and change our old images if we are to provide a solid foundation with room to dream. Rather than portray a God who can be dismissed easily, we must present the God of limitless possibility; a God who reaches out lovingly, but also challenges youth to move beyond their fears and inadequacies. This God gives us the freedom to choose our destiny yet stays involved no matter what the choice entails. This God speaks to teenagers, leads them, listens, confronts, affirms, wants the best — but is always there as a source of comfort and hope. Once they are connected to a concrete person, they can begin to shape the relationship and allow it to shape them. Teenagers need to know a God who continues to mold and fashion them.

VISION OF SELF

Do we provide our youth with an adequate vision of Christian personhood? Do they have a sense of what it means to be made in the image of God, their Creator? Do they see themselves as sons and daughters of God through their baptism into Jesus Christ and the Holy Spirit? We must provide a vision of self-acceptance as well as the ability to claim one's goodness and giftedness if today's youth are to achieve a healthy adulthood. David Elkind confirms that "teenagers need a protected period of time in which to construct a personal identity... a secure sense of self, of personal identity, allows the young person to deal with both inner and outer demands with consistence and efficiency" (Elkind 5).

It is critical that young people grow up with a comfortable awareness of their strengths and limitations. How many of us as adults are still learning to approach situations with self-confidence, self-acceptance, and flexibility? (I know I am!) Our youth need to hear and understand the words of Isaiah: "Do not fear, for I have redeemed you. I have called you by name and you are mine. Since you are precious in my sight, since you are honored and I love you, I will give others in exchange for your life" (Is 43:1,4). There are enough voices that speak otherwise. The voices that tell us that we need to be somebody else — thinner, richer, more attractive, more popular, more successful, more everything — voices opposed to the voice of dignity and trust in our own unique personhood.

Does the advertising that enters our homes and surrounds us in our daily lives depict us as uniquely gifted in our individuality? Or are we failures if we do not wear Sassoon jeans, ooze erotic energy through a new perfume, or have the latest toy or model car or computer software? Do our educational institutions, our corporations, our professions project images of people who are important solely because they hold degrees, amass titles, assume power, wield influence, and control wealth? Are we defined by what we have materially, educationally, professionally? What about who we are and what we are meant to be? (Wright 167)

To be truly spiritual, young people must be challenged to be truly aware of who they are and who they are called to be. "The more we can remove the blocks to an appreciation of who we are and who we are becoming, the truer we can be in our response to the Gospel call to serve others and God" (Hart 3). Nothing is accomplished by running away from ourselves or putting on a new self for each new situation. And yet, what is the Christian vision of self we want to hold out and hold up as a model for our youth? It is the vision that the same Spirit given to Jesus resides in each of us, and that loving ourselves is critical to responding in faith. It is the vision that youth make a difference, individually and collectively, and that self-love provides both the power and the courage to create change. It is the vision of immense potential, because each of us has unique experiences, talents, and gifts that cannot be duplicated. It is the vision of what one person can do to make life meaningful, as seen in the life of Jesus. It is the vision that weakness, failure, mistakes, and hurt are reconciled through death and resurrection.

As youth accept what is real in themselves, it helps them accept the reality of unconditional love. A vision that is real rather than ideal will allow young people to discard masks and fantasy selves and begin defining themselves from within. A Christian vision of self is the Word made flesh within us, empowering us to be and become that same word. "If we teach them the awesome mystery of the person, created in the divine image, we can begin to awaken their own sense of responsibility for the preservation of that image in others… That lesson can give our children hope for a future in which they are neither ciphers in an impersonal system nor demigods enamored of their own power" (Wright 169).

VISION OF CHURCH

A spiritually challenging vision would fall short if it failed to examine the role of the Church, of parish, of community, of People of God, as well as the institutional model we encounter. I firmly believe that our young people are capable of transforming our current concept of church if we don't successfully ignore or push them away first. Young people hunger for a place to belong, a place to express themselves as well as their doubts and concerns. They long for a community that lives the beatitudes, is inclusive and expansive, hospitable and welcoming. Our present faith communities fall short in many cases. We are too concerned with weekly collections and how we "appear," with power and control and whose parish it really is. We have become a dysfunctional family hell bent on keeping secrets and playing who do you trust. And yet isn't the basis of Christian community a divine call? Our Christian communities should be a way of being together not simply for each other, but also for God.

> And still, if we expect any salvation, redemption, healing and new life, the first thing we need is an open, receptive place where something can happen in us… We cannot change other people by our convictions, stories, advice, and proposals, but we can offer a space where people are encouraged to disarm themselves, to lay aside their occupations and preoccupations and to listen with attention and care to the voices speaking in their own center… Hospitality therefore, is such an important attitude. (Nouwen 76)

We are not simply isolated individuals. We are not in competition with one another. We are the body of Christ, and we experience the saving power of God in and through our relationships with others, by being "church." Unless we are united by our vision of the Kingdom, it is easy for our faith life to become a set of beliefs adhered to personally, but not lived communally. We become disconnected, wandering in a desert of our own creation. As a community, we need to confront the issue and address together our meaning and purpose. We must have a sense of direction but provide a diversity of options for how the journey is fashioned. "A parish's direction must be both inward and outward. It has to be inward toward seeking the Lord, making God the center of parish life, but it also has to be outward, toward the conversion of the world and the establishment of God's kingdom." (Rohr and Martos 94)

Young people (as well as the rest of us) need to understand this two-pronged approach as being a focal point of the Church's mission: centered in God and expressed through action for conversion. Certainly our parish communities as well as the wider Church need to be actively committed to achieving this same vision.

The best image to describe such a life-sharing community is a blazing fire. Many persons contribute time and energy to the community, giving up part of their individual existence to maintain the fire. By being willing to give of themselves for the good of the whole, however, the light and life they generate is much more than they could ever produce separately. They receive more than they give to one another and they have enough left over to share with others outside the community. They become, as Jesus said they would, a city on a hill, a light shining on a mountain, a beacon drawing others to themselves. (Rohr and Martos 89)

Young people must be challenged with the vision of both a human church and a dynamic church. They need a place to belong and contribute; to participate with other members of the community in building something of which they can be proud. They need to know what the community stands for and stands against. They need a church whose principles and beliefs can be tested against their own life experiences and make a significant contribution to their worldview. It must be a church that grabs their attention and invites their action on behalf of justice — a church that believes they are important for who they are *now*, not because they are "the future church."

It the goal of youth ministry is to draw young people to responsible participation in the life and mission of the Church, we must know how our community gives and receives life (what are our charisms?) and how our life source focuses our mission. Only a holistic and integrated vision will combine presence, personal growth, and participation of an active faith community. Pope John Paul II claims that "to be young is to be attracted to truth, justice, freedom, peace, beauty and goodness. To be young means to be eager to live; to live joyfully, meaningfully" (*Origins* 3). Maybe our church community needs to be infused with these same values if young people are to claim it as their own. "Take your place in the life of this body, however imperfect it may be. Bring to it your needs, your enthusiasm. Contribute to the expression of the Church's faith and prayer, the special poetic gift and desire to commit yourself that is of youth" (John Paul II, *The Pope Speaks* 370). The spiritually challenging vision of church call us to promote the dignity of all persons in a multi-cultural society, values formed and lived in the style of Jesus, special care for family growth and development, outreach to youth-at-risk, social consciousness grounded in the Scriptures, and the exploration of what it means to be and live as a Catholic Christian in relationship with others. Youth must be invited to be co-creators of this vision and to participate in its realization.

VISION OF THE WORLD

We don't have to look too far to see the opportunities the world provides. There is wealth beyond our wildest imagining.

Our children enjoy leisure and luxury not available to other generations. Economically, scientifically, educationally, recreationally, politically, the world is ours for the taking. And in many cases, that is exactly what we have done! We also know that 10% of the world consumes two-thirds of the world's resources. We experience great poverty as well as great affluence. The earth is abused for the sake of progress, racism flourishes, our defense system is a national priority while our education system declines, political prisoners have been forgotten, and young people are exploited for the sake of a dollar. We claim that we are thriving and still much of what we cherish is dying. More than ever, we need a spiritually challenging vision of the world and our place in it.

> The call of the spiritual life then, the call of ministry, is the call to take all the insights in the life of Christ that we have ever been able to gather back down the mountain to the world of our own time. The call to ministry in this century is the call to be aware of the root causes of suffering in this world and to work a few miracles of our own... If we are really to minister, it is up to us to be transformed and then transfiguring. And then we must set out to do something to cure the causes as well as soothe the symptoms. (Chittister 77,82)

If spirituality is both deeply personal and dynamically interpersonal, the vision must address not only the needs of youth, but the needs of the world in which they live. Young people must learn to be in the world, but not of the world. They must realize the importance of both solitude and compassionate action. What is the cost of discipleship in our ever-changing world? There must be a prophetic approach that is also balanced. And our youth must move from isolation to involvement — from "me" to "us." We must challenge them to attend to God in *all* aspects of their life experience, in *all* the systems in which they move. The vision must be broad and deep, exciting and engaging, captivating the young to attend to the following:

1. **Caring for the Earth**. Young people need a spiritual vision grounded in respect for all creation, interdependence, and stewardship. Our youth need examples of less consuming and more sharing, and an ability to see with new eyes our connection to the earth and our responsibility for its survival.

2. **Global Awareness**. Do we present a "think globally, act locally" mentality? We are citizens in a global world. We can no longer ignore unjust relationships of any kind. Young people must be asked to let go on many levels and to act against international, national, and local suffering and injustice.

3. **Work**. Young people need assistance in choosing a vocation that promotes the kingdom message. Careers that promote happiness, self-satisfaction, the public good, and personal fulfillment must be explored, rather than simply prestigious, high paying, yet alienating or powerless positions. The vision must present work and career as redemptive.

4. **Peace**. Reconciliation and peace were high points in Jesus' ministry. Violence and war are now taken for granted as facts of life. War has entered our homes through the media on a scale never before anticipated. Young people need conflict resolution skills and a vision of peace as a viable alternative to the choices the world presents.

5. **Technology**. Do we really know what we believe and what we don't believe? Or are our lives controlled by the images and information someone decides to share? Young people need to critically evaluate the media's messages, the consumerism, the information barrage, and make decisions based on Christian values. Our technology allows us to prolong and even determine life — how will we address the quality of that life for everyone? Does the Christian vision aid or abandon them in this task?

The list could become endless, but the issue remains the same. We cannot confine the vision to me and God, or me and the church, or even my prayer life. Spirituality encompasses so much more and is so much less at the same time. Joan Chittister says, "You have to be a part of the binding up of the wounds of the world. And you can do it in many, many ways. You can do it by critiquing the world. You can do it by restructuring the world. You can do it by providing alternative models for the world. You can do it by working in the world. How you do it doesn't matter, but you must do it. It cannot not be done" (Chittister 177-178). Maybe we as adults need to absorb this part of the vision before we are able to witness to its value for our youth! Do we practice what we preach?

MOVING BEYOND THE VISION

Luckily, we are a covenant people. God's promises are repeatedly fulfilled — through imperfect people, in an imperfect church and a wounded world. However, throughout the Old and New Testaments the vision was clear, and we have somehow managed to muddy the truth. And so we too wander in the desert and wonder what the promised land really promises. We've lost sight of the vision. We all need it reimaged and rearticulated, but especially our young people. They are searching for meaning and although we can't provide that for each of them, the Christian vision cannot be our best kept secret any longer!

Spirituality is not something we have or don't have. Spirituality is a life process. It is coming in touch with our unique spirit as lived through our life experiences. It is the process whereby we recognize the God of our experiences as well as the God of our faith tradition. It is the process of searching for our own authentic voice so that we can speak with the authority that our experience has given us. Our spirituality takes shape in the quality of our relationships, with ourselves, with others, with all of creation, with God. (Riley)

Our young people have much to say about the God of their experience and tradition. Are we willing to listen? They are hungry for so much more. Will we be able to challenge them with a spiritually challenging vision they can't refuse? If not, we shouldn't be surprised if they look elsewhere!

WORKS CITED

Broccolo, Gerard T. *Vital Spiritualities*. Notre Dame IN: Ave Maria Press, 1990.

Chittister, O.S.B., Joan, *WomanStrength: Modern Church, Modern Women*. Kansas City: Sheed & Ward, 1990.

DiGiacomo, James. "The New Illiteracy." *Church* (Fall 1986): 3-7.

Dillard, Annie. *Teaching A Stone To Talk*. New York: Harper & Row, 1982.

Dorr, Donal. *Integral Spirituality*. New York: Orbis Books, 1990.

Elkind, David. *All Grown Up and No Place To Go*. Reading MA: Addison-Wesley, 1984.

Hart, Thomas N. *The Art of Christian Listening*. New York: Paulist Press, 1980.

Nouwen, Henri. *Reaching Out*. New York: Doubleday & Co., 1986.

O'Malley S.J., William J. "Scripture from Scratch." *America* 4 Feb. 1989: 77-81.

Osmer, Richard. "Challenge to Youth Ministry in the Mainline Churches: Thought Provokers." *Affirmation* 2.1 (Spring, 1989).

Pope John Paul II. *Origins* 6 (May 1986): 3-4

Pope John Paul II. *The Pope Speaks* 29 (1984): 370.

Powell, John. *Fully Human, Fully Alive*. Allen TX: Argus Communications, 1976.

Riley O.P., Maria. *Wisdom Seeks Her Way*. Washington DC: The Center of Concern, 1987.

Rohr, Richard, and Martos, Joseph. *Why Be Catholic?* Cincinnati: St. Anthony Messenger Press, 1989.

Wright, Wendy. *Sacred Dwelling: A Spirituality of Family Life*. New York: Crossroads, 1990.

Chapter 2

Gospel Spirituality

Donald P. Gray

*"This is the time of fulfillment. The reign of God is at hand!
Reform your lives and believe in the gospel!"*

Jesus appears on the Jewish scene as a messenger bearing good news (gospel) from a king. Messengers of earthly kings, of course, generally brought bad news and more bad news, especially for those already burdened and in straitened circumstances. The appearance of this messenger is, therefore, cause for gladness and rejoicing. Although the one whom this Jesus serves and whose interests he represents is already king, there is clearly some difficulty about his actual role, for his reign is at hand and hence not yet fully established. Other rulers, the rulers of this world, have taken control of human life with disastrous consequences as the appalling suffering on all sides attests. The announcement of the good news will, as a result, bring in its wake a terrible struggle between this king and those reluctant to renounce their unjust and lethal power. The battle lines are drawn in advance, and it will prove necessary to choose sides in the conflict now taking shape. To turn a deaf ear to this good news is to have made one fateful choice. To welcome this message and offer hospitality to the messenger is to enter upon a new but costly way of life against the forces of death and destruction.

THE REIGN OF GOD

What does the approaching divine reign entail? Justice and therefore peace. Shalom. Blessing. Well-being. Salvation. The God of Jesus has made the cause of human welfare its own cause. [1] Jesus is himself identified with this divine cause on behalf of human beings. God has set himself resolutely against everything going on in human life that opposes and undermines human well-being. The divine concern is all-embracing, nothing is excluded, everything that belongs to human well-being is included, whether it be bodily, emotional, spiritual, social, political, economic, legal, educational, or environmental. God cares passionately and compassionately about every aspect of the human, and this caring is both active and determined. Here one finds no narrowing of the divine concern to the individual alone, the spiritual alone, the sacral order alone. Here one finds, not an other-worldly hope, but rather an ardent and committed hope for a new age, a time of fulfillment in this world, a future-worldly hope [2] that will include even the most excluded and outcast members of society, namely, the dead.

Jesus invites his contemporaries to look about them for indications of this mysterious divine activity on behalf of a new order, "signs of the times" as he called them. All around them the sick are getting well, the demoniacs are being freed, the sinners are turning to God, the lost are being found, the dead are returning to life. Deep-seated pathology is being replaced by well-being. As John Shea puts it, "No one has seen summer, yet its presence is proclaimed by the budding tree. No one has seen God, yet his presence is proclaimed by the transformed person" (Shea 165).

Jesus makes a "preferential option" in his ministry for the undesir-ables, the rejected, the disenfranchised, the despised, the marginal; in short, for the suffering. He is the physician who seeks out those in need of his assistance. His concern is not with the well, whoever exactly they may be (Mt 9:9-13; Lk 5:27-32). Jesus welcomes those who come to him (Lk 15: 1-2). [3] He rejects no one, turns no one away. Hospitality for outsiders is at the heart of his ministering. What is revealed here, in the judgment of Christian faith, is nothing less than the divine hospitality: God rejects no one, turns no one away, welcomes one and all. In Jesus' compassionate concern is to be found God's compassionate solidarity with and involve-ment in the plight of the suffering. One can only conclude from Jesus' sen-sitivity to human suffering that "God is compassionate, suffering with and taking into himself the pain and oppression of every son and daughter" (Shea 107). Supposed divine invulnerability (impassibility) gives way to the supposition of divine vulnerability (passibility) and pathos. [4] The tragedies of human life bring tears also and especially to the eyes of God. Such a God is no stranger to heartbreak, pain, and grief. Rather he/she is, in the remarkable observation of Whitehead, "the fellow-sufferer who under-stands" (Whitehead 532).

Such a willingness on Jesus' part to stand by the fringe people in human society, indeed, even and particularly the sinners, is at first surpris-ing, perhaps confusing and outrageous. Jesus' behavior in this regard does not by any means find unanimous approbation in his culture. Far from it. He is criticized severely, relentlessly, for the odd, indeed bad, company he keeps. (Holl) Why does he not spend his time among the decent people of his day? He appears to render himself guilty by association. Would a gen-uine man of God consort (even share the table) with such disreputable peo-ple? Not likely! Jesus reminds the uncomprehending that he has come for "the lost sheep of the house of Israel" (Mt 10:6, 10:24; Lk 29:10), not the 99 who have never strayed from the sheepfold (Lk 15:3-7; Mt 18:10-14), if, in fact, there be such thoroughly righteous ones about. (They are, after all, hard pressed to find a representative to stone the woman seized in the act of adultery!)

It is worth reminding ourselves that the Jewish king, representing the interests of Israel's King Yahweh, was expected to show special concern and offer special service to the little people, the lowliest members of society. The most powerful and wealthiest member of society was expected to champion the cause of the powerless and the poor, those who were defenseless and had no one to speak on their behalf. (Senior) Needless to say, kings rarely took such expectations and responsibilities seriously. In announcing the advent of God's reign and acting strictly in accordance with this heavenly King's intentions, Jesus makes it plain that there is a King, the King of the universe, in fact, who takes these obligations and works of love and compassion most seriously indeed and who is determined to see to it that the widow and orphan, as well as the sinner and demoniac, are not uncared for. The God whom Jesus serves and whose rule he announces is, after all, none other than the God of the Exodus, the God who liberated the oppressed and enslaved from Egyptian tyranny, the God who is "immensely and powerfully compassionate" toward those who cry out to him/her. [5] Jesus understands and represents to others the tender feelings of the Father for his injured Children.

Jesus calls out to this tenderhearted God in prayer with the name "Abba." This term was commonplace in daily Jewish life, since it was regularly used by the Jewish child to address his or her father. (It is usually translated into English as "daddy" or "papa.") Its use in a prayer setting, however, was extremely rare. Presumably, Jesus' intention in speaking in this way to the Lord of the universe and in inviting others to do likewise was to commend a certain style of approach to the holy mystery which we call God: that of a child before a kind, loving, and provident parent. For Jesus, Abba and his rule over human life were to be henceforth and forever at the center of the believer's life.

To know Abba is to trust him and to hope in him and to love him. In fact, it is only by trusting, hoping in, and loving Abba that one can possibly know him in any genuine sense. It is a matter of knowing Abba, not merely of knowing about him, and in such matters religious tradition, although of inestimable importance, can never serve as a substitute for firsthand experience, which in actuality, tradition should seek to encourage and support. There can be no real doubt about the fact that Jesus himself lived from such trust, hope, and love. [6] There can be no real doubt that it was this uniquely profound experience of God, however much encouraged and supported by a remarkably rich religious tradition, that provided the abiding ground of both his astounding knowledge of God and his power to reveal that same God in a transforming way. By sharing with one and all, but especially with the outcasts, his trust and hope and love, Jesus offered nothing less than the gift of God himself, and in and through that gift, human well-being (salvation). The needy need not wait until Jesus' death has taken place before they can find true life; it is already available to them now in the present, if they will only accept in gratitude and joy Abba's compassionate concern for them and their well-being. Such acceptance will take the form of a life of faith, hope, and love. It is, nonetheless, clear enough from the Gospel accounts that thoroughgoing transformation of life did not, in fact, generally take place prior to the tragic conclusion of Jesus' ministry and his reappearance after his death. In this regard, the example of the closest disciples of Jesus is quite instructive, for they were apparently unable to enter upon the path of faithful discipleship until they had passed through the harrowing experience of Jesus' death and their own disloyalty to him.

While it is doubtful that Jesus actually predicted his death in elaborate detail as the Gospels suggest, it is highly probable that he not only anticipated an untimely death but intimated as much to his disciples (Senior 140-143 and Brown 61-68). Jesus did not set out to die, but rather to serve and thus to bring abundant new life. All the same, he knew well enough the risks and perils of challenging and confronting vested interests in the name of God on behalf of the well-being of the rejected. After all, many of the prophets before him had been martyred, and only recently the prophet John the Baptist had been executed by Herod Antipas, the political ruler in Galilee. Jesus had counted the cost of ministry, especially a ministry of good news for the wretched, as his disciples certainly had not. While Jesus was in no sense eagerly running toward death, clearly he had accepted death as a possible outcome long before he was actually confronted with its inevitability. Jesus had awakened concern in circles of power among men with significant vested interests to protect; he had stirred up the fears and anxieties of the leadership elite, both religious and political, who at least in their own minds believed that they had much, perhaps everything, to lose should a new order arise. No quarter could be given. Jesus was obviously determined to continue upon his divinely appointed course. Conflict was to be expected from such a confrontation of differing values and world views and death became increasingly probable, perhaps unavoidable. Each actor played out his respective role in the drama, a role assigned not by fate or the stars but by personal choice and human passion. Jesus, passionate for the cause of God, came up against the establishment of his day and was broken on its unyielding resistance to Abba's priorities. Judgement had been rendered, and Jesus was found wanting and thoroughly discredited. Or so it seemed, at any rate.

Initially, the death of Jesus was not luminous with meaning for his scattered and dispirited disciples; it appeared to them, in fact, that it represented the end of all meaning. They had lost not only a beloved teacher and leader but also a way of life and the tasks of discipleship. Moreover, they can hardly have been happy about their own failure to support the master in his hour of crisis and distress. Preoccupied with their own safety, they had deserted Jesus in search of security from the mounting opposition. Jesus had stood his ground; they had yielded theirs. It is not difficult to imagine the extent and intensity of their grief, a grief that was not, as we are inclined to imagine, tempered by anticipation of an imminent resurrection victory over the dark forces of death (Brown 85-86). The New Testament accounts make it quite clear that they had to be won over to resurrection faith in the face of a natural and readily understandable tendency to doubt. The Resurrection occurs, not as a matter of course, but as a stunning surprise. The women went out to the tomb to grieve over the dead one. Never is it even hinted that they visited the place of burial to await the Resurrection. The men were hiding out in dread of the authorities. They were not, it is clear, serenely, even complacently waiting through a period of brief separation until the master should return from the realm of the dead. It is devastation that we find on all sides in the wake of Jesus' tragic end.

In Luke 24, we are told a sad and touching story about the departure of two of the disciples from the capital city just after Jesus' Crucifixion, a story presumably illustrative of the mood of the others as well. As they leave behind not only the holy city but a way of life as well and make their way to Emmaus, they are anticipating nothing. They are utterly without hope. They are joined by a stranger. It is, of course, Jesus himself, incognito. After they have shared with him their grief, he opens up to them their familiar Scriptures from a quite new standpoint, suggesting that perhaps, after all, the death that has left them bereft was not without meaning but somehow mysteriously can be made to serve the saving intentions of God. Excited by this possibility, but still unable to identify the stranger correctly, they prevail upon him to share the table with them. The sharing of stories is to be followed and completed by the sharing of the meal. In the breaking of the bread, they finally recognize him as God, Messiah (Christ), and their Lord. With his sudden disappearance they go out to proclaim the good news to others back in Jerusalem only to be greeted with the good news that Jesus has already appeared to Peter.

This wonderful story provides a splendid insight into the dynamic movement of early Christian liturgy and of Christian liturgy today. We can well imagine early Jewish Christian communities struggling to understand the messianic expectations of their people as detailed in the readings from the Scriptures in the light of the Risen One, who had entered into his glory but who first had to suffer. Undoubtedly, as they listened once again to the stories of the suffering Servant in second Isaiah or to the difficulties of the righteous at the hands of their enemies in the Psalms, their hearts burned with excitement within them. The events of the recent past, death followed by Resurrection and the outpouring of the Spirit, were beginning to make sense, to fall into a pattern. Bewilderment was giving way to insight; desolation was being replaced by hope and renewed expectancy.

If the Scripture readings and the interpretive homily make recognition of this strange crucified figure as the messiah possible, it is especially at the table in the breaking of the bread that he appears to them in his true light. Now they know for a certainty that he is with them still. Trips to the burial site are now rendered unnecessary and useless. He is here among the living. He can no longer be found in the cemetery among the dead, back there in a past that is gone forever. His disappearance from the table does not obliterate the communion with him achieved through the meal; it opens the way for the essential task of discipleship to be taken up: the sharing of the good news that crucified Jesus is risen and is Lord and Messiah, the abiding source of salvation from God.

We know from the Gospel accounts that it was only after the terrible death of Jesus and the emergence of Easter faith that the closest disciples of Jesus were genuinely transformed and brought to courageous commitment to his cause. That process of transformation was already underway in the period of ministry, but it remained incomplete and imperfect. They only partially understood, only partially gave themselves to this new way and the new order that Jesus championed and exemplified. Those who had ministered at the side of Jesus during his lifetime were themselves, after their disloyalty to him at the time of his death, in desperate need of ministry, forgiveness, and healing. Jesus, ever faithful to those whom he had called, was there, unexpectedly and miraculously, to provide the required remedy. It was from this group of earnest but failed disciples, who had been irrevocably touched and transformed by Jesus both in life and beyond death, and that church emerged, ready to continue the tireless work of Jesus in the power of God's Spirit. A new community had been given birth through the Spirit's creative action, as the Spirit had earlier given birth to the Savior himself. A life, and in a peculiar way a death, had brought home to them the enduring and constant love of Jesus' Abba, their Abba, and they could never again be the same. They could no longer accept or live form the unexamined priorities of their culture, their own past. Jesus had shared everything with them, and now everything that had belonged to him belonged to them. They, too, were Abba's children as Jesus had been preeminently his child. That sharing continues in the ongoing ministry of the Risen One present in the power of the Spirit. The invitation to choose life is still open. Loving his own, those entrusted to his care (and he draws no boundaries in this regard), he loved them and still loves them to the very end. That love, manifested in that life and that death, has proved itself redemptive and liberating over the centuries. Although interpreted in many ways and from many different cultural directions, that life and that death have enabled others to find meaning, to endure, and to achieve some measure of understanding of their own lives and tasks as well as their own suffering and death.

The kingdom, proclaimed by John the Baptist and furthered by Jesus came nearer still with Jesus' Resurrection and the consequent transformation of his disciples. A new age had dawned.

REPENTANCE

In summoning his hearers to repentance in the light of the approaching kingdom of Abba, Jesus demanded the most fundamental of conversions, the conversion of the heart to God's compassionate love and thus a far-reaching reordering of one's life-priorities (Senior 85-86). It is one of the basic purposes of human nurturing to establish an order of priorities appropriate to the established cultural situation and reflective of its deepest biases. It was Jesus' purpose, as God's prophet and representative, to expose the highly questionable nature of this order of priorities (even in a dominantly religious culture such as his own) and to propose a radical alternative appropriate to a new and drastically reordered age and reflective to the divine purposes. Jesus evidently understands himself as the authentic and hence authoritative interpreter of God's mind and heart, the exegete of God, as Schillebeeckx calls him (Schillebeeckx 242).

Jesus' own priorities are thoroughly theocentric and adamantly altruistic without leading to an ultimately destructive denigration of the self. Jesus insistently invites his hearers beyond a narrowly conceived range of concerns, largely defined by self-interest and anxiously defended against outsiders. Jesus invites his hearers to live beyond fear which means to live from trust, confident hope, and compassion (Hellwig 53-55, 89-90, 175). Jesus stands unambiguously on the side of change and presents himself as a change-agent in his society. That is undoubtedly what leads to his death. That is still what is disturbing about him. Jesus, realist that he is, recognizes that change costs and willingly accepts that cost on behalf of that new order he refers to as the kingdom of God. Death, he affirms, can serve the interests of life. The God whom Jesus reveals refuses to underwrite the status quo with its widespread injustices and pervasive suffering, but rather restlessly agitates for a new and more just pattern of relationships resting upon quite different premises.

The point needs some emphasis for people living in a period of drastic change, both cultural and ecclesial. We have perhaps for too long associated the divine with stability and order, certainty and security. When purchased at the price of human suffering, these concerns are to be rejected in favor of a new order with all the insecurity and uncertainty that may entail. As Jesus announces the advent of an epoch-making moment of historical change actively promoted by Abba, he meets with increasingly stubborn opposition from those who are able to see change only in terms of the losses they fear incurring. They are not yet capable of imaging the gains, the newness of life, to which the Gospel invites them. A mystery of death and life resides at the heart of the Gospel message, a mystery enacted for the benefit of others by Jesus in his ministry, cross, and Resurrection. Living as we do in a period of challenging change, we are likewise being summoned to participate more profoundly in this paschal mystery. When we experience the fuller life that this mystery brings into our lives, we discover the joy that the good news brings. Apparently for many in the Church, change betokens little more than loss. This grief, visible in anger, depression, and withdrawal, indicates that they are not yet able to imagine the possibilities of larger life that are being offered in these circumstances of apparent death. The grief-stricken need understanding and support to make their way through this difficult passage. This is surely one of the most fundamental and demanding tasks of church renewal, a work of mercy, a work of compassion. Many such works of compassion lie at hand in both Church and culture. Even here, with regard to our traditional corporal and spiritual works of mercy, however, we need to undergo a change of heart, a reordering of priorities, if our hearts are to be made over according to the pattern of the compassionate heart of Abba, if our priorities are to be brought into alignment with the divine priorities.

The requirements of altruism are clearly wider and more demanding that we have traditionally imaged. The love commandment needs to be expanded so as to include the world of nature as well as God and neighbor. The other species on this planet, which might legitimately press certain proprietary rights stemming from their earlier settlement of the land and the seas, are, in fact, our neighbors. They too are injured and have been left half-dead by the side of the road (the roads we have built). They are in desperate need (facing outright extinction as many of them are) of some good Samaritans who will take pity on them and not indifferently pass by on the opposite side of the road. Of course, such compassionate care and commitment will take us out of our way and will require a new effort from us.

A more expansive and inclusive sense of the neighbor in need perhaps provides us with an opportunity to revise in a similarly expansive way our traditional thinking about the works of mercy. Traditionally, these works of mercy (or, perhaps better, these works of care and compassion) have been directed to the victims of sickness, unjust institutional processes, and social violence — those who are injured in either body or soul (or both).

Today we recognize that such expressions of concern, while still indispensable and vitally important, are nonetheless inadequate to the extent that they address symptoms while leaving unaddressed, and thus still in power, the underlying causes. We have come gradually to acknowledge the need for social, political, and economic works of mercy, which seek the reform or replacement of existing structural patterns that keep on producing their victims in ever greater numbers, numbers too great to be satisfactorily coped with by conventional, more privatistic corporal and spiritual works of mercy.

More recently, however, we have advanced still a step farther to the awareness that even these works are insufficient and need to be complemented by ecological works of mercy that seek to speak to the issues raised by attention to the entire community of living beings. What we are observing here is a remarkable and surprising development of consciousness that transcends, but does not by any means ignore or denigrate, the personal dimension of human life in favor of the social and finally of the biological and ecological dimensions of human life.

The good news that the reign of God is at hand comes to us along with an invitation and a challenge to grow steadily into an all-inclusive, welcoming compassion which offers a healing hospitality to all of God's creatures who meet us along the way. It is in this transforming conversion from a dangerous and damaging self-preoccupation and apathy into caring sensitivity and committed service that we find our salvation, our well-being as children of the Abba God whose image we are called to be.

ENDNOTES

[1] For this language, see Hans Kung, *On Being a Christian* (New York: Doubleday, 1976) 214-77; and Edward Schillebeeckx, *Jesus: An Experiment in Christology* (New York: Seabury Press, 1979) 62, 213, 240. Walter Kasper, *An Introduction to Christian Faith* (New York: Paulist Press, 1980) 110, says "The content of faith is a call to a decision to adopt Jesus' cause, which is the cause of God with mankind."

[2] This is Monika Hellwig's way of putting it in *Understanding Catholicism* (New York: Paulist Press, 1981) 177.

[3] See Franz Josef van Beeck, *Christ Proclaimed: Christology as Rhetoric* (New York: Paulist Press, 1979), on "the rhetoric of inclusion."

[4] Abraham Heschel, *The Prophets*, v. 2 (New York: Harper Torchbooks, 1971) speaks eloquently of the divine pathos. His insights have clearly influenced William Thompson's *Jesus, Lord and Savior. A Theopathic Christology and Soteriology* (New York: Paulist Press, 1980) and more recently his *The Jesus Debate* (New York: Paulist Press, 1985).

[5] See Monica Hellwig in *Understanding Catholicism*, (New York: Paulist Press, 1981) 20. Her interpretation of the "burning bush" incident in this context is quite striking.

[6] I have explored this theme more extensively in *Jesus: The Way to Freedom* (Winona MN: St. Mary's Press, 1979).

WORKS CITED

Brown, Raymond. *Jesus: God and Man*. Milwaukee: Bruce, 1967.

Hellwig, Monica. *Understanding Catholicism*. New York: Paulist Press, 1981.

Holl, Adolf. *Jesus in Bad Company*. New York: Avon Books, 1974.

Senior, Donald. *Jesus: A Gospel Portrait*. Cincinnati: Pflaum Standard, 1975.

Schillebeeckx, Edward. *Jesus: An Experiment in Christology*. New York: Seabury Press, 1979.

Shea, John. *Stories of God*. Chicago: Thomas More Press, 1978.

Whitehead, Alfred North. *Process and Reality*. New York: Harper Torchbooks, 1960.

Chapter 3

Growth in the Christian Life

Thomas Hart

A helping relationship in the context of Christian faith is aimed at growth in the Christian life. The question is, what is this growth? Can we be more concrete about our goal? Such definition is crucial to the whole helping enterprise. It is very hard to get to Xanadu if you don't know where Xanadu is.

A lot of ink has been spilled on the question of Christian spirituality. It goes in many directions, but all the radii fan out from a common center, Jesus Christ. Paul names him the new Adam (Rm 5:12-21, 1 Cor 15:42-50), which means he is the second and greater progenitor of the human race. The first three Gospels call him the beloved Son in whom the Father is well pleased (Mk 1:11, 9:7, and parallels), and admonish us to listen to him. John sees him as the Word of God in the flesh (Jn 1:1-18) which means God's whole message to us about life is visible in him. In the same Gospel, Jesus is portrayed as saying of himself: "I am the Way and the Truth and the Life" (Jn 14:6). The answer to the question about growth in the Christian life is then a person, Jesus Christ. We reach the fullness of our human potential as God envisages that potential, in the measure that we are conformed to Jesus. Let us examine, at least briefly, what seems to be at the heart of his way of life and his teaching.

HIS LIFE

The strongest feature of the life of Jesus of Nazareth is that he lives it with God. He speaks of his Father continually, showing an habitual awareness of him in the way he perceives reality and responds to it. One thing he wants above all: to do always the things that please the Father (Jn 8:29), to accomplish his will (Jn 4:34). He is seen regularly at prayer, strengthening the vital bond, sensitizing himself to the Father's leadings in his life. His impact on others produces in them an impression to which they testify in chorus, the Gospels being their testimony: In this man we have met God in a degree that puts Jesus in a class by himself. Jesus, summing up his life in a prayer on the evening of his passion, says: "I have glorified you on earth, having accomplished the work which you gave me to do" (Jn 17:4).

What is surprising is not so much his orientation but the manner in which he lives it out. It is steeped in ordinariness. He does not leave the crowd to go off and live a more ascetic life, nor does he persuade his followers to do so. He does not lay stress on fasting or other ascetical practices, or present celibacy as the distinctive feature of his way of life. On the contrary, he is seen at table in questionable company with sufficient frequency to earn the name of glutton and drunkard, friend to tax collectors and sinners (Lk 7:34). And though he is celibate, his chosen followers, the Twelve are, with the possible exception of John, all married men. Jesus does take time to pray regularly. But the typical situation in which he is found in the Gospels is a social setting of one kind or another. The usual thing he is doing is helping people in some way — now healing, now reconciling, now feeding, now teaching them. He is not a priest, scribe, or pharisee. He takes his stance outside the religious institution of his day, a layman without connections or authorization. But his life is ministry, his milieu all human society.

HIS TEACHING

What does he teach? He teaches exactly what he lives. For one thing, he teaches a contemplative vision of life. All the vehicle of his instruction is the ordinary stuff of this world, seen through to its significance in God. He calls attention to the word of God spoken in the change of seasons, the growth of seeds, the birth of a child, the harbingers of weather change, the storm at sea, the dinner party, the judge, the ruler, the rich man and the beggar, the steward, the householder, the child. He finds lessons of eternal significance in these and many similar earthly realities. He is much more than a skilled pedagogue adapting to the thought-world of his audience. He is a first-rate religious teacher because he is a profound contemplative.

In his teaching he stresses certain things. He attaches great importance to simplicity of life, not laying up treasure on earth, yet not being anxious about the means of life (Mt 6:19-34). His parable of the rich man and poor Lazarus instructs us to share what we have with those in need (Lk 16:19-31). His parable of the good Samaritan makes it both goods and services (Lk 10:25-37). He urges forgiveness and reconciliation, not judging, loving even enemies (Lk 6:32-38). He often reminds people of the shortness of life, the preciousness of the present day, the need to stay awake (Mk 13:32-37). With regard to God, he teaches trust in all circumstances, hope in the unexpected deliverance, confidence in God's forgiveness, and the constancy of his love for all of his children. He stresses the importance of listening to the truth wherever it is spoken and of speaking the truth whether it is profitable or not. Where suffering is concerned, he teaches a mystery: that suffering and dying are not the last word, but the passage to new life. He does not say much in explanation of it, but he teaches that our God is a God at work in the depth and darkness of things, somehow bringing life out of death, good out of evil, meaning out of meaninglessness.

Now if we look back over these teachings, we can see that there is nothing arcane or esoteric about them. They are plain truths, intended not for a select few but for everyone, livable in *all* circumstances and styles of life. He shares them not just with the Twelve, but with the multitudes.

The religious genius of Jesus is to radicalize and to simplify, to get at the root of our relationship with God and to sum it up in a few words. And so, in the last days of his ministry, when a scribe asks him what is the greatest commandment, he pulls his whole teaching and entire way of life together into a single summary rule of life:

> You shall love the Lord your God with all your heart, and with all your soul, and with all your mind, and with all your strength... You shall love your neighbor as yourself (Mk 12:29-31).

No one will say this program is easy, but it is certainly not complicated. It demands absolutely everything of us, all day every day, but the content of the demand is basic and clear.

It is as if Jesus surveyed the religious scene of his day and said to himself: These are good people, but they are all confused. They think God wants religious services, tithes, and the strict observance of law. In fact, he wants their hearts. They think he wants religiosity, complete with sackcloth and a daily regimen. He would much rather see them love one another and share what they have with one another, so that everybody has life. They think he wants them to reject the world and isolate themselves from it, when in fact he wants them to enjoy it and give thanks for it, and to work to make it more human. They think he wants them to live in fear, fear of doing wrong and fear of him, when in fact he wants them to live in joy and freedom. They think he wants them to walk about with their heads down because of all their failures, when in fact he wants them to trust like children in his forgiveness and the dependability of his love. They think they have to earn their way with him and win a reward if they can, when in fact he wants them to accept his acceptance of them as a gift quite undeserved.

And so we find this simple good man in table fellowship with sinners (Mk 2:15-17). We see him helping people out even on Sunday (Lk 13:10-17). We find him attacking the religious leadership of his day for straining out gnats and swallowing camels, adhering fanatically to the traditions of their ancestors while neglecting justice and mercy and faith (Mt 23:23). We find him, not leading public prayers or gathering people for sacrifices, but quietly spending himself to free people from their burdens — their inner demons, their diseases, their guilt — and urging others to help. Just as tirelessly he bears witness to the truth, though he knows what happens sooner or later to people who bear witness to the truth.

Just as the great commandment summarizes his life and teaching in a verbal formula, the last supper epitomizes it in a symbolic action. In giving the bread and the wine, Jesus tries to compress into a pregnant gesture everything his life has meant. Anticipating his death on the next day, and wishing to make it clear that this death is something not imposed on him but freely chosen as the way he wants to express his love for his Father and us, he gives his disciples the bread and wine, after giving thanks, and says: "This is my body for you." "This is my blood poured out for you." It is his own living of the great commandment, and he proposes it as the model for ours: "Do this in memory of me." What he intends is made further intelligible by two surrounding statements, both about choice.

> The ruler of this world is coming. He has no power over me; but I do as the Father has commanded me, so that the world may know that I love the Father. Rise, let us go (Jn 14:30-31).

Greater love has no one than this, that a man lay down his life for his friends (Jn 15:13).

Jesus is the perfect embodiment of what he teaches. And the Eucharist, because it contains the summary of his teaching and his life, remains the sustaining ritual action of the Christian community.

CHRISTIAN GROWTH TODAY

We have looked at the Word made flesh. Now we look at ourselves. The purpose of our lives is to become like Jesus, and not just to resemble him externally. We are to be rooted and grounded in him (Eph 3:17), to be ever more closely identified with him so that we can say, "I live, now not I, but Christ lives in me" (Gal 2:20). Any growth in the living out of the great commandment is growth in Christ. The entire object of Christian spirituality is right here.

To apply these foundational truths to the situation of the Church today, we must advert to historical developments which produced the religious milieu in which most of us were raised. Until very recently, Christian spirituality had come to be commonly understood as the special preserve of a select number in the Church, and it was conceived along ascetical lines. Vowed religious men and women and ordained priests were those who studied and lived Christian spirituality, while the great mass of Christians understood themselves as followers at a distance, people taught, ruled, and sanctified by these others. They kept the commandments and contributed to the support of the church. But they did not think of themselves as called to a serious life of prayer, to what might be called holiness, or to any kind of ministry in the Church. What had insinuated itself into the body of Christ was a two-class mentality, whose foundations in the New Testament it would be very difficult to find.

Into this situation Vatican II spoke a revolutionary new word which was really a very old word. In a departure from recent tradition, the Council played down the distinction between clergy, religious, and laity. It discontinued the language of "wholeheartedness" to characterize those who follow Christ in clerical or religious life, a usage which suggested that those who follow him in other styles of life are less than wholehearted. It used instead the expressions "more readily" and "more easily" to describe how those who are priests or religious can devote themselves to prayer and the apostolate. But it said nothing to suggest that these people are automatically holy just by reason of their state of life, or that those who are called along other Christian paths are automatically deprived of the opportunity for holiness by their circumstances.

The most important Council document, the *Dogmatic Constitution on the Church*, cornerstone of the whole conciliar achievement, is most instructive in its very outline. Instead of beginning, as previous treatments of the Church have, with hierarchical organization and lines of authority, this document begins with biblical metaphors which describe the mystery of the whole Church. The Church is the coming Kingdom of God, a sheepfold, and a land to be cultivated, the building of God, God's family, God's temple, the Holy City, spouse of Christ, body of Christ. The constitution's second chapter is a lengthy development of the biblical metaphor of the church as the people of God. It speaks of the priesthood of all the members, states that all without exception are called by the Lord to perfect holiness, describes the sacramental life which undergirds their life together, then speaks of the Church's mission as a concern and activity involving all the members. It is not until the third chapter of the constitution that there is discussion of what had usually been at the head of the book, namely, office and authority in the Church, the Holy Father, the college of bishops, priests, and deacons. In the treatment of the Council, office and authority are seen as derived from and functioning with the whole Church body rather than somehow being anterior and originating. The next two chapters of the constitution return again to broader themes, the fourth chapter devoted entirely to the laity, and the fifth to "The Universal Call to Holiness." Just to round out this structural analysis, we might note that the sixth chapter discusses religious, the seventh the pilgrim Church, and the eighth the Blessed Virgin Mary. The point of the whole discussion is that the Church is conceived by the Second Vatican Council much more comprehensively than it had been for a long time, the conciliar position being that all who belong to the

Church are called both to the fullness of Christian sanctity and to the apostolate. Just in case this last item should be missed, the Council issues a whole separate document entitled, *On the Apostolate of the Laity*. In the contemporary vision of the Church, therefore, it is hardly adequate to think of the laity as a vast silent majority whose calling is to follow, to be ministered to, and to obey.

The unfortunate effect of the two-class mentality in the Church was that it short-circuited immense amounts of spiritual energy, leaving all kinds of potential for sanctity untapped and countless gifts for ministry unused. The achievement of the Council has been to call this entire dormant portion of the Church back to life, causing a widespread resurgence of interest in spirituality and the emergence of many new forms of ministry.

IN THE CONCRETE

All Christians are called to holiness, and the features of Christian holiness are seen clearly in the life and teaching of Jesus. There is only one basic Christian spirituality, speaking as much to lay people as to priests and religious, demanding the same central things of any lifestyle, in any life circumstances. To what sort of things, then, will the Christian helper be attentive in listening to the person who seeks growth?

Well, that religious sister does not represent Christian holiness very well, who although she spends many hours a day in the service of people, does not pray. She has made public profession as a Christian and engages in the apostolate of the Church, but it is questionable how good her roots are and therefore how fruitful her ministry is. "Apart from me you can do nothing" (Jn 15:5). And that pastor does not represent Christian holiness very well who, although he is a priest and says his breviary and celebrates the liturgy every day, is not very open to receiving his parishioners or listening to them, who typically squelches rather than encourages the initiatives his people take in trying to promote the life of the church. He has not taken adequate account of the importance of love of neighbor in Christian growth, love shown in open hospitality, friendliness and encouragement. Nor does he show adequate sensitivity to the truth wherever it might be spoken. And that layman does not exemplify Christian maturity very well who, although he is regular in his church attendance, contributes to the support of the church, and is a member of the Holy Name Society, spends all the rest of his time trying to acquire a fortune for himself, like the man in the Gospel who builds bigger barns (Lk 12:15-21). It may not be dishonest but has he heard that saying of Jesus: "It is easier for a camel to go through the eye of a needle than for a rich man to enter the kingdom of God?" (Mk 10:25). Where love of neighbor is concerned, has he taken account of the effect of his actions on other people? For it is not only in one-to-one relationships, but in every social structure, that we love or fail to love our neighbor. So much of human misery in the world today is rooted in unjust economic and social structures. And that Christian laywoman needs to do some important self-reflection, who, although she is a daily communicant and is conscientious in her responsibilities toward her family, stoutly maintains, and even works for organizations which maintain that people on welfare are simply lazy, that homosexuals do not deserve even civil rights, and that social activists and protesters are Communists. She lets unexamined assumptions rule fairly large areas of her social conduct, and allows prejudice and bias to stand in for actual association with the people she condemns, association which almost always shatters stereotypes and lets in amazing illuminations.

These are scattered examples, but they demonstrate that Christian holiness is a many-sided and high ideal and a lifetime project. It is not achieved easily, is not ensured within any style of life, and is subject to loss as well as gain over the years. Growth on any side of it promotes growth on all others, but, similarly, regression on any side of it works as a drag on the other sides, and a blind spot in any areas is a serious hindrance to growth in other areas.

Paradoxically, the foundation of any growth is self-acceptance at the point where one is. Here both the self and the helper have a role to play, both needing to make that crucial act of acceptance. Sometimes the person cannot make it for him- or herself. We usually find it hard to love ourselves, conscious as we are of all our shortcomings. Someone else has to love us first. This, of course, is exactly what God is always trying to get across to us — that God does love us first and without any questions.

> This is the love that I mean — not that we loved God but that God first loved us and sent the Son to be the expiation of our sins (1 Jn 4:10).

But we frequently need to see this love incarnated in some human being who knows our story, and that is where a helper comes in, the earthen vessel mediating the good news. Self-acceptance does not, of course, guarantee growth, but it is the first and indispensable step. It grounds the conviction that the project is worthwhile, nay, possible; it tells us that we have materials to work with which could be turned into something.

With this foundation in place, and it may need to be firmed in place conversation after conversation, the work that needs to be done will vary from person to person. One person will need to be helped most in strengthening a life of prayer. Another person will need trust in God in the uncertainties of experience. Some couples need to overcome acquisitiveness and consumerism and simplify their lives. Some parents need help in expanding love from the immediate circle of family and close friends to the wider circle of the whole varied human community. Some people need consciousness-raising about and motivation to correct unjust and life-destroying social and economic structures in our nation and in the world. A young man or woman might need assistance in integrating sexuality into responsible loving. Others will need help identifying and developing their own peculiar ministerial charisms. Sometimes people need help with personal issues of particular urgency at a given time — troublesome relationships, work problems, a particular suffering, the vocation question, difficulties in prayer, sexual identity, important decisions, preparation for death. Any circumstance or situation can be made capital of, particularly those which challenge and stretch the individual the most. Any crisis is a fertile seedbed for Christian growth. God, the life-giver, is present and active in all events, waiting on our cooperation. The norm for growth is always Jesus, who so beautifully embodies the ideal, and whose gift to us is his own enabling Spirit.

One final note. The Christian helper needs to realize that he or she is not only watching and promoting spiritual growth in the other, but necessarily also earnestly pursuing it in his or her own life. This is not only because we do God's work effectively in the measure that we are united to him, but also because we can hardly ask others to do what we will not take the trouble to do ourselves. Jesus never did. And any kind of helping is so largely a matter of modeling. One thinks of the words of Emerson: "What you are thunders so loud I cannot hear what you are saying." Yet even where our words are concerned, we affect others more sometimes by offhand or incidental remarks than we do by our most careful and concerted discourses. The quality of our offhand remarks is largely determined by the quality of our lives.

Chapter 4

Growth in the Spiritual Life

Kathleen Fischer

A recent newspaper headline notes that the average American moves 11 times in a lifetime. This mobility is but one expression of the pervasiveness of change in contemporary life. In all spheres we experience movement as the larger reality, within which there are pauses and plateaus. We think we have family life under control, and we learn that our youngest child is having difficulties in school. We are settled in a new job and then find ourselves unexpectedly laid off and in search of other employment. We experience God's presence and comfort, and then suddenly it is gone. We feel plunged into darkness and absence. We depend on a long-standing friendship, and conflict arises in the relationship.

This realization that our world is a dynamic one, marked at every level by movement and change, has influenced our conception of spirituality. A concern for continuous growth has replaced the search for static perfection that characterized spirituality in previous periods. We no longer envision the spiritual life as a way of drifting in a calm and tranquil sea; rather, we realize it is a voyage under ever-changing conditions. What matters is not so much that we arrive at some destination, but how we make the trip. In the past, perfection was equated with the unchanging; we looked forward to a time when we would reach a state of completion. Now the metaphors of journey and pilgrimage mark spiritual discussions; we are aware that there is no completion that does not open out into new growth. Let us examine the difference this perspective makes in three important areas of spirituality: 1) the meaning of spiritual growth; 2) finding the will or purpose of God; and 3) understanding the role of systems, such as marriage, family, and nation, in our spirituality.

THE MEANING OF SPIRITUAL GROWTH

When an ocean liner sets out to sea, the choices that its crew makes at every stage are guided by the destination they hope to reach. Every journey is governed by its goal. So too, the decisions we make in our spiritual lives are guided by the ideal we hold out for ourselves. At some level, often without being fully aware of it, we have a determined idea of a good or holy person. Perhaps we frame that ideal in terms of love and self-sacrifice, courage and fidelity, or higher stages of prayer. In any case, we constantly measure ourselves against it, telling ourselves that we should be more patient, generous, or prayerful. Ideals of spiritual growth reflect our view of perfection. In the past perfection has been equated with the static and unchanging, with a stable condition untouched by the turmoil of daily existence. Many of us still see perfection as a state at which we will arrive, or where others have arrived, finally free from the unexpected turns and new challenges, the brokenness and incomplete quality of our lives. This concept of perfection undergoes dramatic revision in a spirituality where change and becoming are recognized as more fundamental aspects of existence than the static and unchanging, where to be is *always* to become.

Some spiritualities portray God as interested principally in preserving the laws and rituals of religion in their present form. The worship of God then becomes a matter of defending the status quo. This separates creativity from God and undermines our resistance to evil and our hope for a different future. It alters the spiritual journey in major ways, leading us to remain silent before injustice rather than speak out, to cling to familiar images of God rather than embrace new ones, to hesitate to use our gifts rather than overcome fear and take the plunge.

Once we acknowledge the pervasiveness of change, our experience of the spiritual life becomes one of constant outreach toward the new. We are open to growth but trust in the slow work of grace. Only God knows fully what this new spirit gradually forming within us might be. Opening ourselves to the divine presence enables us to move beyond our given situations and envision possibilities that may be contrary to our surrounding environment. In the midst of hatred and war, we can and must imagine a world of peace and work toward its attainment. In situations of conflict, we can break with patterns of the past and extend forgiveness to those who have harmed us. Within a history of family violence, abuse, and pain, we can choose to stop the cycle of violence, to believe that we are loved and capable of loving others.

In this way spirituality focuses on the dynamic edges and turning points of life. The spiritual life might best be described as an unending conversion experience. Human persons are called to true adventure, together with the risks involved in any quest for love and justice. Within such a spiritual vision, our attention is focused on directions or tendencies rather than on particular actions, since there will always be an unfinished quality to our spiritual lives. This or that individual thought or action — whether I lost my temper today or ignored someone's need — is not nearly as important as are the *patterns* of courage or fearfulness, of openness or closure, that appear in our lives. From such a perspective, the questions I should ask myself are those which reveal the direction I am giving my life: How am I facing the problems that confront me? How am I using my freedom to integrate and transcend my past? The acceptance of life as a process means an appreciation of the open-endedness of both personal and social development. Change is not an enemy; within it can be found God's invitation to fuller human maturity.

Perfection in such a world is modeled on a love that takes risks. Spirituality is a challenge to adventure. The spiritual journey of Thomas Merton was such an adventure. Between his birth in France, his life in the United States before and during his Trappist years, and his death in Bangkok, Merton's life was a search on many levels, always unsettled and unfinished. As a young man he converted dramatically to Catholicism. In the monastic life he broke the mold of his vocation and became a writer. In later years his horizons expanded into social concerns and encounters with Eastern mysticism. As Merton's life illustrates, the experience of time means moving into a future which is really indeterminate; it is not the unfolding of a predetermined story.

In this model of spirituality we are dealing with movement and direction, what is coming to be. There is, then, less fear of mistakes and failures and more concern over reluctance to develop one's potential, or the dangers of contentment with a static position and comfort in the backwater. It is God who enables us to "get unstuck," to see things differently, to dream dreams, and image the new. It is God who enables us to embrace newness within permanence.

FINDING GOD'S WILL

Christians look to Jesus' life for the dominant themes of spirituality, and Jesus' life centers on his desire to do God's will.

My food is to do the will of the One who sent me,
to accomplish God's work (Jn 4:34).

We also want to carry out God's design for our lives. However, attempts to do God's will give rise to some of the major issues in the spiritual life: How do I know what God's will for me is? How is God's will related to my will? Appeals to God's will have been used to provide divine backing for a wide range of human activities — from acts of love and peacemaking to murder, greed, and political ambition.

Many Christians assume that God has a predetermined and detailed plan for our lives, one which has been established for all eternity and which we must now discover and carry out if we are to find happiness and salvation. According to this view, God's will lies outside of and over against us.

Clues to it are found in voices other than our own; we look for signs and sometimes ask external authority to tell us what to do. God's will has little to do with our freedom and personal desires.

The contemporary theological movement called process theology illumines the struggle we experience in making Christian choices. This theology speaks of God's purpose rather than God's will, and its categories enable us to affirm both this divine purpose and human aspirations. To see how this is so, we must take a moment to understand how process thought describes the self becoming.[1]

According to process thought, the basic reality in this world is a movement of self-realization which continually emerges from previous experience. As a self, I am subject or center of feeling, weaving together many different strands of relatedness into my identity. I can only become self-aware and self-accepting through all the relationships that co-create me. This personal awareness is a lifelong process, possible only through my openness to others and their presence. My goal is to develop self-possession within a profound relationality, to become a self-in-relation. All that I encounter becomes part of the fabric of my being.

Both body and spirit are continuous creations, not given substances or things. The person and the cosmos are and always have been in process of being made; the full meaning of the human person is found, not in a complete structure or essence, but in a personal history or process of becoming. Every person thus aims at being someone, at realizing some unification of the self with other things and with the world. How my feelings, thoughts, and physical awareness are shaped depends on the world into which I am born and the way I include it in my becoming.

In this movement toward selfhood, all of the human loves and the divine love play a role, interacting in mysterious ways. Whatever takes hold of my becoming and enters into it is present in some way — the family I grew up with, the friends I have made, the qualities of the country in which I live, the ideas I encounter in books and classes, the values I learn to appreciate. Openness to God, as I shape the welter of relationships in my life into a self, enables the self I am creating to approach closer to the beauty God envisages for it.

God's presence in my life can be described as a persuasive lure, a power that operates as love does, by drawing me closer to its object. Present in this way, God calls creation forward on all levels. Process thought finds that this presence is conveyed in the image of God as the Poet of the World. Just as a poet draws out our response by presenting a compelling vision of reality, so God exercises tender patience in leading us to the divine vision of truth, beauty, and goodness. God's power operates even on levels of life where consciousness is not present, but it is in *human* life that the purposes of God are most deeply augmented or frustrated, since it is in human life that the fullest freedom exists. Humanity has the greatest opportunity to manifest God's presence.

God calls each of us out of lesser patterns of growth and to a greatness we would not ourselves envisage. Like a mirror, God's presence shows each creature its possibilities for greatness. The divine call is toward interest in a wider good, toward a larger self; if we are open to God's purpose in our lives, we should find ourselves moving beyond narrow interests. This is the way the New Testament depicts the reign of God — as a vision of human wholeness for which we are willing to relinquish everything — our possessions, our security, even our view of ourselves as holy.

God's power operates in each person's life through a stream of conditions and events, processes and powers which we only vaguely attend to on a conscious level. Sometimes we become aware how the sudden death of a friend, the chance comment of an acquaintance, or a story that appears in the news enlarges the scope of our love and our life's direction. But the divine purposes are largely hidden from view. Since this touch of God comes at the deepest levels of who we are, centering prayer which takes us into our inner selves can be an important part of seeking to know God's will.

Within such an understanding of God's will, the specifics of following God flow from my deepest longings, my relationships, my health and financial situation, my previous commitments, and the political and cultural context in which I live. God's call is always historically incarnate; it is addressed to the actual situation in which I find myself.

Though we sometimes get stuck trying to know whether God wants us, for example, to work with the handicapped or to work for the homeless, to write or to teach, there is needless anxiety here. God has not decided these things for us. They are matters of our choice; God merely wants us to seek the good. Finding God's will is not a matter of discovering a previously determined plan; it is rather a process of making the best creative choice we can make within our circumstances.

For example, a young woman is struggling to know what career choice would be in keeping with God's wishes for her. She is a shy and quiet person, generally uncomfortable with her adult relationships. On the other hand, she comes alive in the presence of children and can never remember a time when she has not loved being around them. When it is suggested to her that she make these part of her prayer and decision-making, she comes to a peaceful and joyous choice of a career teaching young children, convinced that this is both something that will lead to happiness and something fully in keeping with God's purpose for her. The confidence and improved image of self that come from this work gradually enable her to begin the process of healing her adult relationships with family and friends.

What spiritual growth does is expand the range and depth of my love and my capacity for relationships. It enables me to retain my integrity while incorporating greater contrasts into my life. I can experience and encourage diversity and uniqueness in others without feeling defensive and insecure. In this spiritual vision, I can rejoice when others succeed, seeing their success not as my diminishment but as an enrichment both of me and of the web of existence which sustains us both.

In a world view where reciprocity and mutual responsibility are the norm, becoming adult takes on new meaning. No longer is it equated, as it so often has been in our society, with becoming an independent and solitary individual. Rather, adulthood now requires that we reject both dependence and independence and embrace interdependence. To grow in maturity is to relate more fully with all of life. Interdependence is not something to be feared but an experience we all share as we mutually give and receive from one another.

Discernment of God's will requires careful attending to the reality of our lives as they change and develop. God's purpose is revealed only gradually, since it is a direction and not a final plan. It takes into account all of my responses along the way, responses which influence God's succeeding call for me.

Although we cannot know with certainty that a particular action is God's will, there are criteria for evaluating our Christian choices. As the New Testament authors stress repeatedly, we know that we are dwelling in God's love if we live according to the pattern of Jesus' life, since he is "the image of the invisible God, the first-born of creation" (Col 1:15). Christ gives concrete expression to the ideal toward which God is calling creation. Jesus is described as the path or door that leads to the deeper realities; he reveals the goal of the process of becoming, what it means at the most fundamental level to live in terms of who God is and what humanity is. In Jesus we see how we are to view every situation in terms of God's vision of beauty and truth. We know our humanity in looking forward to the new creation we are to become in view of the possibilities released into the world in the event of Jesus Christ. The vision of Jesus makes people whole, healthy, and strong. Jesus restores people's humanity and life.

The Christian tradition has offered another criterion for evaluating Christian decisions. As expressed by Ignatius of Loyola, confirmation of a choice comes in the form of God's peace, a deep sense of rightness about our choice. Process thinkers would emphasize certain qualities of this peace. Since it results from the experience of God, the peace that accompanies a decision should not only calm turbulence and preserve the sources of our energy; it also bears a quality of movement and expansiveness. We sense that in our decisions we have not escaped life's risks, but rather have found in God the will and power to meet them. In addition, the experience of peace should open us to the larger community, to wider sympathies. Our choices are judged, then, by the way they have enlarged our powers and led to growth in the love of humanity as such. In making choices we are able to remain open to God's purpose while at the same time taking seriously our own aspirations and freedom. This is so because God's purpose is the fullness of both the individual's and the world's potential. It is the divine Poet's vision of truth, beauty, and goodness.

The biblical understanding of sin fits well with this view of Christian growth. In the story of Adam and Eve the entry of sin into the world is portrayed as a breakdown of relationships — of human persons with God, with one another, and with nature. This rupture of relatedness finally culminates in the murder of brother by brother in the account of Cain and Abel. Sin, then, is our refusal to honor the circles of interdependence that support life. It is a refusal to relate. This happens, for example, in our oppression of others because of gender, race, or class; in our destruction of the ecosphere, and in our movement toward nuclear disaster. Redemption, in contrast, is described as reconciliation, as New Creation. Healing is the attempt to restore the nature of relationships to the way they ought to be lived.

This interpretation of sin acknowledges the solidarity of human existence. Our choices have consequences for others and ultimately for the whole social fabric. We ourselves are affected by the tragic situation human beings have created through accumulated decisions. In our decade we are perhaps most aware of this in terms of the cycles of violence perpetuated in our families and communities, where those who have been victims of violence and abuse go on to damage others. Human solidarity has created a state where the selection of the true good is often very difficult; there is a deep tendency to select apparent goods which do not satisfy the human yearning for happiness and wholeness. This social nature of both sin and grace underlies the importance of systems in our spiritual lives, the final topic we will explore in this chapter.

THE ROLE OF SYSTEMS IN OUR SPIRITUALITY

The recognition of systems is an outgrowth of an interdependent world view. We exist and choose as parts of our lives from those broader networks of persons to which we belong: marriages, families, churches, political establishments, economies, institutions of all kinds. A system is like a mobile; when one part of it is touched, all parts are moved. In a system the parts necessarily become changed by their mutual association;

systems are dynamically interacting parts. Thus they have a profound influence on the lives and decisions of their members.

Because a system has an identity larger than the individuals that comprise it, we speak of a sinful system or, in turn, of a system mediating grace to us. Perhaps this can be best understood by beginning with a small system, a friendship or marriage. Friendships and marriages have an identity that goes beyond the individual personalities of the two persons involved. The current focus on co-dependence has helped us understand how this is so. In a healthy friendship the actions of the two persons support self-esteem and creativity in one another. In Christian terms, we speak of their being grace for one another. In a co-dependent marriage the two share the same sickness. An alcoholic individual, for example, is not the only one who suffers from the disease of alcoholism; the whole marriage suffers from it. In interpreting a friendship or marriage in this way, we look not only at its individual members, probing for the sources of health or illness within them. Rather, we focus on their patterns of interactions. How do they express affection and anger? How do they get their needs met and respond to the needs of the other?

Likewise in speaking of a family that is dysfunctional for any reason, we are referring not just to the individuals in that family, but to the family dynamics. A family may consist of husband, wife, and children — the traditional nuclear family — or it may be composed of a broader range of relatives, of people supporting one another who are not blood relatives, of single parents raising children. Whatever its constellation, a family is also a system, and all of its members exercise mutual influence on the spirituality of each member. This influence continues long after they stop living together physically. This means that many of our gifts and strengths come from our families, as well as many of the problems we are attempting to solve and the limitations we are trying to overcome.

This insight into family systems is a way of recognizing the power which the past has over our present. It continues to be the matrix for present choices. One spiritual task is finding new possibilities in the givenness of this past. We need to be open to God in our lives as a source of newness and healing.

Systems touch our lives on an even larger level and have become an urgent concern for contemporary spirituality. We live not only within marriages and families; we also belong to churches, cities, and nations. In addition there are political and economic networks to which we contribute and which influence our lives. Just as sin and grace are embedded in our family systems, so are they mediated by these other systems. It is not enough, then, for me to be concerned with my own prayer life and personal path to virtue. I cannot say that I love God and my neighbor if I remain indifferent to the structures that determine people's lives. I must direct my attention and energy to the redemption of these systems. Since this work is tough to tackle alone, I need the support of others in this effort. Together we need to analyze structural dynamics and develop strategies for action.[2]

We cannot direct our energies to all systems at once. There is hope, however, in the knowledge that they are themselves interconnected. In our time, anti-hunger activists and peace and justice advocates are increasingly aware of the interlocking nature of war and hunger. We are recognizing the common ground of all oppression. This means we need only enter at some point in the movement, and our efforts will link with those of others to strengthen their momentum. When presented with the evil of human systems, it is possible to despair. Systems resist change. Only a deep conviction that grace as well as sin can touch them, will sustain our efforts. Concern with systems is one of the ways we recognize our power to hurt and heal each other. The life in the midst of death, which is the Gospel promise, arises within these connections.

The more fully we enter into the struggle to transform structures and systems, the more deeply do we realize what it means to view the spiritual life in terms of growth and change. We continue to hope, though our hopes are never fully realized. We search for direction in situations that are ambiguous and conflict-ridden. We celebrate incomplete victories and partial successes. We learn, as Alfred North Whitehead has said, that the worship of God is not a rule of safety. It is, rather, an adventure of the spirit. [3]

ENDNOTES

[1] My summary is based on Alfred North Whitehead, *Process and Reality* (New York: The Macmillan Co., 1978), and *Religion in the Making* (New York: World Publishing Co., 1960).

[2] For help in analyzing systems, see Joe Holland and Peter Henriot, S.J., *Social Analysis. Linking Faith and Justice* (Washington DC: The Center of Concern, 1983).

[3] See *Science in the Modern World* (New York: The Macmillan Co., 1967) 192.

Chapter 5

Spirituality and Contemporary Culture

Joan Chittister, O.S.B.

Somewhere there reads the following definition of an American: "Americans are people who are born in the country, where they work with great energy so they can live in the city, where they work with even greater energy so that someday they can live in the country again." Right or wrong, the definition has a great deal to say about the relationship between culture and spirituality — about what you do with what you are — and why you do it.

Two pieces of religious literature indicate with special clarity the essential connectedness of spiritual maturity and cultural consciousness. The first comes from Exodus 3:18. "On Horeb," the Scripture tells, "the angel of Yahweh appeared to Moses in the shape of a flame of fire, coming from the middle of a bush. There was the bush, blazing, but it was not being burnt up 'I must go and look at this strange sight,' Moses said, 'and see why the bush is not burnt.' Now Yahweh saw him go forward to look and God called to him from the middle of the bush. 'Moses,' he said, 'come no nearer. Take off your shoes, for the place where you are is holy ground.' And then Yahweh said, 'I have seen the miserable state of my people in Egypt. I have heard their appeal to be free. I am well aware of their sufferings. I mean to deliver them. So, I'm sending you to Pharaoh to bring my people out....'"

The message is a dramatic one. Just at what would seem to be the moment of Moses' total immersion in the presence of God, God stops Moses where Moses is, to teach him that his holiness depends on finding holiness where he stands and then by taking that energy to other people for their liberation. Moses learns that holiness is made of virtues, not of visions; Moses learns that holiness depends on being for the other; Moses learns that holiness depends on being about something greater than the self; Moses learns that holiness is being present to the presence everywhere it is and even where it seems it isn't.

The second story of culture and spirituality comes from the tales of the Hasidim. An old rabbi of great wisdom, whose fame had spread beyond his own congregation to villages and rabbis far on the other side of the mountains, one day, suddenly, died. The young rabbis were bereft. "Now," they said, "what shall we do when our people look to us for guidance? Without the old master, where shall we get the answers to the great questions of life?" So they decided among themselves to pray and fast until the old man's holiness and wisdom would be infused into one of them. And sure enough, one night in a dream, the old man appeared to one of the younger rabbis. "Master," the young teacher said, "it is good that you have returned. Now, with you gone, the people look to us for answers to the great questions of life and we are still unsure. For instance, Master, they demand to know 'On the other side, of what account are the sins of youth?'" "The sins of youth?" the old man asked. "Why, on the other side the sins of youth are of no account whatsoever." And the young rabbi said, "On the other side the sins of youth are of no account whatsoever? Then, what has it all been about? On the other side, what sin is punished, if not the sins of youth?" And the old man answered slowly and clearly, "On the other side, that sin which is punished with constant and unending severity is the sin of false piety."

The point is clear: Piety is cultural. Holiness depends on our choosing the pieties proper to the times. Culture and spirituality, in other words, are of a piece. As Moses and the old master both knew, the function of spirituality is not to protect us from our times; the function of spirituality is to enable us to leaven it, and stretch it, and bless it, and break it open to the present will of God.

Well, if culture is the way people think and feel and behave as a people, and spirituality is the way we live out the life and teachings of Jesus in this particular culture, at this particular time, then the question for us must become: What cultural realities are challenging the Gospel now, and how can the Gospel best challenge the culture if we, here, now, are really to be a holy people? The history of spirituality identifies three basic responses to culture: the intellectual, the relational, and the performative.

An *intellectual spirituality*, as the scholars define it, is a spiritual life that is creed-centered and concerned with beliefs and committed to union with God. An intellectualist spirituality is good at drawing denominational lines and identifying heretics and maintaining orthodoxy and having personal mystical experiences. The intellectualist wants to stay and contemplate the bush.

A *relational spirituality* is committed to the development of human bondedness as the preeminent model of the Christian life. The relationalist talks a lot about love and the relationalist is willing to stay in Egypt if necessary, bush or no bush, to keep the slaves company in their pain.

Finally, *performative spirituality* is action-centered. Performers in the spiritual life are "Our Father" people. They pray every day, "Thy kingdom come, Thy will be done" and then they do something to bring it about. Performers are people who know that the word is incomplete until it has become transforming action. Performers would prefer to reform Egypt — by carrying the burning bush back there.

The question for us is, what is our cultural situation now? And which type of spirituality is most needed and how do we build it?

Let's look briefly at the cultural situation in the United States from 1960-1988, the era that has formed the spiritual life of most of us. In this period, we have experienced major shifts in the national belief-value system. Family patterns have changed, sex roles have changed, and governments that talked freedom and justice and human rights have been riven with one corruption after another and so became daily less and less credible. The most dramatic transformation of world view that ever took place in human history has taken place in this period. John Glenn, the first American astronaut, took, from outer space, the only picture of the planet that had ever been taken. And he took it with a $45.00 camera that he bought at the local drugstore just before the trip. Up until that moment, the human view of earth and its place in the universe had never been anything else but theory and speculation and educated calculations. Up until that moment, you and I knew where we lived only on the basis of artistic guesses. Now, for the first time in history, we could really see ourselves in all our grandeur — and in all our smallness.

This generation, too, saw scientific progress that was often more threat than help. In these few years, science changed life, changed death, changed family, changed sex, changed birth. And changed war from struggle to annihilation. Until, finally, science has managed, in our generation, to change the very meaning of "meaning." In this era, military security became our highest priority, our greatest expenditure, and our scarcest commodity. Thanks to our "military security," indeed, we have created the end of the world, and we are storing it in the cornfields of Kansas.

In this age, too, we have seen new interest in the wisdom of the East as the wealth of the West lost its power to save. American dominance, isolation, and perfect security ended with the launching of Sputnik. And the rise of a Third World, with its commitment to neutrality, challenged the U.S. notion of its "Manifest Destiny," to be the "city on the hill," "the new Eden," "the covenanted people," as never before in U.S. history.

In this same time frame, integration challenged white supremacy. And feminism challenged the white male system and even the white male god.

And great poverty in the midst of great affluence — the working poor —
this very moment challenges all the American myths ever made about fair
play, and blessing and the Protestant ethic and the American dream and
freedom and justice for all.

And all of this has happened in a society where 10% of the world —
Western Europeans and North Americans — consume, hoard, waste or control two-thirds of the resources of the world. Indeed, social consensus on
values and beliefs has broken down. The annual survey of college freshmen, sponsored by the American Council on Education and the University
of California, finds that in the midst of all of this, unlike their predecessors,
this year's college freshmen are less concerned about pollution, more
approving of abortion, less opposed to the death penalty, more intent on
cohabitation before marriage, less committed to the elimination of racism,
less obligated to help others in difficulty, less interested in environmental
clean-up and control, considerably less concerned about developing a philosophy of life, and extremely more interested in being "very well off
financially."

And all of this while the government spent only $0.20 of every dis-
posable dollar, minus entitlements, in 1987 on human resources — education, employment, job training, social services, health, and fiscal assistance
— but spent $0.64 of every tax dollar Congress has the authority to dis-
tribute on the military.

Indeed, we need spiritual-cultural revitalization. Indeed, the consensus of old values has broken down. Indeed, the spirit is dying in the most
church-going nation in the world. Indeed, the current spiritual-cultural
dilemma looms large. Individualism infects every institution; individualism
has been raised to the point of high art; individualism erases the Trinitarian
model of life in common; individualism runs rampant — to the point of the
pathological — in this society at a time, in fact, when global community is
urgent if both this planet and its peoples are to be saved.

Our current spiritual dilemma, then, lies in how to link the personal
with the public dimensions of life; how to make private spirituality the stuff
of public leaven in a world fiercely private and dangerously public at the
same time. The fact is that simple spiritualities of creed and community and
cooperation are no longer enough. We need now, surely, a spirituality of
contemplative co-creation if the culture is to be Christianized. No — if
Christians are to be Christianized. Genesis insists that the function of
humanity is to nurture and cultivate and care and procreate and have
dominion over. Carrying on God's work in the world is, in other words,
"the spiritual life."

And what does religion have to do with all of that? When culture is in
chaos and society is in upheaval, it may be important to look for a moment

at the process of social revitalization. The anthropologist Anthony F.C. Wallace teaches that major transformations of thought and behavior happen in a society when society discovers that a common set of religious understandings have become impossible to sustain. At that point, Wallace says, the society begins to undergo a "revitalization movement" of four major stages.

Stage one is a period of serious individual stress. In this stage, people begin to question past values and start to establish new patterns of thought and behaviors. They don't think about things as they once thought about things. What the generation before them took for granted, they begin to debate and discard.

In stage two, wide-reaching social stress becomes apparent. What we once called our culture is now barely recognizable, and people begin to decide that their problems aren't personal. Their problems, they decide, are a result of failure in the anchor institutions they had depended on for stability and direction. The churches are out of tune with their need; the schools remote from their life questions; the government corrupt and corrupting. There is political rebellion in the streets, and schism in the churches.

In stage three, though people as a whole recognize a problem, they can't agree on how to cope with this new social situation. Some want to change the system; some want to send in the troops. And they quarrel and divide and blame authority.

Then, inevitably, in stage three of a revitalization movement, a nativist or traditionalist movement arises. Nativists argue that the danger has come from the failure of the people to adhere more strictly to old beliefs and values and behavior patterns. They want the "old time religion," and they find scapegoats aplenty. The economy would be all right if it weren't for unions; marriages would be all right if it weren't for feminism, and the country would be fine if it weren't for communism.

In the fourth, and final, stage of a revitalization movement, Wallace points out, comes the building of a new world view and the restructuring of old institutions to enable it. In simpler societies, the leadership for this rebuilding of the society usually came from a single charismatic person. "And Moses intervened," Psalm 89 reminds us, "and you, O God, turned aside your destruction." In more complex cultures, like our own, multiple spokespersons are needed to lead the people to new understandings about old values. The role of these spiritual leaders is not to repudiate the older world view entirely, but to shed new light on it so that it can be remembered that God's Spirit manifests itself always in new ways to meet new needs. Then, more flexible people begin to understand the experiment with the new consensus so that cultural transformation — the movement from death to life — of an entire people begins to happen.

Finally, not the older generation, not the sojourners who brought old ideas and goals and values and designs from one desert to another with them, but the generation that "grew up with" the emerging insights, the generation that spent their life wandering in the desert and knew no others, comes to maturity. And old institutions find themselves with new leadership. And the institutions are restructured, provided that someone brings them up with the new questions and new insights.

And how do we know it can happen? Because in this country alone we have seen one generation withdraw their allegiance to a king, and the next abolish slavery, and the one after that regulate businesses, and the last empower laborers and this one, now, here, beginning to struggle for liberation and equality and survival." And Moses intervened," the Psalm teaches, "and you turned aside your destruction." What God saves, in other words, God saves through us. Just as God did with Sodom and Gomorrah and Mordechai and Esther and Isaac and Jacob and Joseph and the Pharaoh and every requester of miracles in the New Testament.

We need to intervene for one another. We need a new world view that puts the old one "in new light." But how? And where will this "spirituality of contemplative co-creation" come from in an individualistic culture? And in what way can the religious leaders of our time help to build this bridge from privatized piety to public moral responsibility? I suggest that, we begin to look at the bases of social brokenness; that we ourselves begin to see the spiritual link between the personal and the political, I'm suggesting that we build programs that look again at the seven capital sins, but this time on two, rather than on simply one, level. The level of personal, yes. But the level of the global as well.

Envy on the personal level is certainly a lack of acceptance of self which leads, in its sinful form, to a rejection of others. But at the global level, isn't it ethnocentrism as well? When we uphold criminal governments for our own good rather than recognize the needs of the people of the country, when we impose our values and structures in return for trade, isn't that a form of envy and its failure to accept a thing for what it is?

Pride is, of course, the need to dominate and coerce others on the personal level. But on the global level, isn't it also the mania for national superiority, for being numero uno, for having the best of everything?

Lust is clearly the exploitation of another for the sake of physical satisfaction. We are beginning to recognize it when it's date rape or pornography or selfish sensuality, true, but is there yet enough conscience in us also to see lust as the national passion for the instantaneous gratification that justifies the exploitation of whole peoples so that we can have the cheap cash crops and conveniences we demand that rape their lands and loot their futures? Isn't it the exploitation that comes from lust that leads to the feminization of poverty and the loss of feminine resources and values in a world that is reeling from the institutionalization of masculine values?

Gluttony, the overconsumption of food, leads to waste and bloatedness and misuse of resources on the personal level. But it is also surely at the base of the lack of distribution of surplus to the dying in Ethiopia and the farmers in the Soviet Union. Someone wrote of this culture, "We do not have a war on poverty; we have war on poor people." And what are we Christians doing about it?

We speak of covetousness as a lack of a sense of "enough," and we know that on the personal level that leads to the sinful brink of hoarding or an inordinate desire for unnecessary possessions. But what is the difference between that kind of covetousness and the demon that fuels a suicidal arms race in the quest for superiority?

Anger we recognize as the cultivation of an eschatological sense of righteousness and judgment, of putting ourselves in the place of the patient justice of God. And we teach with conviction about the danger of assuming the right to convict and punish the other. "Vengeance is mine; I will repay," we remind one another. But what has happened to the national moral fiber when whatever evil we say of the Soviet Union is counted as virtue; what about the sin of demonizing our enemies, or our refusal to sign the Geneva arms accord agreements or our inability as a nation to hear the other meaning of "human rights"?

We abhor sloth, in its assumption that anyone has the right to live off the efforts of others, in its laziness and lack of responsibility. But where is Christian leadership in the building of a new world view about the sinfulness of multi-national structures which live off the backs of the poor or give unjust wages and benefits or take the unequal treatment of women for granted, and absorb women's lives at lesser pay for the convenience of others, and then moralize about that kind of domestic servitude? And all in the name of "God's will" for us.

And we go on blindly in our search for goodness. We collect garbage to keep our yards clean, not because the earth was not made to absorb those materials. We turn down the heat to save money, not resources. We car pool because of lack of parking spaces, rather than a lack of personal need or a chance to help another. We counsel and educate for individuality and autonomy and control and independence and security and suicidal defense in a world that needs community and mutuality and cooperation and interdependence and human responsibility and contemplative co-creation. We build small shelters for the homeless and huge rockets to make people homeless. And we go to church. And we go to church. And we go to church.

Yet 70% of all the respondents to a survey conducted by the Williamsburg Charter Foundation, a non-sectarian organization concerned with religion in U.S. public life, said in January 1988, that "It is important that the president have strong religious beliefs and that religion has a place in public life." Well, where is that public religion in private life supposed to come from? When Jacob saw Joseph in Egypt, he said, "Now that I know you live, I can die." And God said to Moses, "Stay where you are. Where you are is holy ground."

Clearly, the role of the spiritual life today is, like Jacob, not to die until we have assured a dynamic and meaningful spirituality for the next generation. It is, like Moses, to recognize where we are as the ground of God's grace. It is certainly to enable us to see life differently so that God's reign can happen in our time.

Chapter 6

An Integrated Spirituality

Corita Clarke, R. D. C.

THE PROCESS OF ONGOING CONVERSION

The challenge of our human, spiritual lives is to become integrated persons. A spirituality for ministry is one which furthers our development in ways that enable us to become holy and whole. Our holiness, as Paul reminds us, is God's desire and God's work in us (1 Th 4:7). We are, in the words of Bernard Lonergan, invited to "a fated acceptance of a vocation to holiness" (Lonergan 240). This acceptance and surrender is the effect of our awareness of God's great, unconditional love for us. The process is one of ongoing conversion, our gradual transformation as we live and pray and minister to and with one another.

Conversion has been described as a subtle "turning" more and more toward God. It involves a change of consciousness which provides an alternative vision or perspective on our life and our world. There are times when this may seem to be caused by a sudden impact, as William Johnston implies when he suggests that two conditions for conversion are a shock and a period of solitude. But the invitation is also present in the seemingly normal conditions of our everyday experience.

The challenge to grow in awareness and *to be really free* is ongoing. It requires honest, attentive listening and authentic struggle before God in prayer and with God in activity. It is easy to agree that love ought to show itself in deeds, but how can we be sure we are really loving and growing as loving persons? We can opt for a just and countercultural life style, but there are then decisions to be made daily as to how to be faithful to this vision.

The paradigm for our journey of conversion is the Paschal Mystery of Jesus. The disciple is called to die on one level in order to rise on another level, to enter into and live the experience of Jesus. This involves a willingness to let go of our control over our lives and to let God lead. It is an acknowledgement that, as Karl Rahner has said, God is addressing us in every situation in our lives. It is much more God's work in us than what *we do*, yet it involves openness to God's Presence in everything and our willingness to respond to the small, and at times, great invitations in each moment. It involves conscious choices that are consistent with our vision of faith.

Living the Paschal Mystery as an inevitable dimension of discipleship involves the Cross. The goal is not self-fulfillment but self-transcendence which comes through love and is often the effect of suffering. Suffering is not sought nor is it a value in itself. Yet it is precisely in moments of pain, disintegration, and breakdown that there can be the possibility for reintegration and breakthrough. Crisis points in life, moments of frustration, disillusionment, darkness, finitude, rejection, etc., can be moments of grace. We are forced to stop, to come back to the source of our life, the roots of our faith, to recognize our finiteness and our dependence on God. We are stripped of our illusions and learn what our real security is and what really matters. We are united to the sufferings of Jesus and with the suffering of the body of Christ throughout the world in this historical moment.

Spiritual writers of our day, as well as those who have preceded us, have spoken of the grace of the Cross in different ways. Pierre Teilhard de Chardin, S.J. speaks of the "divinization of our passivities." James Fowler writes of the "sacrament of defeat." Dietrich Bonhoeffer stresses the "cost of discipleship" and proclaims that there is no "cheap grace." John Futrell, S.J. writes of the passive purifications of our life as God's hollowing us so that we can rely more on God and less on our own resources. In his words:

> Growth in apostolic holiness is a life time process of being hollowed out by the Lord so that his own life of love can fill us with his peace and joy, which will reach other people in proportion to the hollowing. The hollowing is for his presence. Only when all barriers of self-seeking and self-love in our lives and in our apostolic service have been let go we can be filled fully with his presence... (Futrell 12)

The experience of darkness can be in our prayer or in our active lives, or as Constance Fitzgerald, O.Carm., has recently explored, it can be endemic to our culture, a kind of "societal dark night" (Fitzgerald). If we are going to reach a level of integration, we need to name our experience and stay with it in trust. The great virtue here is poverty of spirit. It involves obedience as we listen to where God is in what we are experiencing. It is often prayer in the darkness, in which we stay in faith and hope, learn to surrender, and allow ourselves to be broken open so that new life can emerge. Like the Emmaus disciples, we need to learn that the Cross is part of the story, but not the whole story. We can grow in union with God and in authentic freedom through this process of conversion, which Lonergan insists is possible when I fall in love with God who has loved me before I knew it. It is all God's doing!

ELEMENTS WHICH AID INTEGRATION

As I have indicated, integration does not just happen by our living through different experiences. The more that ministers can be assisted in articulating their experience and in becoming more consciously reflective, the greater will be the degree of unity and meaning in their lives. I will now indicate some specific elements of a spiritual life that should be presented to and explored with ministers in order that at least some of these could become valuable components of their personal lives. These elements are merely outlined here.

1. **Journaling** — Journaling can be very simple, or can be more detailed and complex, such as the method proposed by Ira Progoff in the *Life Context Workshop*. It can be a reflection on one's prayer, on one's daily life, or both. In spite of some initial hesitation or resistance, most people who are guided in the process of journaling find it beneficial. As one reflects in order to write, one taps into a deeper sub-conscious awareness, and in the act of writing, releases this awareness and brings it to consciousness. Very often it is at this deeper level that God is moving us, bringing clarity, and challenging us to grow. A journal can help us to notice patterns and can become a record of how God has been keeping his promises in our life. Soren Kierkegaard has noted that "our lives are lived forward and understood backwards." Journaling can be a tool which assists this self-understanding and contributes to the fuller integration of prayer and life.

2. **The Awareness Examen** — In 1972, George Aschenbrenner, S.J. promoted a contemporary understanding and adaptation of the examen taught by Ignatius Loyola. In his article "Consciousness Examen," he stresses the value of the daily process as a way to grow in awareness of God's invitations in one's life experiences, and indicates how this method is a form of discernment of spirits. The five steps in the examen: thanksgiving, prayer for the light of the Spirit, practical survey of actions, contrition and sorrow, and hopeful resolution for the future are all in the context of prayer. The goal is a deeper awareness of our identity before God in faith and a consciousness of the graces and invitations in every moment. It is a tool which can lead to a mysticism of action and service. Other Jesuit writers have expanded on Aschenbrenner's work and illustrated how the examen can be a profitable mode of theological reflection. Some of these articles will be listed at the conclusion of this chapter.

3. **Spiritual Direction** — There is a renewed contemporary interest in this very old tradition of spiritual guidance. Today it may be called "spiritual companioning" as persons agree to walk and share their faith journey with another. The director is primarily a listener and a co-discerner. The goals for the directee include articulation, awareness, clarification and at times, decision-making. Spiritual direction may be helpful as an ongoing

support in one's life of faith or as a process and relationship entered into at a specific time for a specific goal. It is important for those seeking to grow in prayer, for those in times of spiritual crisis, for those involved in choices or crucial decisions. It can prove very helpful to ministers to have someone with whom to reflect on their ministerial experience and its relationship to their own lives. Spiritual direction aims at assisting growth toward maturity in faith and the fullness of life Jesus promised.

4. **Discernment** — This is a "spiritual art," a quality, a habit, a virtue, and at times, a personal or communal process for decision-making. All of the elements just mentioned, journaling, the awareness examen, and spiritual direction, can assist a person in developing a discerning heart. It requires reflection and sensitivity to the leading of the Spirit and the inner movements of affectivity developed over time. Ignatius' *Rules for the Discernment of Spirits* are helpful and have been made accessible and relevant for contemporary spirituality by writers like George Aschenbrenner, S.J., John English, S.J., Thomas Green, S.J., and others. Discernment presupposes a willingness to be led by the Spirit as Jesus was. It is a unique mode of prayer that integrates both prayer and action and promotes growth in authentic response to God.

5. **Theological Reflection** — I would like to emphasize theolgical reflection as an essential element in assisting integration in the minister. The method of the Whiteheads is an excellent one to follow. However, there are variations on the model and other contemporary models. Ministers should be instructed in a model and practice using it in group exercises during the period of spiritual formation.

Ongoing theological reflection is essential for authentic ministry. In order to approach Jesus' total fidelity to the proclamation of the reign of God, we must keep asking the questions: Where is the Lord in this existential situation? Where is God leading? What does the Gospel have to say to this concern, today in this time and place?

6. **Summary** — Each of the experiences outlined in this section has, as one of its goals, awareness and growth in self-knowledge. Other such tools are available today with a similar goal, such as the Myers-Briggs Personality Inventory, the Enneagram, Focusing, and Dream Workshops. The approach and significance of these could also be shared in a formation program.

Most of the activities explored initially have an inward movement, but it is crucial to realize that the purpose of the movement within is to be able also to move outward in a more authentic way, in responsiveness to God's Presence and leading both within and without.

COMMUNITY

An essential element of Christian spirituality is community, and while that topic warrants a whole study in itself, it is important in rounding out this work to outline a few points. In particular, community forms a bridge between action and contemplation, and so taking time to reflect on the significance of community can also deepen the awareness of the interconnectedness of these spiritual realities. What follows is a brief reflection on community in the early Christian tradition, in the contemporary culture, and in the experience of present day ministers. Some of the reflection activities at the conclusion of this chapter will invite ministers into their own personal integration of the role of community in their lives.

CHRISTIAN TRADITION

Belief in a God who is Trinity of persons is a basic tenet of Christian faith. God is the name of the relationship in love of Father, Son, and Spirit. John tells us that "God is love" (1 Jn 4:8, 16), a statement which Michael and Kenneth Himes call "the most basic Christian metaphor for God" (Himes and Himes 138). The individual person, made in the image of the Triune God, is to find his or her own identity in relationship with others. So also the Church, the sacrament of Christ, is a communion of persons, the People of God, united in faith and in love. Avery Dulles' most recent model of the Church is a "community of disciples," drawn from the New Testament reflection on Jesus' life and ministry and on the experience of the early Church. Jesus himself gathered the first disciples, formed them, and sent them out together, not singly, to proclaim the good news of the Kingdom. It is within community that Christians can live out the injunctions of Jesus to his followers: "By this shall all know that you are my disciples, that you love one another" (Jn. 13:35). "If I, your Lord and Master, have washed your feet, so should you wash one another's feet" (Jn 13-14).

The early Church document, the *Dicache*, described four essential dimensions of the life of the Church: preaching and teaching (*kerygma*), community (*koinonia*), prayer and liturgy (*leitourgia*), and service (*diaconia*). All these were involved in building up the body of Christ, the Church. The various ministries of service were ministries to the community and flowed from the life of the community. Christians' communion with one another was itself a witness to God's love. Within community they could hold together the polarities of prayer and action (Acts 2:42-47).

Subsequent centuries present a history of Church development which varies greatly at times from the idyllic picture given in Acts. However, the goal of Christian community remains an essential component of Christianity. The development of ministry also is understood only in relationship to the community. Gifts and charisms are given to individuals for the service of the Christian community. Historical and cultural realities determine the needs of the community and affect the development of ministries in response to the leading of the Spirit.

COMMUNITY AND CONTEMPORARY CULTURE

The social sciences have enlarged our contemporary understanding of the importance of relationships and of community in the lives of individuals. They have thus, perhaps inadvertently, supported the insights from theology and experience of Christians. In the article previously cited, the Himes brothers state the mutual enrichment of the individual and the community in a Christian view:

> The individual and the community give life to one another: as the individual is more truly intelligent and free, more truly human and so more completely self-gift, the network of relationships in which the individual exists is furthered and enriched; the broader and deeper that network of relationships, the more truly human the community and the individual... Each relationship brings with it responsibilities. In order to carry out responsibilities, rights arise. The fundamental responsibility is to give oneself away as perfectly as possible. The fundamental right is the right to do so. (Himes and Himes 139)

The deep human desire for relationships in which one can both share oneself and be enriched by the sharing of others is noted often in contemporary psychology and sociology, yet at the same time the great difficulty Americans have in forming and sustaining community is evident. The impact of modern culture has had devastating effects on the personal and societal capacity to build and maintain enduring commitments. Robert Bellah and his associates in their perceptive study, *Habits of the Heart*, point out how the "rampant individualism" of our American culture has resulted in the breakdown of familial, ecclesial, and civic communities. Their call for a renewal of "communities of memory and hope" issues a crucial challenge to the Church, and impacts significantly on a spirituality for ministry (Bellah 152-155).

Community can exist in many forms, and individual persons can belong to several groups which provide significant relationships and a sharing of some dimension of life. It is important that expectations for community not be focused on one group of persons for all one's relational needs. Much of the dissatisfaction with community stems from unreal expectations or lack of awareness of the demands of authentic community. While more Americans are becoming aware that patterns of individualism and isolation in our culture do not lead to a meaningful life, many are unwilling to enter into the pain and struggle that are part of the growth into true community. This is true in family relationships, working situations, and ecclesial groups. Community involves a quality of presence to one another, a willingness to share oneself, to be open and thus, at times, vulnerable, and a consistent involvement in the life of the community. When shared ideals and purpose are the basis for community, the experience of shared living can be a great source of support and energy. At the same time, community can challenge and issue a call to authenticity and to sacrifice of personal desires for the good of the whole community. A willingness to give as well as to receive is an essential requirement for those seeking the richness of community.

COMMUNITY AND MINISTRY

A colleague of mine, Dick Westley, quotes Martin Buber as saying, "We expect a theophany of which we know only the place. And the place? The place is called community." [1] Westley uses Buber's insight himself to write of community as "the saving place." Ministers in the contemporary Church have the task of working to facilitate this saving place through their relationships, their service, and their everyday lives. It is through awareness and perception of God's presence in their midst and by personal presence to others that ministers can assist people in the discovery of this revelation, this theophany. In a similar vein, Henri Nouwen states:

> Community develops where we experience that something significant is taking place *where we are*. It is the fruit of the intimate knowledge that we are together not because of a common need... but because we are called together to help make God's presence visible in the world. Only to the degree that we have this knowledge of God's call can we transcend our own immediate needs and point together to him who is greater than these needs. (Nouwen 66)

Christian community witnesses to God's Presence in the living out of Gospel values. Loving, caring, serving, and supporting lead to self-transcendence and on-going transformation of the members. In shared faith, prayer and work, pain and struggle, success and failure, joys and sorrows, Christian community is the locus for God's saving actions. Our vision is expanded and our lives are enriched by the sharing and the challenges. The investment of oneself is both a privilege and a responsibility. Community, in its call to interdependence, is a place of personal, ongoing mutual formation and a witness to the coming of God's kingdom of love, peace and justice.

The Latin American theologian, Gustavo Gutierrez has written that:

> Community life cultivates receptivity for God's reign and also proclaims it; in this reception and proclamation a community builds itself up as a community. (Gutierrez 133)

Gutierrez reflects on the basic Christian communities that have developed in the Third World. We are also experiencing in the United States the powerful effect of such small communities that not only vitalize the members themselves, but also give new life to the larger community of the Church. From his own experience, Gutierrez points out the inter-relatedness of solitude and community. Solitude leads to the hunger for community, and the support of community is essential for one's own personal journey through the desert.

It is not so much *that* we live our lives together that is significant, but *how* we share life that can speak of the coming of the Kingdom in our midst. The actual experience is both difficult and rewarding. The authenticity of love, the reality of acceptance and belonging, the experience of forgiveness and reconciliation, all contribute to spiritual growth. The minister not only is called to facilitate this grace-filled environment, but is also energized by it for service. Ministers are invited into ministering to community, and also to ministering that flows from community.

There are situations today in which ministers are alone in their particular call to service. The dangers of isolation and loneliness are very real. Ministers should be encouraged to form a network of supportive relationships of peers, friends, and family, and to make definite scheduled times for being with significant others, even when it entails distance and some time away form the ministry situation. Also, in their ministerial setting, ministers, as disciples and persons who are called to be Church, have as a primary task, building community where they are. Robert Kinast writes of "occasion-centered communities" which are formed in the midst of shared action (Kinast 156). In his analysis of the role of lay ministers in the Church in the present and in the future, he defines the role as "caring for society," and he suggests that the effect will be the formation of "communities of those who care." Contemporary cultural realities challenge ministers to be creative in response to the possibilities for community.

Prayer is an important element of Christian community. The community will benefit from the contemplative prayer of the individual members, but the prayer of the community is also essential. Liturgical prayer is a prime source of a community's life. Both in liturgy and apart from liturgy, shared reflection on the Word of God in Scripture is key to the community's life and mission. Contemplation of the Word leads community members to call one another to faithfulness to the Word in action. In this sense, community is a link between prayer and action.

Communal prayer also flows from reflection on the ministerial action. Intercession is a natural response to the needs of others. Thanksgiving and praise reflect awareness of God's working in both ministry and community. Discernment in prayer is a necessity for determining direction for further action. Presence to one another and to God in communal prayer enables each member of the community to be a beneficial Christian presence wherever they are.

This section began with the idea that our vocation to Christian community came from our relationship to our Triune God. Trinitarian life is one of mutual self-gift in love. What does this call us to as we attempt to live in love and praise of our God? Robert Imbelli suggests that it means:

> celebrating the common life of God and contributing to the common life of humankind. Christian contemplation and action, Christian worship and mission, Christian sacrament and sacrifice all conspire toward their fulfillment in the blessed Name of the Triune God. From this Name they derive their inspiration: in this Name they achieve their integration — the in-breathing and out-breathing of Trinitarian Presence. In this Presence we are no longer strangers and aliens. We receive the freedom of the city and become fellow citizens of the saints. (Imbelli 233)

REFLECTION ACTIVITIES

1. Choose a Scripture passage that was significant for you in your past or present experience, at a particular moment of decision or a critical time. Be there, enter into the Presence of the Lord into the scene from the Gospel or whatever setting. Let the moment unfold again. What was the focus? Recall your feelings, the emotions associated with the time. What did you experience? learn? share with the Lord? What did you have to lose? What have to let go? What change or movement occurred within you? What did you gain? How were you enriched? Were you aware of a movement from unfreedom to liberation or healing? How was the Lord with you? How present? What did your heart know?

Stay there with the Lord and share your present feelings with him. Return to the Scripture passage. Does it still speak to you today? Is it where you are? Do you have any new insights or convictions?

Write down some of your reflections after this prayer time.

2. We say that our Christian life is one of ongoing conversion, of living out the Paschal Mystery of dying and rising. Recall a period of time in your life that you now see as a real conversion experience. Reflect on the process as you experienced it. Can you name the growth and new life you experienced? Where is God inviting you to grow now? What is the cutting edge?

3. What are your main supports for your ministerial life? From what "wellsprings" do you draw refreshment? Are there untapped resources you might explore?

4. What communities or groups do you belong to now? How do you experience the need for support from community? How has community

assisted your spiritual growth? How has community supported your outreach in ministry? Are there any further steps you might take regarding your participation in community?

5. Pray one of the following passages from Scripture: Psalm 138, Psalm 118, Isaiah 54:9-10, Ephesians 3:14-21. As you become aware of the blessings and gifts of your life, let your heart respond to God in gratitude and love.

6. Jesus said "I have come that they might have life and have it to the full." (Jn 10:10) In prayer, share with the Lord your desires for this fullness of life. Ask to see the obstacles to that fullness in you. Listen to what God wants to do for you, to be for you. Let God tell you!

ENDNOTES

[1] Martin Buber, quoted in Dick Westley, *A Theology of Presence* (Mystic, Ct.: Twenty-Third Publications, 1988) 64.

WORKS CITED

Aschenbrenner, S.J., George A. "Consciousness Examen." *Review for Religious* 31, (January 1972).

Bellah, Robert, et al. *Habits of the Heart: Individualism and Commitment in American Life.* Berkley: University of California Press, 1985.

Fitzgerald, O.C.D., Constance. "Impasse and Dark Night." *Living With Apocalypse: Spiritual Resources for Social Compassion* Ed. Edward H. Tilden. San Francisco: Harper and Row, 1984.

Futrell, S.J., John. "Growing Older Gracefully." *Human Development* 3.3, (Fall 1982): 12.

Gutierrez, Gustavo. *We Drink From Our Own Wells.* Maryknoll NY: Orbis Books, 1984.

Himes, Michael J., and Kenneth R. Himes. "Human Rights, Economics, and the Trinity." *Commonweal* 14 March 1986: 138

Imbelli, Robert. "Trinitarian Politics." *Review for Religious* 48 (March/April 1989): 233.

Kinast, Robert L. *Caring for Society.* Chicago: Thomas More Press, 1985.

Nouwen, Henri. *¡Gracias!* San Francisco: Harper and Row, 1983.

BIBLIOGRAPHY

1. *Conversion*

Fitzgerald, O.C.D., Constance. "Impasse and Dark Night." *Living With Apocalypse: Spiritual Resources for Social Compassion.* Ed. Tilden Edwards. New York: Harper and Row, 1984.

Futrell, S.J., John. "Growing Older Gracefully." *Human Development* 3. 3 (Fall, 1982).

Green, S.J., Thomas M. *When the Well Runs Dry.* Notre Dame IN: Ave Maria Press, 1979.

Johnston, S.J., William. *The Inner Eye of Love.* San Francisco: Harper and Row, 1978.

Robb, S.J., Paul V. "Conversion as a Human Experience." *Studies in the Spirituality of Jesuits*, May 1982.

2. *Reflectivity*

Aschenbrenner, S.J., George A. "Consciousness Examen." *Review for Religious* 31, No. 1 January 1972.

Haughey, S.J., John. "Hindsight, Prayer and Compassion." *Living With Apocalypse*: *Spiritual Resources for Social* Compassion. Ed. Tilden Edwards. New York: Harper and Row, 1984.

St. Louis, Donald. "The Ignatian Examen: A Method of Theological Reflection." *The Way*, Supplement No. 55, Spring, 1986.

3. *Community*

Foley, Gerald, and Timothy Schmaltz. *Laity in Community: Holiness of Ordinary Life.* Kansas City: Sheed & Ward, 1988.

Gutierrez, Gustavo. *We Drink From Our Own Wells.* Maryknoll NY: Orbis Books, 1984.

Kinast, Robert L. *Caring for Society.* Chicago: Thomas More Press, 1985.

Whitehead Evelyn E., and James D. Whitehead. *Community of Faith.* New York: Seabury Press: 1982.

Chapter 7

The Spirituality of the Minister

Thomas H. Groome

"Spirituality is a mysterious and tender thing, about which we can speak only with difficulty" (Rahner 143). So wrote Karl Rahner toward the end of his life with a wisdom that comes, I imagine, only with the years. Rahner's counsel seems especially appropriate for parish ministers. "Things spiritual" are our stock in trade, and we readily fall into the easy talk of any salesperson. We are more prone, however, to speak glibly about it for others and less likely to reflect on the kind of holiness asked of us by the very form of service that we render. Yet our attempts to be spiritual guides must surely be grounded in our own spiritual journeys. It is not possible to lead people out (e-ducare) religiously if we are not traveling in that direction ourselves.

The current spate of literature indicates that the spirituality of the minister is becoming a cutting-edge topic in our field, not indeed as a new issue for us but an old one rejoined with renewed vigor. [1] But the religions of the West have never had a tradition of the guru, and, if Rahner is any indication, it would seem that the older one gets the less likely one is to presume expertise on matters spiritual. On the other hand, all of us have been struggling along on our own spiritual journeys and hopefully allowing our praxis to both shape and be shaped by them. That praxis may well be our best resource of further insight and direction for the ongoing of the journey. I hope that the style with which these reflections are offered and the questions interspersed throughout will elicit your reflection upon your own praxis and your dialogue around this crucial issue for us — our own spirituality. I begin then with some focusing reflections to set the stage for our more particular theme. [2]

Spirituality is a most nebulous affair to define. Perhaps the nature of it belies the notion of a definition, but we need at least a "working description" to bring with us throughout these reflections. One description I appreciate is that of James Michael Lee who writes, "A person's spirituality is the way in which one mobilizes oneself religiously in the total and actual living out of one's daily activities" (Lee 7). While I could add dimensions to Lee's description, I appreciate it because at least it is holistic, practical, and historically oriented rather than confined, esoteric, and other-worldly — the latter being sentiments that people so often associate with "spirituality." [3]

> *You might want to pause here and ask yourself, What are my most basic sentiments and associations when I hear the word "spirituality?"*
> *What are some of the stories behind what the world elicits from you?*

With a description of spirituality as the way we mobilize ourselves religiously in our daily activities, we can recognize immediately that all the great religious traditions are calls to a spirituality of some kind; all of them sponsor their adherents to mobilize themselves religiously in their engagement with life and the world. Thus, people of all religious faiths are called to a spirituality. It is my intuition, too, that at a foundational level the various spiritualities promoted by the great religious traditions have a good deal of commonality among them. There is also a particularity, however, to the spirituality of each tradition, and I am convinced that the Christian, Jewish, and related traditions (e.g., Unitarian Universalism) share a common spiritual *modus operandi*. In these/our traditions of spirituality, we are called to be holy as our God is holy (see Lv 19:22). What then is the holiness of our God?

First, a central theme of our Scriptures and traditions is that God takes the initiative in love toward all humankind and is actively present in our lives and history with the best of intentions for us. Conversely, by that initiative God calls us into covenant with Godself and invites us to respond freely to God's loving initiative by living as God's people. Our spirituality arises from the divine/human encounter in history and invites a freely chosen (because true love always sets us free) and lived response to that encounter. There is a profound correlation, then, even a synonymy, between our spirituality and right living. It is also important to note here, because some of our particular communities would appear to have forgotten it at times, that spirituality and the call to holiness include all humankind; it is not only for an elite few. [4]

Second, our Scriptures and traditions make it clear that to live as God's people and thus to be holy means to live in right relationship with our God, with ourselves, and with each other. [5] The "holiness code" of Leviticus 19 opens by calling us to be holy as our God is holy but then proceeds to elaborate (19:3-37) that that means placing God first in our lives, living with love and justice toward our neighbor, and especially toward the downtrodden and marginalized of society, as toward ourselves (v. 34). But living in "right relationship" is also one of the biblical understandings of justice. In other words, the quest for justice and our spirituality cannot be separated. They are two sides of the same coin—our call to holiness of life.

We hear that oneness summarized in the Hebrew Scriptures with the beautiful words of Micah 6:8. The response that God asks of us—the spirituality to which we are called—is "only this, to act justly, love tenderly and walk humbly with our God." And in the Christian scriptures the heart of spirituality as right relationship is given a similar summary for us by Jesus in the Great Commandment: "You shall love the Lord your God with all your heart, with all your soul, with all your mind and with all your strength … You shall love your neighbor as yourself" (Mk 12:30-31). The very structure of both summary statements indicates that spirituality and justice—both being right relationship — can never be separated from each other.

Our traditions also reflect the conviction that it is only by living in such loving relationship with God, ourselves, and others that we not only become holy but also become whole. We become who we are called to become, people who are fully alive as the glory of God in whose image we are created. In the phrase of Josef Goldbrunner, then, "holiness is wholeness." Our spiritual journey is the lifelong process of saying yes to God, yes to our own best selves, yes to our neighbor with love that demands justice, and yes to our responsibility of doing God's will toward all creation.
What is your description of spirituality?
How do you understand the call to holiness within your own faith community?
What or who has most shaped your understanding of your spirituality and call to holiness?

COMING CLOSER TO HOME

All the members of our faith communities are called to a spirituality and holiness of life at least something akin to what I have described above. As members of those communities, we are so called as well. But now we must move even closer to home, to our identification within our faith communities as ministers. In our communities, we are somehow commissioned with and engaged in the task of sponsoring people, with God's help, into right relationship with God, themselves, and others. We must ask, then, does the service we render in our communities of faith give some particularity to the kind of holiness to which we are called? Does our praxis require of us and indeed form us in a spirituality that is uniquely ours? In other words, is there "a spirituality of the minister?" I believe there is, that the work we do demands a particular expression of holiness from us even as rendering that service may also be the best source for our own spiritual growth.

An anecdote: Recently I was asked a question that helped to deepen my awareness that in fact our own spirituality is at the very heart of who we are. The questioner was a young woman who, with little background in the field, was about to begin graduate studies in religious education at Boston College. She was intent on discovering how she might best prepare herself for what was now to be her chosen ministry. The context was a conversation with me as her academic advisor about course selection. I suggested a variety of courses in our curriculum from which she might choose. She seemed reluctant, however, to make choices. Finally, in what I later discerned to be her search for some principle of selectivity, she asked me, "But what do you think is at the heart of religious education?" I asked what she meant by "heart." She responded, "What really makes it happen—especially when it is done well."

     * *How do you respond to her question? Why?*
     * *What are some of the implications of your response?*

I knew that I could say "the grace of God" and be theologically accurate, but she was obviously asking the question from "our side" of the covenant. In that academic context I was first tempted to emphasize the importance of knowing the history, theory, and practice of religious education and the importance of some field experience. I considered the need for sound biblical and theological formation. I thought of the importance of her understanding the sociology of knowledge and the psychology of learning. All these resources and many more are important, I believe, to the success of the enterprise, but none of them nor all of them combined seemed to be the "heart" of it all. Eventually, having had many "idols" leveled by her question, came my response: "The heart of religious education is the heart of the religious educator." We both sensed that we had stumbled on the truth.

It is imperative, then, that we attend to our own spirituality and to the particularity of it as ministers. What then is this spirituality of the minister? What are its recognizable characteristics? What does it ask of our hearts?

     * *How do you name the characteristics of the holiness that is*
     required of you? You might want to take a piece of paper, pause a
     while, and complete this sense: For me, the spirituality of the minis-
     ter requires...

Some further questions:
     * *As you look at what is required of us spiritually, what are some of*
     the difficulties, problematics, and obstacles in your context to living
     into that kind of holiness?
     * *Why are the obstacles there and how can they be surmounted?*

OUR HEARTS AS THE HEART OF MINISTRY

To outline my own reflections on what is particular to the spirituality of the minister, I return to this metaphor of "heart." It seems a particularly appropriate one for us since we are ever engaged, by God's grace, in the spiritual process of enabling people to write the covenant "upon their hearts" (Jr 31:33), hearts, not of stone, but of flesh "that they will live according to my statutes, and observe and carry out my ordinances; thus they shall be my people and I will be their God" (Ez 11:20).

To me the metaphor of "heart" immediately suggests *passion, generosity, love,* and *commitment.* I will reflect on what these four dispositions require from the heart of the minister, thus indicating the kind of operative spirituality to which I believe we are called. You, of course, will add to these reflections from your own praxis.

PASSION: FOR THE PEOPLE

Our ministry requires from our hearts that we bring a deep passion and caring for the well-being of those we serve. Does our praxis have a humanizing effect in people's lives? Our ministry is to enable people "to make and keep life human" (Hannah Arendt's phrase). This requires of us a radical commitment to ministering in a humanizing way, in a way that promotes the wholeness of shalom and the fullness of life for all (see Jn 10:10).

This passion for the people requires primarily that we treat them as *subjects*, as responsible historical agents who are co-learners with us on their spiritual journey "home" to God. Treating them as subjects requires that we have a deep reverence for them as human beings.

That we treat our co-learners as subjects is not inevitable. Much of our prior socialization in ministry could lead us to presume that our students are "objects" who are to be formed (as good Catholics, Presbyterians, Orthodox Jews, or whatever), rather than as people who are to be subjects of their own faith and grow through right relationship in the faith community into their own unique identity before God. Indeed much of ministry in general would seem to be marked by an I/It relationship. To have a true passion for the life of our people requires that we relate to them as subjects, with an I/Thou (Buber) relationship of mutuality and respect between co-learners. Because of our socialization to the contrary, treating our co-learners as subjects calls us to constant vigilance and examination of consciousness (two necessary disciplines on any path to holiness) concerning the mode of our actual being with the people we minister to and with.

A spirituality whereby we relate to our co-learners as subjects and embody a passion for their life's well-being means, concretely, at least three things. First, to honor them as subjects we must invite them into dialogue with themselves, with ourselves, and with each other. This means providing opportunities that enable them to speak their own word, to name their own reality, to tell their own stories. Second, it means that we develop the discipline of listening to them, of truly hearing what they are saying both explicitly and "between the lines." And, this is my third point, the listening that honors them as subjects also requires confronting them in love, asking them critical questions that are consciousness-raising and that deepen the level of the dialogue, inviting them to imagine new possibilities beyond what they presently perceive. Without that kind of gentle challenging in love, we are failing to take them seriously as subjects.

    ** What are some of the implications of passion for the people for your ministry?*

GENEROSITY: THE GIFT OF HOSPITALITY

Hospitality is considered a virtue in all of our faith communities. We are to recognize the universality of God's love by giving genuine welcome to all who come among us. The hospitality required of the minister, however, pertains especially to the kind of environments that we create. These environments must be ones of true welcome and genuine openness, places where people can find that safety in space and time that promotes their own subjectivity, their coming into right relationship, and their discovering of God's presence in their lives. Padraic O'Hare has published a very fine essay, "Hospitality as a Paradigm For Youth Ministry," to which I am greatly indebted for the insights on hospitality here. With adaptation from O'Hare's categories, I believe we are asked to give the gift with generosity of psychological, intellectual, and ecclesial hospitality. [6]

Psychological Hospitality: O'Hare describes this as a "deep-struck spirit of acceptance and compassion for the groping pilgrim" and goes on to explain that it requires self-transcendence. I see such self-transcendence as a form of *kenosis*, the kind of self-emptying that Paul attributed to Jesus (Phil 2:7). It expresses itself as a form of empathy, an ability to "cross over," generously to let go and enter into the place of the other. We need to cross over and enter into true solidarity with others, try to hear what they are hearing and to see what they are seeing. Without such empathy, we will not offer them the psychological hospitality that all pilgrims need; we will fail to touch what needs to be nurtured and healed along the way.

Intellectual Hospitality [7] : Here I refer to our responsibility to provide an environment that invites the participants to grapple with and question their faith, that enables people to come to see for themselves what their religious tradition means for their lives. This, too, requires a kind of kenosis from us in which we indeed profess our own faith commitments but not as a form of hardened ideology to which they must submit for acceptance, i.e., to experience hospitality. The hospitality here requires a letting go of what Foucault called "knowledge control," a giving up of our claims to epistemic privilege and sponsoring people instead to their own knowing and choices in faith. Such intellectual hospitality also requires our openness to be called in question by others and to learn from them.

Ecclesial Hospitality: By this I mean that our ministry praxis (i.e., our operative spirituality) is to help create an open and welcoming community of faith. As *ekklesia* has roots in *ekkletoi* (the Hebrew is *quahal*), meaning "those who are called out," so our religious leading out is to call people into what Elizabeth Schussler Fiorenza describes as "an inclusive discipleship of equals." [8] We are to prepare for communities of faith that are marked by inclusivity, mutuality, collegiality, and genuine respect, where there is a welcome for all, saints and sinners alike, to feel at home.

** Look at the environments and events you create in your own ministry. In what ways are they marked by the gift of hospitality?*

LOVE: FOR THE TRADITION

Both of the characteristics of our spirituality outlined above and the fourth one to come are expressions of love of some kind. Thus it is somewhat arbitrary on my part to use this central activity of the heart to express our attitude toward the tradition. And yet by doing so, I intend to highlight the spirituality that the tradition asks from the heart of the minister. As ministers within our faith communities, entrusted with the sacred mandate of remembering and handing on the faith handed down to us, I believe we are called to a profound love for our tradition. We are to cherish it as a gift that brings life to us, have faith in its possibilities to be a source of meaning and life for others, and hope that it can ever renew itself and be rediscovered by others as holding the potential of God's self-disclosure in truth for their lives. Our tradition will be the source and measure of the identity in faith to which others come, the symbol system through which they are to grow into right relationship with our God, themselves, and others. The more we cherish the tradition and effectively make it accessible to them, the more likely they are to be sponsored in their own holiness of life. My point here could be misinterpreted, so let me way more clearly what I do and do not mean.

Our love for the tradition does not mean simply repeating it as if it is a reified or fossilized thing; that would be the surest way of killing it. Handing on the tradition does not mean asking people to repeat our past in their future. Rather it is the making present of the gift out of which they can create their own future as a faithful people together. Nor does our love for the tradition require that we canonize it or propose it as perfect or complete. Rather, our love for the tradition requires us to bring retrieval, suspicion, and creativity to it; retrieval to uncover the subversive and life-giving memories that are in it, but can be forgotten; suspicion to recognize its distortions and the ways it has been used to legitimate oppression and injustice (sexism, racism, militarism, etc.); and creativity to renew and expand our present understanding and living of it because it will always have a "surplus of meaning" (Paul Ricouer's phrase) for us. Such love of the tradition calls us to pray and study our way into an ever deepening appreciation of it. It requires a firm commitment of us to renew ourselves and our faith communities to more faithfully reflect the truth of our tradition, because both are capable of being poor reflections of it.

** What do you see as the implications of this love of the tradition for us?*

COMMITMENT: TO THE REIGN OF GOD

The symbol of God's reign is rooted deeply in the consciousness and commitment reflected in the Jewish Scriptures (*malkuth Yahweh*) and in the life praxis of Jesus (*basilia tou theou*). It is a symbol of God's intentions for creation: that all people are to come to wholeness and fullness of life by doing God's will on earth as it is done in heaven. The Reign of God is a statement of our purpose. It reflects how we are to minister. It reminds us of how essentially practical our faith traditions are — that they are not systems of ideas but ways of life to be lived that help to create freedom and justice for all. Remembering Lee's description of spirituality as how we mobilize ourselves religiously in our daily activities, the Reign of God calls to our hearts for commitment so intent, that people may mobilize themselves to live as if God rules in their lives and in our world.

In a sense, this fourth echoes the first dimension of our call to holiness: seeing to it that we are life-giving for all. But here we are raising up this commitment of our hearts to God's reign as providing us with the overarching hermeneutical principle by which we interpret and explain the tradition itself, and by which we interpret and critique our own historical reality. It provides us, too, with the vision toward which we constantly invite people to decision — decisions that are to be lived on personal, interpersonal, and social/political levels and that promote justice and peace, love and freedom, wholeness and fullness of life.

** What does it mean for you to commit to the values of God's reign?*

To summarize, the spirituality of the minister requires of our hearts a passion for the people, the gift of hospitality, a love for the tradition, and a commitment to God's reign. The level to which they are reflected in our ministry will be both the measure and the source of our own holiness.

Some further questions for appropriation and decision:
** What would you agree with, disagree with, or add to this description of the spirituality of the minister?*

** From your own reflections and this essay, what has emerged for you as the identifying marks of the spirituality of the minister?*
** What is the next step in your own spiritual journey as a parish minister?*

Post script: Throughout our dialogue in Washington, it was significant to note how many times people spoke of "a person who lived it" as a major influence in their faith formation. That, too, is what these reflections have attempted to state: that our own spirituality, the state of our hearts, is the heart of religious education.

ENDNOTES

[1] Among the recent works I have found most helpful are James Michael Lee, ed., *The Spirituality Of The Religious Educator* (Birmingham AL: Religious Education Press, 1985), a fine collection of essays; and Parker Palmer, *To Know As We Are Known* (San Francisco: Harper and Row, 1983), a powerful essay on the correlation between "knowing" and "loving." Iris V. Cully, *Education For Spiritual Growth* (San Francisco: Harper and Row, 1984) is not directed specifically to the spirituality of the religious educator per se but is very insightful regarding the overall spiritual purpose of religious education.

[2] As many of the participants recognized, the structure I gave to our learning occasion in Washington was based on the general style of a shared praxis approach. These opening remarks served somewhat as a focusing activity.

[3] The description that emerged for me in the aftermath of our dialogue in Washington is as follows: "Spirituality is our conscious attending to God's loving initiative and presence in our lives, and to the movement of God's Spirit that moves our spirit to commit ourselves to wholeness for ourselves and for all humankind by living in right relationship with God, ourselves and others, in every dimension and activity of our lives."

[4] There has been a marked popular assumption in my own tradition of Roman Catholicism that holiness/spirituality is primarily for people who are ordained or are in vowed religious communities. In light of that, I consider Ch. 5 of the Second Vatican Council's *Dogmatic Constitution on the Church* (Lumen Gentium) to be a major breakthrough toward a more inclusive understanding of spirituality. The very title of that chapter, "The Call of the Whole Church to Holiness," is itself significant.

[5] My own awareness of spirituality in the Jewish and Christian traditions as a mode of right relationship has been heightened by the work of Dr. Katherine Zappone. See her doctoral dissertation, *Reconstructing Relationality: Spirituality in Religious Education*, Boston College, July 1986.

[6] See Padraic O'Hare, "Hospitality as a Paradigm for Youth Ministry." Occasional Paper, No. 10. The Center for Youth Ministry Development, 1986. Available through Don Bosco Multimedia.

[7] O'Hare uses the category of "Ideological Hospitality" here but writes "The chief tool of ideological hospitality is 'intellectual hospitality.'" This is a toleration of the young peoples' (he is talking about youth ministry) groping, stumbling, and contradicting as they move to conscious expression of their loyalties" (parenthesis added) 7.

[8] See Elizabeth Schussler Fiorenza. *In Memory of Her.* (New York: Crossroad, 1983.), especially Chapter 4.

WORKS CITED

Lee, James Michael. "Lifework Spirituality and The Religious Educator." *The Spirituality of the Religious Educator.* Ed. James Michael Lee. Birmingham AL: Religious Education Press, 1985.

Goldbrunner, Josef. *Holiness is Wholeness and Other Essays.* Notre Dame IN: University of Notre Dame Press, 1964.

Rahner, Karl. *Concern For The Church.* Edward Quinn, trans. New York: Crossroads, 1981.

Chapter 8

Spirituality for the Future

Leonard Doohan

The beginning of a new era offers an appropriate time to look ahead and to review the past. Ahead lies the year 2000 and the beginning of the third millennium of the Christian era. Behind us, in the wake of the Second Vatican Council, lies a period of more than 20 years of historic efforts to renew Christian living.

Therefore, this is a particularly appropriate time to review Christian spirituality and to try to distill the characteristics that are especially helpful for trying to live as Catholic Christians. I will offer ten characteristics that I think we will need in the decade ahead. Some are perennially important, others are new emphases.

The first of these characteristics is a renewed sense of the importance of baptism. Christianity used to be an inherited aspect of life, uniformly lived by entire families, cities, and even countries. Now, however, faith is a matter of personal choice, less an inherited tradition. It is a commitment made after an awareness of what the responsibility of baptismal dedication implies.

Furthermore, there is a healthy awareness among a growing number of Christians that baptism implies the building of a community of faith, based on the word of the Lord, and lived with a sense of gratitude and Christian liberty. Instead of the passive approach to faith of past decades, we see approaches to church, family, work, social and political issues that are motivated by a growing sense of baptismal responsibility. This rediscovery of baptismal vocation is like a new Pentecost, challenging each of us to end the isolating of religion to a Sunday service and to integrate baptismal awareness and commitment into every aspect of life.

Spirituality does not refer primarily to the efforts we make as Christians but rather to what God is doing in us. *Therefore, a second hallmark of contemporary Christian spirituality is the awareness that life is a grace and gift from God.* God's baptismal call to us is not just words but rather is filled with power. It is effective in us. The active involvement of today's Christians needs to be complemented with attitudes of openness, receptivity, and awareness of our emptiness without God.

The Father, Son, and Holy Spirit are the very life that constitutes Christian spirituality. This comes to us in the liturgical life of the Church and also in personal prayer. In a world that increasingly stresses activity, achievement, success, and involvement, Christians will need to pause, withdraw, receive, and abandon themselves to Divine Providence. This requires stillness, quiet, reflection, and meditation that cultivate a sense of wonder, awe, inspiration, and concentration on the life-giving power of God.

Since growth in Christian living is principally the work of God, the second characteristic, which helps keep the others in perspective, is the daily lived awareness that life is grace.

We live in a future-shock society. The changes of every five to ten years are now equivalent to the previous impact of a generation. In times past, we could consult an authority figure such as a pastor for decisions on difficult faith or moral issues, but rapid change and the decrease in numbers of clergy make this more difficult. Changes in business practice, politics, social development, finance, medical practice, and sexual issues are very rapid and what is ethical and what is unethical is difficult to identify.

In a time like ours, Christians must learn to form themselves for right and true judgment of conscience based on the sources of faith and the moral norms of personal Christian convictions. As circumstances change, conscience must evaluate differently and at times arrive at different conclusions. *Thus we have the third characteristic of a spirituality for our time: forming one's conscience primarily through self-evaluation, prayer, prudence, knowledge of our faith, and the consensus of faithful Christians.*

The last 50 years have seen significant developments in our awareness of the importance of work for our spiritual development. People cannot sanctify themselves in their spare time but only in the major periods of each day, one of which is work. The seemingly ordinary conditions of working life are very special, for it is normally in daily labor that a person is a partner with God in the betterment of our world. After all, the Church's mission is not to itself, but to the service of the world.

Like everything that is good, work can be used to exploit, punish, oppress, and degrade. It can also lead to personal growth and to community and social benefits. Life proves itself Christian in the events of one's working life, where genuine personal, social, and world progress are directly connected with a spirituality of work. In their attitudes to work, Christians show their endurance and voluntary acceptance of hardship, their reaction to temptations to sin that come in times of work, and their struggle-filled efforts to build good relationships at work.

For most Christians the toil connected with work is a sharing in the sufferings of the Lord. Fidelity to Christian values is more severely tested at work than in any other normal time of each day, and yet here Christians are generally alone in their profession of faith. *Work is truly a basic component of contemporary spirituality. This is the fourth characteristic of a contemporary spirituality.*

A fifth characteristic is a commitment to participation in community building at all levels: family, church, political, and international. A new kind of Christian is emerging, neither fanatical nor extreme, but committed and willing to struggle. People work harder at family life and development than in any previous generation, and success is evident. Others have committed themselves to public office in politics, finance, education, or administration. Many others are today's peacemakers in what has become for them a Christian challenge and spirituality.

Community building is also seen in parish renewal efforts and commitment to committees, parish councils, diocesan pastoral councils, and national or international organizations. All these forms of community building will intensify in the next decade with the increase in the numbers of basic ecclesial communities, neighborhood groups, networking, and group development.

The sixth characteristic of a contemporary spirituality is a healthy approach to the joys of life. We are the only generation in the history of humankind that has two lives: a working life and a leisure life, and the latter, too, will be integrated into Christian growth.

As our own country in particular gives more emphasis to the good things of life, to leisure and free time, to the joys of sexual love, to ever new forms of entertainment, culture, health, and wellness, the Christian challenge will be to permeate these joys with Christianity and to enjoy the blessings of God's creation. This is not only good in itself, but also an excellent preparation for the celebrational dimensions of liturgy, the ecstasy of prayer, the intimacy of family life, and a joyful optimistic outlook.

Christian spirituality has witnessed many methods of prayer, frequently requiring time and lifestyles unavailable to all the baptized, but reserved exclusively to the contemplative monk or nun. This is no longer the case. Any period of intensified prayer, personal or liturgical, consists of basic attitudes that cannot be switched on or off, but must be life attitudes lived throughout each moment of the day, and intensified in so-called prayer periods. Genuine prayer requires that the Christian be one who lives true charity, gives prime time to the more intense periods of prayer, and chooses a place for prayer that is conducive to an experience of the Lord.

Since the quality and growth of prayer are principally the work of the Lord, growth is not earned by commitment to exceptional methods, nor is it restricted to vocational commitments. Rather, the Christian's contribution consists in attitudes cultivated in remote preparations: those basic attitudes that enable a person to be still and available to the Lord, facilitate an openness to the Spirit's inspiration, lead to concentration with Christ, and prepare for the rich religious experience of silence in God. *A greater appreciation of the universal call to prayer is a seventh characteristic of spiritual growth in this decade.*

As the eighth characteristic of contemporary spirituality, I see an increase in commitments to new kinds of church forms or groupings. Parish renewal projects and parish or interparish retreats emphasize conversion and renewal as an ecclesial experience. Paralleling the parish-based renewal efforts are the spiritual movements that are characterized by sharing in faith, witness of mutual charity, and the community thrust of the members' lives. Another current trend, likely to increase in the immediate years ahead, is the movement of family spirituality which fosters the realization of being a domestic church.

In the decade ahead, one of our aims in church life will be to facilitate dialogue and eventual integration of the vision of church that comes down from above, from Church leaders, with the insights and vision that come from below, from all the baptized. In the past our vision of church filtered down to the people, but in the years ahead it will percolate upward to Church leaders. Church life is now focused on local small groups that are the foundation of national and international churches. The 1990s will see greater interest in the strength of these local foundational churches.

A ninth characteristic is the dedication to Christian service of others. Not only are we more clearly aware of who we are as church, and more fully appreciative of the world in which we live, but we see service to that world as an integral part of our spirituality. Christian ministry, so powerfully developed in recent years, will more frequently be ministries to the world: humanizing our lives and societies, cultural and educational development, defense of human dignity, rights, justice, and economic wellbeing.

This outreach in service is not made from the "haves" to the "havenots," but rather is consciously provoked with an awareness of mutual need. To serve others is a prime way of personal enrichment, and in satisfying the needs of others, one satisfies one's own need to reach out. Those who work for the social betterment of others may never heal society of its sin, but will certainly bring healing to their own sinful, selfish lives.

A final characteristic is prophetical responsibility. "Prophet" is one who speaks on behalf of God words of challenge and confrontation, consolation and encouragement, hope and reconstruction.

Christians will become more public in their condemnation of society's injustices: misuse of wealth, abortion, pornography, consumerism, abuse of others, oppression, misuse of power and government, and so on. They will also increasingly be the visionaries who can give reasons for living and hoping amidst the pains of modern life. Furthermore, they will become the agents of reconstruction, peace, and universal community values.

This prophetical ministry is an extension of service. It is a personal or organized struggle against the injustices of structured society. Already there has been much involvement in social justice issues — just salaries, rights of minorities, defeat of sexist positions, opposition to unlawful government, correction of legal injustices, abuse of the environment. These prophetical challenges have produced change and have been educationally valuable to those involved. They will intensify, making political involvement a major component of contemporary spirituality.

In sum, as we move toward the year 2000, our lives as Christians will be supported and strengthened by a renewed focus on our baptismal vocation, an awareness that life is grace and gift, and by responsible commitment to conscience formation. Spiritual growth will integrate work, community building, the joys of life, and the celebrational elements of prayer and worship. Christians will be intensely conscious that they are a church that serves and prophetically challenges each generation. These are characteristics I believe we will need in the years ahead.

Chapter 9

Perspectives on Spirituality: A Sampler

CREATION PERSPECTIVES

Creation spirituality challenges each believer to be both a mystic and a prophet. In other words, it affirms both prayer and action. The mystical dimension invites each of us to see God's presence everywhere, to live in wonder and in trust. The prophetic dimension invites us to face the pain and oppression of the world and to become agents of healing and transformation. Prayer and action must flow in and out of one another.

First, creation spirituality invites us to see all of life as holy.

Second, creation spirituality sees human beings as blessings.

Third, creation spirituality emphasizes that life is a gift.

Fourth, as a holistic spirituality, creation spirituality deals with sin and suffering and death.

Fifth, creation spirituality, has a very strong horizontal dimension.

Alexandra Kovats
(Creation Spirituality 6)

Reinhabitating the North American continent on the basis of the mutual enhancement of the human and the natural is a task to which the Church in America might well dedicate its energies. Even our concerns for international peace and social justice can be realized only within the context of a common care for the endangered planet. The renewal of religion in the future will depend on our appreciation of the natural world as the locus for the meeting of the divine and the human. The universe itself is divine manifestation. The splendor and beauty of the earth in all its variety must be preserved if any worthy idea of the divine is to survive in the human community.

Thomas Berry
(Spirituality and Ecology 162)

Creation spirituality unleashes vitality, creativity, and playfulness. It is generous, mutually affirming of diversity, and non-competitive. Unlike fall-redemption spirituality, it does not set up competitive dualisms between males and females, celibate and married, heterosexual and homosexual, white and black, Christian and non-Christian, us and them. It is egalitarian and pluralistic, rejoicing in the many-ness of beings that interconnect in a rich cosmic community. It allows us to lay aside our defenses, our needs to control, dominate, and destroy the other. It is the spirituality that is needed for an ecological, peacemaking, and just world community.

Rosemary Radford Ruether (169)
("Matthew Fox and Creation Spirituality: Strengths and
Weaknesses.")

Spirituality embraces not just our relationship with God and other persons, but with all of nature as well. Convictions that set us over against nature need to be converted to a spirituality of ecological interdependence.

Kathleen Fischer
(*Reclaiming the Connections* 40)

On the religious level this new ministry calls for a developed theology of creation and a spirituality which is sensitive to the presence of God in the natural world — locally and worldwide. Rituals that celebrate God's presence are vitally important in order to reconnect us in an integral way with the natural world. We should try to develop these for our homes, basic Christian communities, parishes, dioceses, national Churches and the worldwide Church. This will call in creative powers which at present lie dormant in the community of the Church.

We will not be successful in our efforts to develop a new attitude towards the natural world unless we are sustained and nourished by a new vision. This vision must blossom forth from our understanding of the world as God intends it to be. We can know the shape of this world by looking at how God originally fashioned our world and laid it out before us.

Sean McDonagh
(*The Greening of the Church* 202, 213)

This universe itself, but especially the planet Earth, needs to be experienced as the primary mode of divine presence, just as it is the primary educator, primary healer, primary commercial establishment, and primary lawgiver for all that exists within this life community. The basic spirituality communicated by the natural world can also be considered as normative for the future ecological age. This spirituality is grounded in the basic characteristics of the universe as manifested from the beginning: the unique and irreplaceable qualities of the individual and the inseparable bonding with every other being in the universe. These constitute the ultimate basis of a functional spirituality for the human community just as they constitute the functional cosmology of the human community.

Thomas Berry

CULTURAL PERSPECTIVES

We Mexican-Americans, in our Latin American sense of *familia* and *carnalismo* (brotherhood), have a great contribution to make. The *familia* gives its members a deep sense of security because they experience that they are someone special: loved, desired, valued, and respected simply because they are who they are — not because of what they ought to be or could become, but simply because they are who they are. No masks or games are necessary, for no matter what happens, one belongs. *La familia* is not the house where people reside; it is the bond that unites persons and allows them to experience that innermost and existential sense of belonging. I am never alone; I am part of the *familia* and the *familia* is part of me. Intimacy is natural because it is the ordinary behavior from the first to the last days of life — we touch, we joke, we caress, we converse…we can cry and sing, fight and love…yet in spite of everything, we are the *familia.*

The joy of Mexican-Americans is one of their most obvious characteristics. They love their fiestas and everyone is welcome to participate. Neither destitution nor wars can dampen their festive spirit. Even in the midst of suffering, there is a spontaneous joy that is not easily found elsewhere. Outsiders notice it and comment upon it. It is obvious in liturgical gatherings, spontaneous in home life, and carefully planned into commemorations of historical events. In their sorrows, disappointments, reverses, and struggles, there is joy. It is evident in the eyes and smiles of their children, in the playfulness of their youth, and in the inner peace and tranquility of their elderly. In the midst of whatever happens — triumph or tragedy — they rise above it to celebrate life.

It cannot be adequately explained but it can certainly be sensed, for it is nothing less than the joy of the experience of new life within them — not yet fully realized but certainly beginning. It is through the ongoing synthesis of traditions that his new life is gradually coming into its fullness.

Virgilio Elizondo
(Galilean Journey 111, 120)

Touching the heart of a people means touching their spirituality in a tangible, visible way. It means bringing all of the happiness and pain, laughter and tears, joy and sorrow, to God in celebration.

Can't it be said that this is the true paschal mystery: the living, dying and rising of Jesus as he lives, dies and rises in this people? Can't it be said that this is the true Spirit of God set free within this people? Can't it be said that this is bringing the true faith of the people alive in this time and in this place?

Arturo Perez
(Popular Catholicism: A Hispanic Perspective 14)

White Christianity and white theology have been so concerned about orthodoxy (i.e., the right kind of teaching) that they have grossly neglected "ortho-practice," the right kind of practice. Black spirituality and black theology must be concerned with the process of developing ortho-practice, the right kind of practice (i.e., a life style which helps us to be in action the people of God). Black spirituality must be holistic, for holiness is nothing but wholeness. We cannot be holy without being a whole person. Wholeness involves loving oneself and one's people. Wholeness involves acting for oneself and one's community. Holiness involves being concerned about all aspects of life. Therefore, black spirituality must involve the whole person embracing all aspects of black life. We must learn to pray as if everything depended upon God and work in all aspects of life as if everything depended upon our lives.

Albert M. McKnight, C.S.Sp.
("Black Christian Perspective of Spirituality")

We are blessed because we are black and as such have immediate access to the gift of negritude, the gift of blackness, the gift of soul. This gift is no simple thing. It is a manifold gift, a many faceted jewel. It is a cultural thrust which facilitates not only the way that we excel in the arts of singing and dancing and praying and preaching, but also enables us to relate humanely to God, and helps us to live in harmony, in a non-exploitative way with all of God's world.

Specifically because it facilitates soulfulness, and spiritual inspiration, and inspirational celebration, negritude is a gift that could greatly bless the worshipping church. Indeed it is a grace that the worshipping church desperately needs.

Clarence Jos. Rivers, Jr.
("The Gift of Being Black and Catholic")

Without a doubt, the agency for gospel liberation and the strongest asset of the black community is "black love." It is the chief attribute of the black family, and that which predicates pride of ancestry and willingness to include prodigal children, outcasts, the pariah, the stranger, and even the oppressor within the fold of its embrace. Historically, black love has enabled the momentarily crushed spirits of black folk to look beyond the immediacy of present suffering to a God who has never forsaken them in the hour of anguish and despair. It has been the religious aspect of black love that has prompted black Christians to consider the worth of all human life, born and unborn, legitimate and "illegitimate;" single or several times married; old, unemployed, young, and inexperienced — all in terms of the accomplishment of God's will expressed in the here and now. "Love one another as I have loved you" is an invitation that the black family has accepted and acted upon in ways that may be clearly differentiated from those of white families who are also Church.

…But behind black Christian love is the Christ who teaches that bitterness must be dispelled with *effective* compassion and *affective* justice toward the oppressors who also need liberation through the redemptive power of God.

Toinette M. Eugene
("The Black Family that is Church")

The Native Americans look for many meanings and signs from the Great Spirit's creation. Non-Indians use the term Mother Nature. Indian people believe that "Mother Nature" can be a living bible from which one can see, hear, touch, feel and learn a great deal. Nature or Mother Earth was made by the Great Spirit; therefore, there are obviously many revelations that the two-leggeds may learn if they simply have the sense to look.

We, the American Indian, had a way of living that enabled us to live within the great, complete beauty that only the natural environment can provide. The Indian tribes had a common value system and a commonality of religion, without religious animosity, that preserved that great beauty that the two-leggeds definitely need. Our four commandments from the Great Spirit are: (1) respect for Mother Earth, (2) respect for the Great Spirit, (3) respect for our fellow man and woman, and (4) respect for individual freedom (provided that individual freedom does not threaten the tribe or the people or Mother Earth).

We, the Indian people, also believe that the Great Spirit placed many people throughout this planet: red, yellow, black, and white. What about the brown people? The brown people evolved from the sacred colors coming together. Look at our Mother Earth. She, too, is brown because the four directions have come together. After the Great Spirit, *Wakan Tanka*, placed them in their respective areas, the *Wakan Tanka* appeared to each people in a different manner and taught them ways so that they might live in harmony and true beauty.

We believe that *Wakan Tanka* loves all of its children equally, although the Great Spirit must be distributed at times with those children who have destroyed proven value systems that practiced sharing and generosity and kept Mother Earth viable down through time. We kept Mother Earth viable because we did not sell her or our spirituality!

Ed McGaa, Eagle Man
(*Mother Earth Spirituality* 204, 33, 205)

FAMILY PERSPECTIVES

Family sacramentality flows from the sacramentality rooted in life. To limit an understanding of the family to a functional analysis misses life's deepest dimensions which both begin and end in mystery. But within the unfolding mystery of salvation, key ways in which the family reveals God's presence can be discovered. This is particularly evident in the family's communal life, its growth in holiness, and its ability to give selflessly out of love for one another.

Robert Hater (*Holy Family* 54)

If a family is *ecclesia*, then it is first of all to be a community, an intimate network of personal relationships. As a Christian community, the family is also to be of service to one another and to those outside the family who have special needs. The family is also to be a community which prays and ritualizes its faith in ways natural to families. Because the spirit and life of the family are guided by the Gospel, the family finds itself inclined to adopt attitudes and values which are sometimes counter-cultural. The ways God speaks in the Gospel, in the Church, and in the event of our times leads families today to a new understanding and awareness of the impact of human sexuality on families and on the family roles of men and women. Single parent families find themselves confronted by unique challenges to be guided and sustained by the Spirit. The domestic church, in its various forms, is called to proclaim the Gospel, to be a light on a hilltop and the salt of the earth.

The life of the family is itself holy. It is a mistake to act as if we must make it holy by artificial means. The family is a faith community — or is called to be such. All that need be done is to look at the life of the family and to discover the naturally sacred events that already take place there. The family recognizes the sacred character of these events and takes simple steps to celebrate that sacred character through prayer and ritual.

Mitch and Kathy Finley
(*Christian Families in the Real World* 16, 40)

The spirituality of family is not only concerned with recurring patterns, but also with the changing texture of the here and now; with the rapidly expanding minds and bodies of children; with the vigilance of maintaining healthy intimacy in marriage; with the challenges of young adulthood and mid-life; with birth and death.

Our family lives need times of wonder. These are difficult to find when we are frantic with activity and separated from one another in the process. We do not need to be hermits to experience the deep disclosure of presence and sacred time available to us when we play unpurposefully together, when we are silent together on a meander through the forest, or when we simply sit and enjoy the gentle lapping of the ocean as we lie on the beach and with our fingers make furrows in the sand.

Wendy Wright (*Sacred Dwelling* 41, 50-51)

There are many things families can do to make a peaceful environment by taking the time and making the commitment. They can learn skills in nonviolent communication, really listen to one another, learn to phrase their talk in ways that are not confrontational or accusing but that invite dialogue. They can establish family meetings in which decision-making within the domestic church is shared. They can learn negotiation skills and allow their children to resolve their own conflicts, acting as models rather than as arbiters. Families can remember that gestures of touch (the family hug, resting on each other's arms, being carried and protected) are disarming and healing as well as affirming and are part of the art of peacemaking.

Wendy Wright (*Sacred Dwelling* 177)

A family spirituality first conditions the "being" of the family; it is more about what the family is, than about what the family *does*. A family spirituality involves a simple, lived dedication to Christ in the real world. It is about prayer, faith, serving others, and so forth, of course. But because it is about such, it is also about laughter, about being foolish in the eyes of "the world," and about a great affection for a good party.

A family spirituality is one that is in-process, undergoing transformation even as it transforms us and the life we are. As a family we are not the same now as we were last year — or last month — and neither is our spirituality, our continuing efforts to follow the lead of the Gospel in ways that make sense for our time and our place.

Mitch and Kathy Finley
(*Christian Families in the Real World* 136-137)

SOCIAL PERSPECTIVES

True spirituality — the authentic religious journey — can never be an escape from life's problems. God, the sacred center at the source of all authentic spiritual journeys, must be met in the midst of life, not in escape from life. Today we live in a *global* age — an age of planetary exploration and communications and new global interdependencies. Our spiritual journey — our search for life in God — must be worked out now in a global context, in the midst of global crises and global community. Our spirituality must be a global spirituality.

The question is not *whether* there will be a new human order. It is rather, *what kind* of order? On what values and world views will it be built? Will it be a world order based on power and domination over the earth and each other? Will it serve a few at the expense of many? Will its successive stages lead to increasing hunger, war, deprivation, and dehumanization? Will it be an order where increasing wealth flows into the hands of a few? Or will we decide to journey on a path toward a world order that serves all humanity as a whole? Will it be a liberating and humanizing world order? Will it help us become more fully human and more fully human community?

Patricia Mische
("Toward a Global Spirituality")

Structural justice, interpersonal respect, and personal integrity all come together at the heart of an integrated spirituality. The area where they meet may be called '*Shalom*', the biblical word which means all-embracing peace in every sphere of life:
 — the peace of being in harmony with nature and the cosmos;
 — peace based on justice and reconciliation in society and the world;
 — peace in our relationships with family, friends, and community;
 — a deep personal peace arising from being at home with oneself;
 — and opening oneself up to experience peace as an utterly undeserved gift of God, a peace that passes all understanding in all or any of these areas of life.

Donal Dorr
(*Integral Spirituality* 5-6)

The spirituality being born in Latin America is the spirituality of the church of the poor, to which Pope John XXIII called all of us, the spirituality of an ecclesial community that is trying to make effective its solidarity with the poorest of this world. It is a collective, ecclesial spirituality that, without losing anything of its universal perspective, is stamped with the religious outlook of an exploited and believing people. The journey is one undertaken by the entire people of God. It leaves behind it a land of oppression and, without illusions but with constancy, seeks its way in the midst of a desert. It is a "new" spirituality because the love of the Lord who urges us to reject inertia and inspires us to creativity is itself always new.

A spirituality is a walking in freedom according to the Spirit of love and life. This walking has its points of departure in an encounter with the

Lord. Such an encounter is a spiritual experience that produces and gives meaning to the freedom of which I have been speaking. The encounter itself springs from the Lord's initiative. The Scriptures state this repeatedly: "This is why I told you that no one can come to me unless it is granted him by the Father" (Jn 6:65). "You did not choose me, but I chose you" (Jn 15:16).

This is what many Christians are now learning in Latin America. To be followers of Jesus requires that they walk with and be committed to the poor; when they do, they experience and encounter with the Lord who is simultaneously revealed and hidden in the faces of the poor (Mt 25:31-46). This is a profound and demanding spiritual experience that serves as the point of departure for following Jesus and for reflection on his words and deeds.

There is no aspect of human life that is unrelated to the following of Jesus. The road passes through every dimension of our existence, as we saw in the biblical models discussed earlier. A spirituality is not restricted to the so-called religious aspects of life: prayer and worship. It is not limited to one sector but is all-embracing, because the whole of human life, personal and communal, is involved in the journey. A spirituality is a manner of life that gives a profound unity to our prayer, thought, and action.

Gustavo Gutierrez
(*We Drink From Our Own Wells* 29, 35, 38, 88)

Thus the kernel of this spirituality consists in an orientation of one's own life not toward oneself and in behalf of oneself, one's group, or one's church, but toward the poor of this world, just as they themselves genuinely shift from a concentration upon their personal or group ego. This is the spirituality necessary for consistent service to the reign of God, the object of our service. It is a most effective mediation of the demand of Christian love to service and not be service. It is the option of living one's life in order that the poor of this world may be done justice, in order that life may come into being, and in order that the human order of things, overwhelmingly the producer of death, slow or violent, may produce life instead.

Jon Sobrino
(*Spirituality of Liberation* 177)

The Church's social teaching tells everyone that the Christian religion does not have a merely horizontal meaning, or a merely spiritual meaning that overlooks the wretchedness that surrounds it. It is a looking at God, and from God at one's neighbor as a brother or sister, and an awareness that "whatever you did to one of these, you did to me." (Mt 25:40).

Archbishop Oscar Romero
(*The Violence of Love*)

September 23, 1979
The great need today
is for Christians who are active and critical,
who don't accept situations without analyzing them
inwardly and deeply.
We no longer want masses of people
like those who have been trifled with for so long.
We want persons like fruitful fig trees
who can say yes to justice and no to injustice
and can make use of the precious gift of life,
regardless of the circumstances.

March 9, 1980
"God's reign is already present on our earth in mystery.
When the Lord comes, it will be brought to perfection."
(Vatican Council II, *The Church in the Modern World* 39).
That is the hope that inspires Christians.
We know that every effort to better society,
especially when injustice and sin are so ingrained,
is an effort that God blesses,
that God wants,
that God demands of us.

Archbishop Oscar Romero
(*The Violence of Love*)

[This March 9 passage is from Archbishop Romero's last homily. He was assassinated as he concluded the homily.]

When we look prayerfully at our society in an effort to see what God is doing and revealing and inviting us to do, we also see signs of hope, seeds of resurrection. God is working patiently, persistently, creatively through less than perfect social institutions and movements worldwide. Wherever effective and loving compassion are taking shape in institutional structures and social policies, the Spirit of God is at work.

In this socio-economic context, God seems to be calling us to personal conversion through helping with the fundamental institutional and changes necessary to enable millions of the poor and marginalized to begin to take control of their own lives and participate more fully and equally in society.

James E. Hug, S.J. and Rose Marie Scherschel
(*Social Revelation* 45, 46)

Without expecting our intervention to have immediate or spectacular consequences, we must have the courage to work for peace at every chance and stimulate others to do the same. Great peace thoughts and expectations will have to be 'applied' problem by problem, stage by stage, every day anew, with courageous tenacity, in spirt of all disappointments and incomprehension. Peace is the art of standing fast, of persevering, and the ability to believe that this work does make sense, even if one cannot see the results immediately. The peacemaker must help to open up ways for the future and take the risk of not being right until tomorrow.

A spirituality of peacemaking which is attentive in this way will enable us to manage the tensions inherent in struggling for peace and justice in a world wounded not only by personal sin, but also be sinful attitudes and practices expressed through social, economic, and political institutions.

(Peace Spirituality for Peace Makers 18)

WOMEN'S PERSPECTIVES

Instead of valuing the differences that God has given us, it seems to me that we create, artificial differences to hide from the vision of God. We create vain fears to avoid living creatively out of love. Within them we take up extreme positions, choosing to make too clear a distinction between what is certainty and what is doubt, between what is sacred and what is secular, between having a vocation to some sort of formal ministry and not having such a vocation, between whatever is clerical and whatever is lay. A middle road does exist between each of these alternatives and this middle way is one that heals rather than exaggerates divisions. It enables both women and men to reclaim themselves as people God knows and loves and in whom God recognizes the divine image. It honors the vision of God.

Lavinia Byrne
(Women Before God 71)

God's presence and revelation amid all life's processes is not immediately apparent. To discover it requires that we cultivate a consciousness that continues to seek meaning — God's meaning — within the events of our lives. In this search, women's experience is particularly important because it often calls into question the dualisms that shape our traditional view of the holy: sacred/secular, spirit/body, contemplation/action, church/world, and spiritual/natural.

These dualisms have inhibited our ability to recognize the sacred in the secular, our body as the incarnation of our spirit, the church as part of the world. They have tried to limit the presence and action of God to a very narrow range of human experience. Could this be the reason so many women do not think of themselves as having a spirituality? Furthermore the dualisms have clouded our realization that we, by our very lives, give shape to God's on-going creative presence and continuing revelation in human history. We also have the power to inhibit God's activity.

Maria Riley, O.P.
(*Wisdom Seeks Her Way* 4)

Wisdom not received, wisdom neglected, becomes wisdom of dubious worth, finally no wisdom at all. Too many women long ago stopped believing in the worth of the gift they have. They stopped listening for the inner word of divine mystery trying to find its voice through them. Now, within these past two decades many women have begun growing in their capacity to hear the word and to recognize the embrace of divine love in their lives. But too many women are still voiceless about spiritual matters. No longer deaf to the word spoken in inner stillness, such women remain mute, unable to talk about what they have heard.

Does it really matter that men and women have mutually respectful words to speak to one another about God when we gather for prayer? Most certainly it does matter. It is the whole Church which has a call to contemplative living, to seek the face of God and to worship in spirit and in truth. Christian contemplatives make the journey "up the path of speech." All true contemplatives begin the journey with the pious intention of seeking God, but the great discovery of the journey is that on the way we find ourselves. For in the beginning, before we lost our way, we were created male and female as God's images.

Mary Collins
(*Women at Prayer* 43, 45)

This spirituality, then, is ultimately a passion for life, and it reaches beyond the mere expression of self to the survival of the human society and the regeneration of social structures. There is another side to passion that complements holistic love for creation, and that is rage and anger. We have to be capable of outrage for the sake of the reign of God. There is a wonderful Greek word that recurs in very interesting places in the New Testament that combines the meaning of boldness with passion — I believe the word is *parrhesia*. When that word appears in Scripture, its moral context is always one of conflict. It's a word you find in Luke and John and Acts, especially. It is a gift of the Spirit. It is a gift of audacity that overcomes fear, shyness, weakness and above all, self-doubt. It is precisely this *parrhesia* that patriarchy has repressed in women and that must erupt today — a sense of outrage against injustice, of boldness in confronting the abuse of power, of passionate witness in the face of all forms of violence.

We will have to be a people who believe in the possibility of change. This requires that another characteristic of our spirituality be *imagination*. I think probably of the many things that I've learned from my years of working in government, the most discouraging has been the failure of the imagination which seems to doom our system to go on repeating the past, going in circles, repeating the old agendas, replicating the old logic — whether it's legislation or foreign policy — we keep coming up with non-solutions. Certainly my work with human rights abuses taught me something about the lack of imagination, the mindlessness, and the compulsiveness that is responsible for so much terror. It really did change my notion of evil.

The exodus has begun. The age of the patriarchs is over. They will be left behind in Egypt. And so, to believe in Exodus is to hope, it is to believe that the God of history is the God of Surprise, and is leading us somewhere. It is to understand also that the way to the promised land and to the new covenant is through the wilderness. That's why we need *passion, resistance, relinquishment, imagination*, and *solidarity*. Only those gifts and deep prayer will sustain us on the journey. It is to believe that if some women are disobeying the Pharaoh's commands, we should take note; it may be divine grace breaking through our defenses.

Madonna Kolbenschlag
(Women in the Church 205-206, 208, 213)

WORKS CITED

Berry, Thomas. *The Dream of the Earth*. San Francisco: Sierra Club Books, 1988.

———. Thomas Berry "Spirituality and Ecology." *The Catholic World* July-August 1990: 159-162.

Brockman, S.J., James R. *The Violence of Love: The Pastoral Wisdom of Archbishop Oscar Romero*. San Francisco: Harper & Row, 1988.

Bowman, F.S.P.A., Thea, ed. *Families: Black and Catholic, Catholic and Black*. Washington DC: USCC Commission on Marriage and Family Life, 1985.

Byrne, Lavinia. *Woman Before God*. Mystic CT: 23rd Publications, 1988.

Collins, Mary. *Women at Prayer*. New York: Paulist Press, 1987.

Dorr, Donal. *Integral Spirituality*. Maryknoll NY: Orbis Books, 1990.

Elizondo, Virgilio. *Galilean Journey: The Mexican-American Promise*. MaryknollNY: Orbis Books, 1983.

Eugene, Toinette M. "The Black Family that is Church." *Families: Black and Catholic, Catholic and Black*. Ed. Thea Bowman, F.S.P.A. Washington DC: USCC Commission on Marriage and Family Life, 1985.

Finley, Mitch and Kathy. *Christian Families in the Real World*. Chicago: Thomas More Press, 1984.

Fischer, Kathleen. *Reclaiming the Connections*. Kansas City: Sheed and Ward, 1990.

Gutierrez, Gustavo. *We Drink from Our Own Wells*. Maryknoll NY: Orbis Books, 1984.

Hater, Robert J. *Holy Family*. Valencia CA: Tabor Publishing, 1988.

Hug, James, S.J., and Scherschel, Rose Marie. *Social Revelation*. Washington DC: The Center of Concern, 1987.

Kolbenschlag, Madonna, editor. *Women In The Church*. Washington, D.C.: The Pastoral Press, 1987.

Kovats, Alexandra. "Creation Spirituality." *Praying No. 25* (July-August 1988): 5-7.

McDonagh, Sean. *The Greening of the Church*. Maryknoll NY: Orbis Books, 1990.

McGaa, Ed, Eagle Man. *Mother Earth Spirituality*. New York: Harper Collins Publishers, 1990.

McKnight, C.S.Sp., Albert M. "Black Christian Perspective of Spirituality." *Families: Black and Catholic, Catholic and Black*. Ed. Thea Bowman, F.S.P.A. Washington D.C.: USCC Commission on Marriage and Family Life, 1985.

Mische, Patricia. "Toward a Global Spirituality." *Whole Earth Papers No. 16*. New York: Global Education Associates.

Peace Spirituality for Peacemakers. Belgium: Pax Christi International, 1983.

Perez, Arturo. *Popular Catholicism: A Hispanic Perspective*. Washington DC: The Pastoral Press, 1988.

Riley, O.P., Maria. *Wisdom Seeks Her Way*. Washington DC: The Center of Concern, 1987.

Rivers, Jr., Clarence Jos. "The Gift of Being Black and Catholic." *Families: Black and Catholic, Catholic and Black*. Ed. Thea Bowman, F.S.P.A. Washington DC: USCC Commission on Marriage and Family Life, 1985.

Ruether, Rosemary Radford. "Matthew Fox and Creation Spirituality: Strengths and Weaknesses." *The Catholic World*. July-August 1990: 169-172.

Sobrino, Jon. *Spirituality of Liberation*. Maryknoll NY: Orbis Books, 1985.

Wright, Wendy. *Sacred Dwelling: A Spirituality of Family Life*. New York: Crossroads, 1990.

Part Two

Overview

PRACTICAL APPROACHES

This section proposes some concrete arenas in which to address adolescent spirituality and some practical methods for enhancing young people's spiritual growth. In Chapter 10 we return to the insights of **Sharon Reed** as she identifies directions for adolescent spirituality. Using the theories of William O'Malley, Charles Shelton, and Michael Warren, she weaves a picture of the impact of imagination, relationships, and life structure on the world of adolescents. She suggests ten practical approaches for addressing their spiritual dimension and some realistic expectations for youth ministers.

In Chapter 11, **Maria Harris** examines education and spirituality. She identifies five paths or criteria for educators: taking care, taking steps, taking form, taking time, and taking risks. Throughout her essay, she integrates practical examples and questions to encourage creativity, imagination, and renewal in the activity of educating.

Austin Fleming reflects on "Spirituality and Liturgy" in Chapter 12, including the experience of intimacy and our need for it in worship. He examines liturgical ministries and their contribution to our concept of spirituality. He proposes some real challenges for the involvement of young people in worship, beyond our current "audience" mentality. **Thomas N. Tomaszek** concludes this chapter by offering 19 suggestions for improving worship with youth.

In Chapter 13 **Kathleen Fischer** emphasizes the importance of prayer intrinsically tied to our life experience. She speaks of contemplation as "the attitude of heart required by an interrelated world view." She offers some practical suggestions for nurturing our contemplative lives, coupled with a wonderful perspective on intercessory prayer. "Prayer takes us toward God, others, and the world by uniting us with the ground and center." **Jacquelin Bergan** and **S. Marie Schwan** conclude this chapter by offering practical approaches for helping youth (and adults) pray.

Fischer's vision of solidarity is magnified by **James McGinnis** in Chapter 14. He calls all of us to simplify our lifestyle and commit ourselves to discipleship. He examines some very practical ways young people can be involved in expressing a preferential option for the poor and connecting with the earth. He also identifies ways that we can support each other in this process. "We need to root out the obstacles in our lives that keep us from risking and from loving more deeply. Being too comfortable can dull our sense of urgency and passion for justice." **Thomas Bright** concludes this chapter by offering practical activities for youth that connect justice, solidarity and spirituality.

Finally, in Chapter 15, **Gregory Rohde** suggests the possibility of "Spiritual Direction with Adolescents" as a beneficial means of guiding and companioning them on the spiritual journey. Adolescents need an opportunity for critical reflection on the values, relationships, and concerns that occupy their attention. They also need the growing sense of God's presence in their life and a nurturing of this presence through deepening prayer and involvement. He identifies specific characteristics required of adults involved in this direction relationship and implications for strengthening youth ministry.

Hopefully the directions and approaches suggested in this section will build on the framework provided in the earlier foundations section to enhance our commitment to adolescent spiritual growth.

Chapter 10

Directions for a Spirituality for Adolescents

Sharon Reed

If I could now answer all the questions I've been asked about how to raise children, I'd say 'I really don't know. I honestly don't know whether it's better for you to be strict or permissive, demanding or acquiescent, whether you should spank or restrict or understand. I simply do not know. Not as a psychiatrist, not as a parent. But whatever you do, do the best you can. Just please do it in the sense of participation in growth. Watch with awe as your children's petals unfold. Marvel at the growing. Be with them in it as fully as you can.' (May 39)

I must admit I would offer the same advice to youth ministers questioning how to foster and nourish the spirituality of young people entrusted to them. I honestly don't know the "right" course to follow, the "best" programs to offer, or even "the way" most adolescents will respond in a given situation. To some extent, I'm grateful for that, because it means that grace cannot be programmed. It means that adolescents and spirituality are not things that can be controlled or manipulated to successfully complete some aspect of my job description. They are persons and processes that have a life of their own, and I am the one lucky enough to be called to participate in their growth—"to be with them in it as fully as I can." And so once again, we return to the ministry of presence, and still we question whether presence is good enough. Isn't there something more we can and should be doing? Gerald May suggests we can "watch with awe" and "marvel," "but whatever you do, do the best you can." *And the dialectic appears: awe and action, appreciation and involvement, being and doing, mystic and prophet, contemplation and participation.*

Can we work towards a spirituality balanced between attending to the presence of God in awe and appreciation, and acting on behalf of that God-presence in the service and promotion of justice? Will contemplation move us toward action and is our action grounded in contemplation, and do young people see evidence of the validity of both? And do we as adults refuse to be observers, but active participants in the same spiritual growth process as our youth? We have much to learn together.

> The natural growth process in children will occur... in most cases, in spite of us. We seldom kill our children by trying to grow them. What we do kill is our simple awareness of the natural growth process. Being so interested in taking credit for the growth and carrying the burden of it, we fail to see its wonder... Seeing it, marveling at it, we can at the same time be an integral, active part of it. (May 41)

Our spiritual growth is no different than natural growth. It will occur in spite of all our efforts. The loss will come if we get so caught up in focusing on the spirituality of our adolescents that we fail to see its wonder. Caught up in its wonder, we cannot help but be integrally involved in fostering its growth!

Although much time and attention has been given to practical directions for spirituality and how to nourish our young people's hunger for God, little has been written on spirituality and youth ministry. However, almost everything we attend to in youth ministry somehow impacts their spiritual selves, whether it is catechesis, retreats, liturgy, leadership, leisure, service, family programs, or advocacy. All are intricately intertwined, fostering and transforming their spirituality. "Spirituality is a process of walking through life with the Lord's presence, teaching, and power as the basis for everyday living" (Hill 101). Therefore, all we do in youth ministry should call young people to reflect on how they organize their lives before God, both through appreciation and action. We need to provide a balance of these as we seek to foster that same faith growth, regardless of the methods or programs we use.

William O'Malley, S.J. focuses on the lack of religious imagination in our ministry with the young.

> There is a natural potential within every human person, even nonreligious persons, that responds to the numinous and sacred in nature and art, and, if grace builds on nature, we can begin our movement toward the spirituality that deals with God by sensitizing children early to that more accessible and less intimidating union with the powerful and invisible forces all around them (that are, in fact, the aliveness of God.). (O'Malley, "Spirituality" 393)

O'Malley believes young children should be exposed to centering and meditative prayer while they are "less defensive and more imaginative" ("Spirituality" 393). Learning should always be an adventure in curiosity where they can discover their own answers. Storytelling and myth and fable should be used frequently, and youth should be encouraged to develop and create their own. Since image so dominates media and advertising and education and politics, and yes, even church, youth must be allowed to explore their own images. They should be encouraged to image God, self, family, a reconciled world, heaven, and all the spiritual questions they wish to pursue. He is all for "breaking down left-brain biases" ("Spirituality" 394) and seeing the world and God from a right-brain vantage point for a change. Adolescents, he believes, would then be more prepared to understand the stories of Scripture and the truths which they contain. "Our audiences remain comfortably complacent in the face of a message that was calculated to upset, to provoke a total reversal of values: a conversion. There are many causes for that complacency, but I believe the root cause is that they have never really learned to read that message for themselves" (O'Malley, "Scripture" 81). O'Malley advocates retreats and other community experiences where young people come to grips with their own vulnerability, their own beliefs, their own selves. Young people crave excitement and stimulation. Why should not they find the discovery of God in their own day-to-day lives stimulating? Maybe because they have never been taught to look for God there!

O'Malley does not seek to disregard doctrine or formal catechesis or skill development, but simply to open our eyes to the fact that the world makes a wonderful classroom for conversion, and that we have to trust young people's experiences and allow them to reflect on them. "According to Jesus, they are always in the Kingdom. Teach them to feel it, enjoy it, revel in it, perhaps even remain in it" ("Spirituality" 393).

More than anything, young people must not be subverted in search of their souls. In the era of the "good life," young people must know that money, power, jobs, and possessions don't always equal happiness. And maybe that is hard to see because they have lost their capacity for wonder and awe and blessing and hope. Maybe it would be nice if we could take the offensive with young people and their spirituality instead of them always being on the defensive. Let's examine our prayer, ritual, liturgy, advocacy, and presence with young people and evaluate how imaginative we have been. Maybe we will recognize the ultimate value of awareness and be able to model that with young people.

> Awareness is a space giver. An open window, letting the fresh air in. It unties the knots and loosens the tension. Awareness with full acceptance is like pure sunlight shining in a cellar, making it possible for healing to happen and growth to take place. One has to do nothing with it. (May 102)

I think William O'Malley would agree with the need for fresh air and awareness. Young people need to appreciate their spiritual selves as in-process, dynamic, always changing. The other given is that we as adult ministers are not in control of what their spirituality looks like in the end. We can only open up the possibilities and allow them to make the choices. But the possibilities are endless, and so far we have only offered a select few. "To achieve a teen-age spirituality, we must first prove to our young the undeniable existence of their souls. Then perhaps we can show them the One for whom those souls were made" ("Spirituality" 394).

Charles Shelton, S.J. seems to take William O'Malley's approach one step further. For Shelton, spirituality "is concerned with personal response to and growth in the Lord. Concretely, this response to God's call takes place in the context of prayer and one's efforts to proclaim the Kingdom of God through service to one's brothers and sisters" (Shelton 8). Shelton prescribes the two-pronged approach to spirituality of contemplation and action, personal meaning and deepening relationships, and consolidates his perspective of adolescent spirituality into four characteristics (Shelton 9-10).

1. **Christ-centered**. Focuses on the personal invitation of Christ to follow him. Therefore, adolescents seek a strong personal relationship with Jesus at the same time they are realizing its implications and demands.

> Those of us who work with young adults and youth need to be willing to fall in love—with Our Lord and with them. We need to see in everything we do with them an opportunity to introduce them to this radiant, strong, infinitely attractive Person who stands at the center of everything the Church is or does and who waits with urgent longing just for them. Then we will have given them Someone infinitely worthy of their attention and devotion... In giving them Christ—we will be giving them the truth—and sooner or later, that is something to which each of us must return. (Maas 7)

This relationship with Jesus is absolutely critical to the spirituality of the developing, discerning adolescent.

2. **Relational**. Adolescents' personal experience of Jesus is lived out and realized in all their relationships, but especially family, peers, special friendships, and significant adults. Community is a priority.

3. **Future-Oriented**. Although rooted in the present, adolescents are continually trying on values, roles, ideas, and strategies for the future. Although learning to "be" themselves, they are also focused on "becoming" for the future.

4. **Developmental**. Adolescence is a particular life-stage complete with its own insights and perspectives. Adolescents must be given all the time they need to come to an understanding of the scope of their spirituality. We adults also need to understand this developmental stage if we are to be fully present to all the dynamics as they unfold.

Shelton believes that the ultimate question for adolescents is how the person of Jesus Christ makes a difference in their lives and relationships and how this person deepens their commitment to the Gospel message. During the adolescent years, the understanding of Christian values ebbs and flows, thus the integration of these values is often a slow, painful process (for both youth and those who minister to them!). Ultimately, "maturing adolescents gradually experience a deepening commitment regarding what they believe and what is important in their lives" and "gradually come to understand that what they believe is inherently tied to what they do" (Shelton 339). Thus, adolescents consistently need to examine the challenges of Christian commitment and discipleship, "to ask more questions and to think more critically of themselves, of others, and of society" (Shelton 341).

However, it continues to be the adolescent's overriding concern with relationships — with self, Jesus, others, and the world — that serve as the foundation for their developing spiritual identity. It is the experience of God in and through these relationships that allows young people to see themselves as graced and gifted and called to respond in their own, unique way. This can only happen if we take them where they are and enter into their experience rather than try to bring them to where we are. As a church, we need to recognize the special contribution adolescents make to the collective wisdom, precisely because of their world view at this stage of development. Shelton challenges us to harness their spirit and perspective as a means of re-energizing the spiritual life of the community (not to mention ourselves, individually!).

Michael Warren adds a different emphasis to the perspective of O'Malley and Shelton. He seeks a connection between spirituality and justice:

> One cannot approach the question of Christian spirituality, particularly in cultures tied to an economics of consumption, without careful attention to lifestyle. The challenge of finding an appropriate spirituality is partly the challenge of finding an appropriate lifestyle. Second, the crisis of the human spirit in our time is the crisis of knowing what things to pay attention to... Any sidestepping these twin religious challenges of attention and behavior would betray the inner core of spirituality. (Warren, *Faith* 88)

For Warren, when we address the spirituality of young people, we are addressing "a systematic way of attending to the presence of God" (*Faith* 90), and once we do that, we cannot separate spirituality from the world in which they live. "A spirituality is a way of walking, a particular way of being in the world" (*Faith* 95). Therefore, Warren believes we must pay particular attention to the life structure of young people — to their need for immediate gratification, to the violence and self-destructive behavior, to their uncertainties about the future, to the place of success and money, to their disconnectedness — and offer some viable alternatives. These forces "are reversible only through the sustained effort of a community of people proposing in a loving way a different set of values and a different way of living from that of the prevailing culture" (Warren, *Liberation* 88). A spirituality for young people needs to stress eager anticipation and the hopeful expectation of a better future—one that young people help to create. It is a spirituality that attends to God through the poor and suffering and connects rather than separates people. Warren presents a spirituality of solidarity and unity and interdependence where young people are encouraged to see beyond the barriers their own life structures impose. This, of course, will require imagining the world in a new way, taking risks, and substituting unity in God in place of blatant individualism.

> The question of course, is whether the Gospel's imagining of the world is able even to challenge or override the imagination incessantly offered through the printed, visual, and aural word. My own sense is that for most persons it cannot, at least not without the help of groups of disciples actually living out the risks of fidelity. Without the countervailing help of a visible, audible chorus, most persons in our society will not be able to sing the song of Good News. (Warren, *Faith* 105)

Young people recognize the problem, even if they see no solution. And the more we call them to pay attention to the messages and images of their life structure and see them as either destructive or life-giving, the more they will be able to respond appropriately. Adolescents need to take action to express their convictions as much as to achieve a goal. Only by calling attention to what is and imagining what could be, will youth and youth ministers be able to move in the direction of creating a new reality based on the kingdom message. A spirituality for adolescents must entice them into the world to make it better. It is disturbing to think that the call of Jesus is the call to be uncomfortable, to be unwilling to settle for what is. But the message of Jesus is intrusive and unsettling. In the words of Joan Chittister: "our ministry is to continue the work not only of Jesus, the healer, but also of Jesus, the prophet... Our ministry must be not only to comfort but to challenge; not just attend to, but also to advocate; not just of vision, but of voice; not only to care, but to change" (82).

We are being asked to model a spirituality of courage and compassion, not one or the other. We are being asked to liberate ourselves before we attempt to liberate the young or the world. But the focus has to be more than me and God and has to include the actual, concrete ways we choose to live our lives. Our young people have become victims of their culture—thus, the preferential option for the poor and young is a concept we can no longer ignore. To speak of nourishing spirituality and at the same time placate, dismiss, or overlook their needs is blasphemy. We must espouse an integrated spirituality for our youth, "a spirituality of expectation, attentiveness, and connectedness.... a commitment to the reversibility of evil with all the strategies of resistance such a commitment will involve. Perhaps here there is an agenda for youth ministry that will take a long time to exhaust" (Warren, *Liberation* 89).

Regardless which of these three perspectives you adhere to (O'Malley, Shelton, Warren), there is a need to establish some direction for adolescent spirituality; otherwise it will be a topic yielding much discussion but little action. Regardless of whether you hope to assist young people in discovering God in the ordinary or to motivate them to act on behalf of God in the world, we have already wasted too much time. The waters of baptism seem to be running dry and all we have to say is, "I thirst" and we will be given living water in abundance. What are some concrete ways we can share that living water with adolescents and quench the thirst of the rest of the community at the same time? We must be with them in it as fully as we can and do the best we can to nourish the good work God has begun. Consider the following ideas:

1. *Stress the relational aspects of faith, centered on the person of Jesus Christ.* Introduce young people to the Jesus of the Gospels and the cost of discipleship. Examine how the Paschal Mystery is experienced in their families, in their parish communities, with friends, and in the world. Surround them with adults who love and respect them as they are.

2. *Help young people see all of life as sacrament.* Break open the symbols of religious experience and celebrate ritually. Go slowly and use what is natural to fully involve young people. Allow them to express themselves and their faith in ritual celebrations. It can be a powerful experience.

3. *Allow time for storytelling and faith-sharing.* They personalize and internalize our God experiences.

4. *Invite young people into responsible participation within the faith community.* Young people's need to become and belong must be satisfied within a community that cherishes their presence. You don't need to create new roles for them—welcome them into already established ministries. They have much to offer RCIA, sacramental preparation, liturgy, social concerns, parish council, RENEW, religious education, and more. As they have been gifted, they will gift others.

5. *Bring religious imagination into all aspects of prayer, Scripture, ritual, liturgy, and catechesis.* Introduce youth to new prayer forms and worship opportunities, both individually and communally.

6. *Introduce young people to experiences of silence, solitude, and reflection, as well as social action.* Integrate these throughout the year

rather than consolidate into a "course" or "program" format. Justice issues need to be confronted and dealt with accordingly.

7. *Challenge young people to clarify their values using their faith as a guide.* Help them to see Gospel values as countercultural and to make good choices.

8. *Never underestimate the power of presence to young people.*

9. *Assist adolescents in attending to the spiritual dimension of their lives.* What are the priorities, demands, and benefits of living a spiritual life? Nurture and encourage their faith growth in a holistic, balanced manner.

10. *Above all, encourage them to be gentle with themselves.* They have all the time they need to make mistakes and learn from them. Our spirituality unfolds over a lifetime. They cannot have God mastered or figured out or all the questions answered by the end of high school. There is no formula for holiness.

It is not a matter of not having a spirituality, but what kind of spirituality our young people will have. If we are willing to join them on the journey, chances are we will all uncover aspects of God-in-us we never imagined. If we are willing to let go and let God be in charge, a whole new direction may be revealed. We do know that imagination, relationships, and life structure are key elements that continue to need attention. We cannot afford to be complacent, for there are many enticements vying for our youth. If we are not willing to make youth a priority, something or someone else surely will.

We cannot be responsible for designing their spiritual lives, but we can be involved in the shaping. We can influence their spirituality even though, thankfully, we cannot control it. Adolescents' spiritual growth will happen in spite of us. Yet God still wants and needs us involved as instruments, potters, guides, healers, teachers, companions, eyes and ears, and yes, even learners. It has been a long time since many of us watched with awe — and it has been even longer since we jumped in with both feet. More than anything, young people need the freedom of graced trust that allows transformation to happen. Adults cannot give that to them, but we can experience glimpses of it together. We are all called to this deeper union with God so that we can actively care for each other and the world. Maybe we can begin by accepting young people as they are, where they are, and affirm their ability to transform our Church into a kingdom community.

Spiritual perfection is not found in the fulfillment of any rigid blueprint. It is found rather in the surprising moments of meeting between God's active grace and our spontaneous willingness. All of us know such perfect moments. They are moments lived out of the heart, found scattered through the day like manna falling in the desert. They may be very simple and ordinary moments. Perfection is like that (Edwards 14).

WORKS CITED

Chittister, Joan, O.S.B. *WomanStrength: Modern Church, Modern Women.* Kansas City: Sheed & Ward, 1990.

Edwards, Tilden. *Living in the Presence.* San Francisco: Harper and Row, 1987.

Hill, Brennan. *Key Dimensions in Religious Education.* Winona MN: St. Mary's Press, 1989.

Maas, Robin. "Something to Rebel Against: Freedom and Limitation in the Formation of Christian Identity." *Network Paper 37.* New Rochelle: Don Bosco Multimedia, 1990.

May, Gerald, M.D. *Simply Sane.* New York: Crossroad, 1990.

O'Malley, S.J., William J. "Scripture From Scratch." *America* 4 Feb. 1989: 77-81

______. "Teenage Spirituality." *America* 29 April 1989: 390-394.

Shelton, S.J. Charles M. *Adolescent Spirituality.* New York: Crossroads Press, 1983.

Warren, Michael. *Faith, Culture and the Worshiping Community.* New York: Paulist Press, 1989.

______. *Youth, Gospel, Liberation.* San Francisco: Harper and Row, 1987.

Chapter 11

Education, Imagination, and Spirituality

Maria Harris

We teach best when we are most truly ourselves. Thus, I extend here an invitation to imagination. I extend it to the individual teacher who is reading this essay and who is asking, "What counsel would you give me? What paths might I follow?"

I will attempt here to make suggestions appropriate to teachers who want to work out of their own imaginations. Each teacher's response will necessarily be idiosyncratic; nevertheless, some general principles or criteria can help guide us in the journey. I will be naming five criteria which may also be thought of as paths to take or moments in which to dwell. Although presented in sequential order, these criteria are not only relegated to one another, they also necessarily overlap. I will also suggest exercises to accompany each criterion. In order, the criteria (paths) are: 1) taking care; 2) taking steps; 3) taking form; 4) taking time; 5) taking risks.

TAKING CARE

The initial criterion for any teacher is the criterion of taking care. The starting point of the teaching act draws not on material resources — those will come later — but on spiritual ones. Care is an attitude, a way of being toward the other, a decision in favor of reverence and respect. Taking care implies we will not hurry into the teaching situation. Instead we will be at pains to be still, to be silent, to be quiet and give ourselves the opportunity to survey what lies before us in the teaching activity. Care is what the Vietnamese monk, Thich Nhat Hanh, refers to as *mindfulness*. For teachers, care is the activity of being mindful of ourselves as teachers, of our students in their unique personhood, and of the subject matter that will be the third partner in our relation.

The most practical procedure I can suggest for taking care is to urge the disciplines of spirituality: meditation, prayer, periods of stillness. With my own students, before we engage together with subject matter, we often spend ten to fifteen minutes in quiet receptivity and awareness. "Sit back in your soul," I urge them. Then, drawing on the work of Jose Hobday, O.S.F. I explain, "And the way to sit back in your soul is to sit back in your body." Amazingly, they do. We sit quietly, and often it is possible to touch and feel and smell the quietude and openness that enters the room. After a brief time we are able to begin work together on the topic of the day. Invariably, those first moments create a receptivity to the material at hand.

Such an exercise is not limited only to teachers of religion or theology. I am aware of professors of management and physics who do the same. I am aware, too, of teachers of six- and seven-year olds who also begin with such moments of taking care, urging the children to start the lesson by first going into their "heart room." [1] These moments are akin to the Jewish notion that on the Sabbath, the Creator of the world "draws breath." Taking care is the teacher drawing breath before the actual teaching activities begin.

Taking care does not actually start when we arrive in the classroom, however. It begins in our moments of preparation or, to use Mary Tully's term, our moments of previsualization of the teaching situation. I have often been struck by our (teachers') unreserved use of taking care *after* teaching, that is, our use of techniques for evaluation (or *post*visualization). The kind of taking care I speak of is the partner of that work, often left out in the rush to cover material. It is the work of using forms that create a readiness: using forms for *pre*visualization.

EXERCISES FOR TAKING CARE

Below are three simple exercises teachers might use to embody the moment of taking care. The first is toward care for ourselves as teachers; the second is toward care for our students; the third is toward care for our subject matter.

TAKING CARE OF OURSELVES AS TEACHERS

Begin with a meditation, such as Martin Heidegger's "Myth of Care." Care, it is said, was walking along the river one day, picking up earth and thinking, "Wouldn't it be wonderful if there could be human beings?" But because Care couldn't *make* human beings, didn't have the power, Care asked the Holy One to take the earth and breathe life into it. And the Holy One did. Afterwards, the following decision was made. Since the Holy One had breathed life into human beings, the Holy One would receive them when they died: the Holy One was where they were going. Because they were made from the earth, from the *humus*, they would be called *human*.

But because Care had thought of them in the first place, Care would possess them all their lives. [2]

Such a meditation could then be accompanied by taking care to reflect well on the story, and then by asking ourselves questions like the following:

* Where am I, as a teacher, called to embody Care in the class I am teaching today?

* Where does what I am planning to teach today make my students more human? In what ways does it help them give form to their universe?

* Then, after reflecting briefly on each class member, ask: To what in my students' humanity will I address special care today?

Taking even three minutes to meditate on the responses to each of these questions can enhance the teaching activity immeasurably. In a brief space of nine or ten minutes, we will have taken care.

TAKING CARE OF STUDENTS

Care for our students is demonstrated primarily in our naming of the students. I would argue that regardless of class size or age (adults, graduate school, little children), the teacher is responsible to know the names of every student with whom she or he works. If name tags are needed, so be it; a folded card at each student's place, set on top of the desk or taped to it can also be used. Whatever method is used, the point of the naming is to allow class members to be addressed as the persons they are, specifically, and not as generic or interchangeable "students." Being addressed as who one is enables a subject-subject relation, a communion of intersubjectivity, a feeling on the part of students that they are *seen*. Being addressed by name by someone who has taken the trouble not only to find out, but to remember what a student is called is a symbol of care for the student in the teaching situation. Such naming then creates the possibility of the student's willingness to accompany the teacher on the journey of learning, for the teacher has already begun that journey by, to use Soren Kierkegaard's phrase, "going to the place where the learner is," and discovering the learner's name.

TAKING CARE OF SUBJECT MATTER

Care for the subject matter can be addressed in a related way. If the subject matter were to speak, what would it say of itself? [3] If it were to be in dialogue with us, what would that dialogue sound like? Taking a few moments to record even a half-page of dialogue can lead to revelation of subject matter we did not know we knew.

But these listenings will be in concert with the greatest respect we can show to subject matter: Finding out all we can about it. As reverent, careful teachers, it is our responsibility to do research, to study, to meet the material for preliminary conversations, to be prepared. Then, and only then, are we ready to introduce it to students and to invite them toward engagement with it.

Taking care is a means of insuring that the teacher acts as a contemplative, intensely involved in seeing, attending, looking. It is a means of insuring that the teacher acts as an ascetic, who, by keeping a respectful distance, is at pains to do no violence to the student or the subject matter. It is a means of readying the teaching self to be a *creator*, by drawing together the elements needed in the act of teaching. And it is a means of moving toward making teaching a *sacrament*, an activity to be performed with the attentiveness given to ritual; a ground to be entered which is assumed to be holy.

TAKING STEPS

The teacher should receive the invitation to imagination as one would receive an invitation to a dance. The reason for the insistence on this metaphor of the dance may at first appear simple, but it implies a profound philosophy of education. This philosophy is based on the following assumption: The core of things is not substance, it is rhythm.

The influence of modern physics has helped teachers understand something of this philosophy, as we discover that all matter is constantly in movement. Modern physics has also assisted many in a return to the rhythms of the universe and to the startling rediscovery of the rhythm of our planet in its daily rotation on its axis, as well as its yearly rhythmic revolution around the sun. These discoveries, in turn, return us to recognize the rhythms in our lives: the rhythm of our own bodies — our circulatory, respiratory, and digestive rhythms that keep us alive; our human living that occurs in a context of the ebb and flow of tides; the movement from autumn to winter to spring to summer; our rhythmic patterns of waking at dawn and resting at sunset. We are surrounded and helped and nurtured by rhythm.

Rhythm in education is a theme with a rich grounding. In 1929, in the classic book *The Aims of Education*, philosopher Alfred North Whitehead described the rhythm of education as having three steps: romance, precision, and generalization or synthesis. [4] The first step is romance. In his view, romance is the moment of first apprehension where the subject matter has the vividness of novelty, holding within itself unexplored connections with possibilities half-discovered by the wealth of materials. In this step, knowing is not dominated by systematic procedures.

In the step of precision, in contrast, the width of relationship is subordinated to exactness of formulation. Precision is a challenge to set some limits, to refine, and to deepen rather than broaden, at least for the time being. It is the challenge to stand back and contemplate, to reflect, and to ask serious questions, especially questions of analysis. [5] It is a challenge to recall that, if one is to reach the final step — synthesis or generalization, where the return to romance occurs — one must slow down and take time to reconnoiter. Classified ideas and relevant technique, which become coupled with the wonder and idealism of first apprehension (romance), are the rewards of precision.

Synthesis is the third step. It is the circling back stage — analogous to a dance, but a dance farther along in time. Subject matter at this step is deeper and more beautiful, because this step is the coming together — the synthesis — of the loveliness of romance and the chastening, studied, ascetic attitude that precision has brought to the subject at hand.

Urging the teacher to take steps is the follow-up to taking care, in the sense that the teacher has now taken on the activity of teaching for himself or herself. The great temptation here, however, is to make the first steps in teaching ones of precision where systematic procedure dominates. My plea actually enhances systematic procedure. That is, if systems, procedures, processes, and tasks are to be learned, these are more appropriate and fitting *after* the step of romance; after time has been taken for diving in, wrestling with, rolling around in, dialoguing, and interchanging with material which is not yet ready to be systematized. The rhythm of education must be respected; otherwise, the process will be short-circuited and in danger of premature closure and conclusion.

EXERCISE FOR TAKING STEPS

The following three exercises can help us step both more lightly and gently as well as be more in harmony with the rhythm of teaching and education.

Stepping Around

Let the beginning of a teaching session be a "go-around." The students can be asked to do sentence-completion activities that directly address the subject, yet preserve the romance of first apprehension. If, for example, the subject for the day is morality, people might begin by giving names and then adding something pertinent to the subject. For example, "I'm Mary Jones, and one person who is a symbol of morality for me is ___________________." or "I'm Dick Walsh, and one image of the moral life for me is ___________________." or "I'm Annie Dillon, and one industry I consider moral in today's world is ___________________." The point here is that story, symbol, and image are ways of fleshing out the texture of a topic, and of teasing out the meanings in a topic. A "go-around" can preserve the richness of first apprehension. And, although I have used morality as an example, any topic might initially be addressed with such an exercise. For example, "I'm Susan Johnson, and for me faith is

___________________; hope is ___________________; war is ___________________; adulthood is ___________________; and so on.

Stepping to the Rhythms of Story and Ritual

The steps in the rhythms of teaching can be applied to whatever subject is at hand, by way of assignment. For example, if a group is studying a novel such as *The Color Purple* by Alice Walker, we might develop a series of questions that moves through contemplation, engagement, form-giving, emergence, and release:

* As you *contemplate* the main characters, who comes first to mind?
* With which character did you find yourself most *engaged*?
* What did the author do to *give form* to this character?
* In what scenes did you find your understanding of this character *emerging*?
* As the book ends, what do you expect will happen next to this person? (release)

But the steps in the rhythm of teaching might also be used in the design of a story, which is our own story, perhaps even our own biography or life story, just as we have used it for the novel. In that case, the steps may be more intense and involving, and may call for more student engagement. For example:

* Write a story where the main character or characters move through these five steps.
* Create a story where you are the main character moving through these steps.
* Tell your own story in terms of this dance.

Again, the steps might be used in the creation of rituals, such as the Yom HaShoah ritual that commemorates the Holocaust, or indeed any ritual activity around a course of study, thus:

* What about the Holocaust do we wish to contemplate?
* With what aspects of the Holocaust will our ritual be engaged?
* What forms, shapes, patterns shall be use in designing the ritual?
* How and when will it be presented?
* What will be the hoped for or intended outcome? [6]

Addressing an event of the magnitude of the Holocaust is perhaps more appropriately done by taking time for the entire rhythm of teaching to unfold rather than an immediate move to the how and when of its presentation. This in turn allows for romance, precision, and synthesis or for the rhythm that begins in contemplation and concludes in release.

Stepping Back and Forth

In the preparation and presentation of subject matter, we need, as teachers, to be sure of a constant forward movement and then return if we are to be responsive to the rhythms of education and teaching. Therefore, in any previsualization of a class session, a third exercise is to imagine the subject matter both as presented to students and as received back from them. Rhythm demands this back-and-forth character; therefore, the time must be spent not only with teacher-talk but with student-talk as well. But subject matter must also be handed over in a way that challenges students to hand it back. This is not done in the form of exams, or repetition; but as the result of the teacher who carefully hands something on, and then asks:

* Now, how might you pass this along?
* If you had been the one presenting it originally, what would have been your first step?
* In what ways would you formulate this question?
* To whom would you be willing to teach it, and what might you expect from them in return?

The point of this exercise is to help teacher and students move through rhythmic steps of forward and back, outward and inward, invitation and response, and to remain conscious all the while of the fact that teaching and learning are not linear and in one direction. Teaching and learning are organic, bodily actions, far more understandable in a context of repetition, return, diving into and pulling out of, and coming to points of rest and quiet before moving on to the next step.

TAKING FORM

When viewed as an activity of religious imagination, teaching is the incarnation of subject matter that leads to the revelation of subject matter. Taking form, then, has much to do with incarnation — especially incarnation that leads to revelation. The criterion of taking form involves three decisions: to take form seriously, to take form as a starting point, and to take form into account. Without central attention to form, the teaching enterprise is in danger of failure.

The exercises below are examples of giving form to subject matter in the actual teaching situation. However, any imaginative teacher will also be aware of form in two wider contexts. These are the world itself, and the place where the teaching occurs, usually a classroom. First, the imaginative teacher will have an educated sensitivity to forms of learning and teaching that are politically, socially, and economically oppressive. This sensitivity will be characterized by the continuing movement to look *for* and then *at* the dominant world view, the set of values and behaviors taken for granted and accepted as natural — that which may be called the dominant ideology of a society—as these are represented in the teaching situation (Kennedy 8).

Thus, the point I am making here is the necessity for all teachers to work at awareness of the questions of how the *forms* of politics, economics, social location, and ideology influence the teaching of any subject matter. I am also arguing that the imaginative teacher include as many points of view as possible as well as an ever-expanding awareness of the existence of opposing viewpoints.

A second, wider context, whose forms has profound influence on the teaching act, is the physical and psychological form of the place where the teaching occurs — what Eisner calls the implicit curriculum — what might be understood by the term *environment*. We learn differently when we sit in straight rows looking at the backs of the heads in front of us than we do when we sit in circles, looking at faces. We learn differently when we are in a room with light and air — or are in the open air — than we do when we are inside a room with poor or no ventilation. We learn differently when we have color and decoration in our surroundings than when the walls are bare. We learn differently when a team of teachers, rather than one person, presents material to us. But we also learn differently depending upon our relations to the others in the situation, both the teacher and those who are our peers. We learn differently if the language of instruction is our second, rather than our first; if the examples used are not germane to us; if all the authorities who are cited as experts represent another sex or race or geography or even thinking pattern from ourselves. Each of these is a set of *forms*, and the teacher needs to take these forms with great seriousness as agents incarnating subject matter, in an implicit and subtle way, but nevertheless in very powerful way.

EXERCISES FOR TAKING FORM SERIOUSLY

The most direct influence of form comes in the shape, design, and incarnation of the subject matter itself: verbal form, earth form, embodied form, forms for discovery, art forms. Therefore, the following exercises for taking form seriously draw on the two counsels: 1) use all the forms of poetic speech on which you can draw; 2) use drama and mime in ways that incorporate body, earth, and the possibility of surprise.

Poetry

Use poetry. For example:
* Ask students to respond to questions in Haiku form.
* Ask students to find poems on whatever topic is being studied.
* Draw on the work of actual poets, such as Kenneth Koch. [7]

In my own classes, I have often used the work of Kenneth Koch, a New York City poet, who has written about his work in teaching poetry to grade-school children in poor sections of the city, as well as to nursing home residents. [8] Koch gives creative directions to his students. He tells them, for example, to write lies (it is a wonderful thing for a child to get permission to lie, even briefly), to write wishes, to write dreams. One of his richest suggestions, one I have often used, asks participants to complete the phrase "I seem to be _____________, but really I am _____________" with a word or phrase. When I use this, I direct them to fold the paper, unsigned, and place it in the center of the room. Another class member chooses one of the papers and then reads it aloud with reverence and with care. As people sitting in a circle read a paper they have chosen from the larger pile, one after the other, the exercise invariably has two results: 1) it creates a community from what had been just a group; 2) it helps participants realize that they are far more alike than they are different. The anonymity allows for a wide freedom of expression since people often write what they are reluctant to speak aloud.

Drama and Mime

It is a rare subject that cannot be learned through pantomime, embodiment, and creative dramatics. Most teachers are aware of that fact but feel constrained by time. Yet the use of drama "fixes" insights in ways that accompany and enrich conceptual material. A presentation of *Fiddler on the Roof*, for example — or even a few scenes from the play — might teach more about the pain involved in commitment and conviction than a more discursive course. *The Roar of the Greasepaint, the Smell of the Crowd* or *Gideon* can teach much about the nature of dependence on the Holy One.

The revelation toward which such incarnation of form might lead is the depth of subject matter beyond and below the surface; depth open to human beings especially through the forms of poetry, song, sorrow, beauty, gesture, and most of all, other people. Taking these forms seriously gives teachers new opportunities to draw on their contemplative, ascetic, creative, and sacramental imaginations.

TAKING TIME

If the incarnation of subject matter is done with care, that incarnation can lead to revelation. Take time. For revelation is a gradual unfolding in the sun, inevitably, necessarily, as tomcats stretch; revelation is closely related to human birth and does not happen except in its own time; revelation cannot be guaranteed; revelation must be waited upon. Waiting for and upon revelation implies a willingness to dwell in patience with subject matter, even to see the values of darkness and unclarity of which Robert Graves writes:

He is quick, thinking in clear images;
I am slow, thinking in broken images.

He becomes dull, trusting to his clear images;
I become sharp, mistrusting my broken images.

Trusting his images, he assumes their relevance;
Mistrusting my images, I question their relevance.

Assuming their relevance, he assumes the fact;
Questioning their relevance, I question the fact.

When the fact fails him, he questions his senses;
When the fact fails me, I approve my senses.

He continues quick and dull in his clear images;
I continue slow and sharp in my broken images.

He in a new confusion of his understanding;
I in a new understanding of my confusion. (Graves 80)

EXERCISING FOR TAKING TIME

For the teacher, the interpretive keys for learning how to take time so that revelation might fostered are found in self-conscious reflection, questioning, and probing the images of temporality. The exercises that follow are designed to help teachers become involved with each of these areas.

Self-Conscious Reflection

I use different "talking papers" to help teachers probe the meaning of revelation in teaching. One of these talking papers has five questions, each with enough space after it for the person to take notes, and then to engage in conversation with another student or teacher or with me. These questions are as follows:

* Have you had a major moment of revelation in your life in response to teaching? If so, describe it.
* What did you learn?
* How did you learn it?
* What difference, if any, did it make in your life?
* Has it made any difference in your own teaching?

Although in my experience, teachers' answers to these questions vary, most teachers do respond that they have discovered revelation happening to them in two circumstances.

The first circumstance usually took place when teachers were themselves students, and a teacher *took time* with them, saw them as individuals, recognized the possibilities in the work they had done, and became catalysts to reveal them to themselves. In my view, these are examples of indirect communication. Content was not delivered; instead, these people as learners were delivered to themselves.

The second circumstance or situation that teachers responding to the above questions refer to concerns their own teaching. Their accounts tend to center around the times when they used forms for discovery, time at which the forms they used to incarnate subject matter did not predict what the outcome would be. I think, for example, of how a sixth-grade teacher introduced her geography class to caves. She did so by re-creating her classroom (environment) by turning it into a series of caves (by turning over furniture, by darkening the room, by asking the children to exercise their imaginations). As the teacher tells it, the learning about caves was far greater than anything she could have prepared from the textbook.

Questioning

In addition to self-conscious reflection, exercises can be directed to questions and questioning. If it is true that the place where the learner is, is the place of the question, then, as teacher, we need to probe the meanings of questions and to create for ourselves and our students a repertoire of kinds of questions. The context of learning to question is best described by Rainer Maria Rilke's well-known passage:

Be patient towards all that is unsolved in your heart and try to love the questions themselves like locked rooms....Do not now seek the answers; that cannot be given you because you would not be able to live them. And the point is, to live everything. Live the questions now. Perhaps you will then gradually, without noticing it, live along some distant day into the answer (Rilke 33).

Once that context has been established, we can move on to levels of questioning and explore deepening levels such as those illustrated below:

Set One: Types of Questions
Informational: listing data, facts, specific content
Comprehension: asking about the meanings of context
Application: asking for places where the content applies
Analysis: distinguishing meanings in the context
Synthesis: making connections about the context
Evaluation: asking for judgments about the content

Set Two: Types of Questions
Receiving/Attending: asking about awareness of a content
Responding: asking where the greatest interest is, about what is intriguing in the context
Valuing: asking whether students accept, agree, reject the content, and why
Organizing values: asking students to reform the content on their own terms, with their own criteria

Characterizing values: asking students what their own approach to the content would be, how they would describe the subject matter at hand [9]

We teachers can destroy the contemplative imagination by insisting on hurry. We can turn the ascetic imagination inside out, where instead of insuring students space, it becomes an intrusive, unwelcome probe. We can unknowingly eliminate the conditions of waiting and receptivity central to the creative imagination. If we refuse to "take" growing time, sleeping time, learning time, we shut the door on the sacramental imagination and cut off our students' capacities to discover the Holy surrounding them in everything. I am returned to such reflection (often with chagrin and embarrassment) whenever I reread a poem given me by one of my students. The student, Thomas Evans, was a man who, like me, had great affection for Martin Buber. Indeed, he titled his poem-request "After Buber," and the request pleaded for my allowing revelation not only to be in *its* time, but in *his* time, not mine. It said:

> Teacher, be consciously active
> In helping me select a human world
> Out of the "purposelessly streaming education by all things."
> Yet cast but a glance — lift but a finger — act "as though you would not,"
> For it is my mysterious personal life at risk,
> And I must direct the fashioning.

TAKING RISKS

The *Oxford English Dictionary* defines risk as "hazard, danger, exposure to mischance or peril." The major danger to which the risk-taker is exposed is loss. And yet, I offer teachers one final criterion to act as counsel and as catalysts to their activity: Take risks. Take risks even if they result in great loss. The vocation demands it. For teaching is the incarnation of subject matter that leads to the revelation of subject matter. And the true revelation of subject matter is the discovery that we, as human beings, are called to be subjects in the world. We are called to exercise the grace of power in the direction of recreation.

For thousands of years the relation of risk-taking and loss has been with us, and history indicates tremendous odds against the risk-taker. But I would argue that the risk-takers are the ones who have contributed most to human re-creation and transformation, often — perhaps most often — under the risk of death. Regretfully, when the choice between gaining the whole world and losing one's soul or taking the risk of losing the world and gaining one's world is set before us, the latter is chosen — is risked — less often than it might be.

Still, if the teaching act is directed toward others discovering and claiming their own powers, teachers must take risks. Even more specifically, risk is required when the powers to be discovered and claimed are not only the powers to receive and to love, but also the powers to rebel, to resist, and to reform. Receptivity and love, yes; rebel, resist and reform, no — or, at the very most, perhaps. Yet the powers of rebellion, resistance, and reform grow out of receptivity; and if they are exercised humanly, they have a dynamism within them that leads to love.

EXERCISES FOR TAKING RISKS

All five powers are critical for the re-creation and transformation of the world. The following exercises are designed to foster the development of these powers.

Exploring Risk-Takers

Since our courage is often developed from studying and musing on the lives of others, make a list of risk-takers, the risks taken, the tasks accomplished, and the losses incurred. Assign their biographies, suggest that people interview these risk-takers if they are still living, or, if they are deceased, interview people who knew them. See either how many teachers can be listed as risk-takers, or where teaching was a central element in the lives of the risk-takers on the list. See how many risk-takers can be found in the world of art. (The risk-takers need not be famous; part of the exercise can be ferreting out the names of little known risk-takers, those in one's own family or community.)

Exploring the Outrageous

In order to explore the themes of resistance and rebellion, build a unit with students on the theme, "It's Outrageous" (a suggestion of artist-teacher Deborah Rose). Rose describes the exercise:

The kickoff is a party. Invitations instruct the students (teenagers in this case), to dress outrageously and to bring outrageous tapes of music. The first activity is part interviews, using questions such as "What is the most outrageous thing you have ever done?" "Who is the most outrageous teacher you have?" "What performing group do you consider totally outrageous?" Dinner consists of build-your-own-tacos, outrageously-gooey cheese nachos, and make-your-own totally outrageous sundaes. During dinner, a rock video provides entertainment — we played part of a "Live-Aid" concert. Any number of outrageous, ridiculous games can be played at such a party, with crazy prizes.

The following week, discussion begins with "What do we mean by outrageous?" The students generate a list of examples. Then they examine the root, or heart of the word, *rage*. Soon everyone begins to see the connections between a Live-Aid concert and outrage against world hunger. From that point, the group can make lists of things that enrage them. From there they can create a program and projects for an entire year. One possibility for Scripture study would be a discussion such as "Is Christianity outrageous?" "Was Jesus Christ outrageous?" (Rose)

And for teachers taking risks, I would add: Are you outrageous? Are you ever outraged? What is the appropriate focus of your rage? To what resistance and reform does it impel you?

Exploring Power

A third exercise, to which I was introduced by Paulo Freire, helps teachers and students explore their own power and uncover powers they might want to develop. Each participant needs at least 15 minutes to do the following:

* Choose an image, gesture, symbol, book title, or the like that represents your power as a teacher (or student or citizen).

* Tell the others in your group (two or three others seem a good number) what the image is, *and nothing more*.

* For 10 minutes, listen to what others see in the image you have chosen; for these 10 minutes, you are to be a listener.

* After 10 minutes, engage in conversation with your partners, sharing your initial reasons for choosing the symbol, commenting on what they saw that you did not see, and describing any revelation to which their comments have led you about yourself.

I have used this exercise for several years now, and it has proven to be an extraordinary way of discovering powers within. The additional point to include in using it here would be a last question, a final question after discussion:

* What risks will these powers enable you to take?

CONCLUSION

These five criteria (or paths) — taking care, taking steps, taking form, taking time, taking risks — are among those to which teachers might look as they respond to the invitation to bring their own imaginations to bear upon the activity of teaching. The criteria are questions, not answers; suggestions, not demands; counsels, not commandments. Nevertheless, I believe that they have within them much dynamism, much energy, much life. Listen to this ancient prayer to the Creator Spirit, the Divine Source of Imagination:

Come Holy Spirit,
Fill the hearts of those who would be faithful,
Kindle in them the fire of Love.

Send forth your Holy Spirit
And they shall be created
And they shall renew the face of the Earth.

I believe the Spirit is waiting to be summoned by teachers who are willing to take care, take steps, take form, take time, and take risks. Outcomes cannot be guaranteed, but the power of imagination is such that if it emerges from our lives, a fire is enkindled and begins to burn. And that fire enables movement in the direction all teaching moves, the direction of re-creation. When re-creation happens, the face of the earth is renewed.

A profound vocation, the vocation of teaching; a profound vocation, the vocation of religious imagination. For it can lead to incarnation, to revelation, and to the grace of power. And these, in turn, can lead to the re-creation of the world.

ENDNOTES

[1] See Mary Terese Donze, *In My Heart Room* (Liguori, MO: Liguori Publications, 1982) for examples of such exercises with children.

[2] See Maria Harris, *The D.R.E. Book* (New York: Paulist Press, 1976) for further commentary on the Myth of Care, drawn from the work of philosopher Martin Heidegger.

[3] For elaboration on this exercise, and for similar exercises, see the teacher's guide to the videotape program "Teaching and Religious Imagination," by Maria Harris (Allen TX: Argus Communications, 1985).

[4] See Alfred North Whitehead, *The Aims of Education* (New York: Macmillan, 1929), chapter 2, "The Rhythm of Education."

[5] See chapter 6, above.

[6] Examples of such rituals can be found in Franklin Littell, *The Crucifixion of the Jews* (New York: Harper and Row, 1975), 141-53. See also Eugene J. Fisher and Leon Klenicki, *From Death to Hope: Liturgical Reflections on the Holocaust* (New York: Anti-Defamation League of B'nai Brith, 1985).

[7] See the following books by Kenneth Koch: *Wishes, Lies and Dreams: Teaching Children to Write Poetry* (New York: Random House, 1970); *I Never Told Anybody: Teaching Poetry Writing in a Nursing Home* (New York: Random House, 1970); and *Rose, Where Did You Get That Red?* (New York: Vintage, 1974).

[8] See Koch, *Wishes, Lies and Dreams* and *I Never Told Anybody*.

[9] See Francis Hunkins, *Involving Students in Questioning* (Boston: Allyn and Bacon, 1976) and *Questioning Strategies and Techniques* (Boston: Allyn and Bacon, 1972).

WORKS CITED

Graves, Robert. "In Broken Images." *Collected Poems*. London: Cassell, 1975.

Hanh, Thich Nhat. *The Miracle of Mindfulness*. Boston: Beacon Press, 1976.

Kennedy, William Bean. "Christian Education and Mission into the Twenty-First Century." *Theodolite* 7.6 (1986): 8.

Rilke, Rainer Maria. *Letters to a Young Poet*. New York: W. W. Norton, 1934.

Rose, Deborah. Unpublished Paper. Newton, MA: Andover Newton Theological School, December 1985.

Walker, Alice. *The Color Purple*. New York: Washington Square Press, 1982.

Chapter 12

Liturgy and Spirituality

Austin Fleming

This chapter concerns itself with spirituality and the liturgical ministries, including the ministry of the assembled believers whom other ministers serve.

The broader context for this discussion will be the experience of intimacy, and the desire for it, in our worship life. "Intimacy" is a live commodity in the business of marketing religious life. Books, tapes, and retreats trumpet the value of, need for, depth, and experience of intimacy in the life of Christians. The approach here will be more basic and less strident.

SPIRITUAL INTIMACY

Not at issue here are spatial or stylistic notions of intimacy in the worship environment or experience. Our concern is rather with the *spiritual intimacy* that is more an affair of the heart than an ambience. Spiritual intimacy may be supported by a particular environment or worship style, but it does not root itself in anything save the encounter with our gracious, loving, and merciful God. Perhaps it is for this reason that the faithful elders in our communities, steeped in years of prayer and devotion, often adapt more easily to ritual and environmental change than do their middle-aged offspring: our elders root their faith in their experience of a faithful and saving Lord, more than in the trappings that adorn the community's celebration of that salvation.

The spiritual intimacy of liturgical prayer is born of those moments that we call conversion: the turning of our hearts to God who made us, who redeems us, and who sustains us. We speak here of those face-to-face and heart-to-heart moments when the Lord's presence in our lives is unmistakable, unavoidable, and deeply powerful. For some these moments are few, but they are not forgotten. This experience of intimacy marks the difference between knowing *about* God and *knowing* God.

WORSHIP NOURISHES INTIMACY

The liturgy does not so much produce or "confect" such moments as much as it nourishes and sustains them. The power of God's love, which draws upon our hearts, is not confined to or restricted by the celebration of liturgical acts. Indeed, it is this spiritual intimacy that draws us *to* divine service; it is that prior relationship upon which liturgy thrives. The best example of this can be seen in the stages of the Rite of Christian Initiation of Adults: the celebration of baptism is the sacramental and communal culmination of the work that the Lord began in the hearts of the neophytes long before they were admitted to communion at the Lord's table. Worship does not invent spiritual intimacy; it sustains and nourishes it.

This is not to downplay the power of the liturgical act in our individual and communal intimacy with the One who dwells in unapproachable light. In the Christian scheme of things, the sacraments and the liturgy of the hours are the premier moments when God's people gather to remember, to find present again, and to celebrate the saving deeds of the Lord in our midst. The intimacy between Creator and created in Christ knows its fullest expression in the church, the assembly of believers. Apart from the work and prayer of the church community, the believer is like the branch cut off from the vine, left to wither and die.

There is the story of the preacher who asked his congregation to not worry so much about the salvation of their individual souls but to image that they would be called to account as a *parish* on Judgment Day. Said the preacher, "If you live as a *people* who are to be judged, you will have not need to worry about your selves." The preacher helps us to put in context the relationship of spiritual intimacy to the life of the community and its worship.

INTIMACY AND MATURITY

It is in the intimacy of communion with other believers that we come to know the height and depth of God's love. Our individual intimacy with the Lord is brought to full growth in the church community; without the community's support and fellowship, we are undernourished. Spiritual intimacy with the Lord yearns to express and share itself with others, for the Lord's intimacy with each of us draws us into that people named as the Lord's believers. True spiritual intimacy comes to maturity in the assembly, the work, and the lift of God's people. It was through the *people* of Israel that the Lord was first revealed, and it is the believed *people* of the new Israel who are saved in the mystery of Jesus dying and rising. "You shall be my people and I will be your God" (Ez 36:28).

THE PHARISEES' PROBLEM

The intimacy of which we speak is as inescapable as the Lord who calls us to it. The divine Lover who pursues and seduces us will not easily be put off. The embracing arms that seek us out are wide with mercy and strong with compassion. A look at the Gospel shows that these same arms welcomed every sinner and outcast imaginable. Only the Pharisees seemed to stand outside the pale of this embrace: for them was reserved the Lord's anger and curse. Why? Because the Pharisees used the Law and its ritual not to free the people but to hold them bound, to load on their backs burdens too heavy to carry, burdens that they themselves would not lift a finger to ease. In particular, table and Sabbath laws were the downfall of those who could not see beyond the power of structure and style. We who study and exercise the law of ritual in our own times would do well to study Jesus' relationship with the Pharisees and his approach to the laws that they so "religiously" kept.

INTIMACY AND HONESTY

Worship demands of us and calls us to this inescapable intimacy with the Lord. The intimacy of divine service requires that we be honest as we stand as worshipers before the Lord who made and saves us. In prayer we find ourselves in the light of the One who is all truth, who searches our heart and knows our every secret. This is the heart of who we are as God's people and the secrets we would prefer to keep in our family closet. When we gather for worship, the heart of who we are as a community is laid bare for the Lord and all of us to see. A married couple may hide their problems from the sight of all, and even from themselves, but these same problems cannot escape revelation in the intimacy of their conjugal relationship. In much the same way, the hidden sins of each community may be closeted for six days of the week, but come the intimacy of Sunday worship and these same problems will reveal themselves, in a myriad of ways, in the Sunday assembly. Our sins of neglect, of infighting, of pettiness and jealousy, of anger and resentment and division — all of these are laid bare and made public as we process to that reconciling table of the Eucharist, knowing deep within us how great is our need for the Lord's mercy in our parish family.

A FELLOWSHIP OF REDEEMED FELONS

Those charged to preach the Gospel in our assemblies have an awesome task indeed. Nothing less than the preaching of the Gospel will bring us to acknowledge both our sin and our need to be renewed by that intimacy that only the Lord's mercy can establish. We need to learn to leave our gifts at the altar and to go first to be reconciled with our brothers and sisters. As a people, the intimacy we share is the intimacy of felons who have been pardoned by the world's Judge. Through, with, and in the company of our Sinless Brother, who was judged and executed as a felon for our sakes, we offer praise and thanks for the great deeds the Lord has done for us. Pardoned and rejoicing, we are sent forth to minister the mercy of such intimacy with our brothers and sisters.

A SPIRITUALITY FOR LITURGICAL MINISTERS

Not too long ago, ministry was understood to be the business of bishops, priests, and those in religious life. All other work in, for, and related to the Church was done under the title, "apostolate," as in the "lay apostolate." Came the 1960s and we discovered that ministry was everywhere and it belonged to everyone. We learned, at last, that ministry is the work appropriate to *all* who are baptized in the mystery of Christ Jesus: "If we have died with Christ, we believe that we are also to live with him" (Rm 6:8), and if we are to live with him, then we are also to *work* with him.

We speak of the "ministry of the baptized" as the primordial Christian ministry. In the celebration of baptism, the one who anoints and seals with the gift of the Holy Spirit addresses these words to the neophyte:

Mary, born again in baptism
you have become a member of Christ
and of his priestly people...
The promised strength of the Holy Spirit
which you are to receive
will make you more like Christ
and help you to be a witness
to his suffering, death, and resurrection.
It will strengthen you
to be an active member of the Church
and to build up the Body of Christ in faith and love. [1]

Moments after we are born again in the waters of baptism, we are charged to take up that priestly work — the ministry of Jesus. We are named as witnesses to the whole of Christ's Paschal Mystery: his suffering, dying, and rising.

EACH OF THE BAPTIZED IS CALLED

How we live out this ministry of the baptized is in some way the same for all of us and in some other ways different for all of us. The sameness consists in the work of all Christians to give thanks and praise to God for all that is given us and especially for that justice that is ours in Christ; we live out our thanksgiving by doing the work of justice in our communities, our nation, and in the world. The difference lies in how each of the baptized is called by God: most to that unique and intimate ministry that married life is, others to a single life marked by a freedom to minister to so many in so many ways; some to vowed life in a community of ministry; and some to that ordered ministry of preaching and leadership. But in all of these, baptism is the sacrament that brands the individual as one who shares in the Lord's ministry.

PARTICULAR MINISTRIES

In addition to these four major vocational ministries, there are a variety of particular ministries in the life of the Church. Indeed, there is a tendency in our own times to name every task a ministry. Consider those communities that have dubbed their refreshment committee "the Coffee and Doughnuts Ministry." In a church community where every activity is a ministry, the definition of this term can become so obscure as to be meaningless.

This is not to deny that the whole body of the Church and its life are truly ministerial realities and that each of the baptized is charged with the ministry of living a Gospel life. But when we speak of "the ministries" and intend an individual or group set apart for the service of others, then we must distinguish between those who serve and those who are served. Neither is this to deny that the whole church community thrive on a network of ministries. Those in one ministry serve their brothers and sisters in another, who in turn serve those who serve them. Such complementarity is the genius of our life together.

WHY THE RUSH?

The caution about naming every task as ministry comes from a wariness of any neo-clericalism that may be afoot upon the holy ground of our life with God. Perhaps the language is already too strong, but one wonders why it is we scramble to "anoint" all persons and tasks as ministers and ministries. Might we not puzzle over the fact that the ranks of the liturgical ministries tended to fill up much more quickly than the ranks of the justice and peace ministries?

For our purposes here the focus *is* on those ministries that attend our worship life. There is a certain ambiguity about these servant tasks and this ambiguity deserves our attention.

Can you think of any other situation, event, or community where:
— the *servants* make a grand entrance?
— the *servants'* names are often printed in a program that refers to the invited guests as "All"?
— the *servants* are guaranteed seats at the head table or in the front rows?

— the *servants* are the most visible and distinguished individuals?
— the *servants* are, often, seen *and* heard?
— the *servants* are the first to be served from the banquet table?
— the *servants* are the first to leave?

THE TEMPTATION OF POWER

Ambiguity abounds here and the potential for misunderstanding is as wide as the space in which these ministers serve, as long as the aisle down which they process, and as close as an apple dangling at arm's length from a tree in the middle of an ancient garden. Our first parents reached not for a piece of fruit but for the power promised in its picking. The serpent had assured them that if they ate the fruit of this tree they would be like gods. In other words, the ambiguity that surrounds the public service of the liturgical minister is ripe with temptation. As vice is basically virtue run amuck, so the minister's temptation to power and prestige is basically one's service seduced by the desire to be served. In another, though recent, age we called this sin.

All this business about ministry is rehearsed so that we can begin to see how great a need there is for understanding *spirituality* in liturgical ministry.

MINISTRIES AND SPIRITUALITIES

The proliferation of "ministries" in our church is equalled only by its complement of supporting "spiritualities." Thus, we read of a "spirituality for lay ministry"; a "spirituality for the ordained ministries"; a "spirituality for social justice ministry".... The list seems endless, though we have yet been spared a "spirituality for the coffee and doughnuts ministry." What we have said thus far about ministry prompts us to take a careful look at this plurality of spiritualities. If Christian ministry is, at the core, a *baptismal* ministry, does it not follow that a spirituality for ministry is, at the core, a *baptismal* spirituality?

For example: the ministry of the pastoral musician is rooted not in the singing of one's song or in the playing of one's instrument, but in the musician's share in the dying and rising of Christ. The baptismal share in the Paschal Mystery of Christ calls the individual to surrender his or her talents to the service of the baptized community. In the same way, the spirituality of the pastoral musician flows not from the particular service rendered God's people in the liturgy, but from the musician's share (through baptism) in the service Christ rendered us in the great Paschal liturgy of his dying and rising. The difference in each case is that the particular ministry and its spirituality are *expressions* of that root ministry and spirituality (Christ's) that belong to and oblige the Christian through baptism.

We press this point for two reasons:

1) ministry and spirituality rooted in baptism are, of their nature, always subject to the dying and rising of Jesus and therefore subject to the Church that is his body;

2) ministry and spirituality rooted, not so much in baptism but more in a particular expression of baptismal commitment, runs the risk of segregation from the community it wants to serve and from the broader Gospel mission of that community.

To understand the risk in the second reason we will need to appreciate the value in the first.

A BAPTISMAL SPIRITUALITY

Spirituality can be simply defined as the art and discipline of the presence to the Sacred. This includes, but is so much more than, the quiet intimacy with God that one might experience in prayer or on retreat. The notion of "presence to the Sacred" is radically transformed in the Paschal Mystery of Jesus. God's Word become flesh for our salvation renders "sacred" the whole of creation; to be "present" to all that is sacred is to be enmeshed with it, as Jesus in his suffering and dying was enmeshed with our humanity. A baptismal spirituality, then, brands and heals us with the sign of the Cross, the tree of new life. The fruit of the tree in Eden provided a temptation to grasp for power. The harvest of the New Creation is ours in Christ, surrendered and emptied for our sakes. Though we are bathed in the light of the Resurrection, our lives and ministry stand always in the shadow of the Cross: To paraphrase the Psalmist, (Ps 62), "in the shadow of your wings, we sing for joy."

A spirituality deserving of the name baptismal is one that renders us present to:

— the mystery of Jesus dying and rising in our lives;

— the Spirit who moves our hearts to prayer;

— the presence of the Risen Christ in his body;

— the whole of creation, which cries out to be reverenced;

— the poor and oppressed, on whose behalf we empty our selves in the work of justice;

— the mercy of God that is our peace and our integrity.

"Your attitude must be that of Christ. Though he was in the form of God, he did not deem equality with God something to be grasped at. Rather, he emptied himself and took the form of a slave, being born in [our] likeness" (Ph 2:5-6). This is the spirituality of God's Servant and of God's servants. We do not live as our own masters, and we do not die as our own masters for while we live we are responsible to the Lord and when we die we die as the Lord's servants (cf. Rm 14:7-9).

As worship is our most honest stance before God, so baptism discloses the truth of our relationship with God in Christ and orients us to that ministry that is the Servant's and the servants'. Baptism and the spirituality we draw from it are always ecclesial (communal) affairs. Though it is the individual who is plunged into the waters of baptism to die with Christ, it is into the waiting embrace of the baptized community that the individual rises with Christ. From that moment the individual ceases to live in isolation. The baptized are enmeshed with Christ's body, the Church, and the mesh is one of mutual service.

In short, the value of a baptismal spirituality is its fidelity to that saving ministry of Jesus which constitutes us as the redeemed and redeeming community.

SPIRITUALITIES OF "LATER ORIGIN"

Ministry and spirituality rooted not so much in baptism but more in a particular *expression* of baptismal commitment run the risk of segregation from the community to be served and from that community's broader Gospel mission. This is a strong statement and deserves some elaboration.

By spiritualities of "later origin," we refer to those that justify and support particular ministries within the life of the community. Such spiritualities are valuable insofar as they spring from a baptismal spirituality as the particular ministry in question springs from the baptismal ministry. The problem arises in this way: in terms of our baptismal ministry we are all equals while the particular expressions of our common baptismal ministry may seem to separate us into ministries of greater and lesser importance, value, and esteem. What we easily lose sight of is that *all* ministry is important, valuable, and esteemed precisely because it is a share in the *Lord's* ministry. To be sure, ministries are different in kind, but they are equal in value because it is the same Lord who calls each of us to service.

> ...I do not want to leave you in ignorance about spiritual gifts... There are different gifts but the same Spirit; there are different ministries but the same Lord; there are different works but the same God who accomplishes all of them in everyone. To each person the manifestation of the Spirit is given for the common good.... But it is one and the same Spirit who produces all these gifts, distributing them as he wills (I Co 12:1, 4-7, 11).

SPIRITUALITY AND THE PASTORAL MUSICIAN

For example: the value of one's ministry in music lies not in the song one sings nor in the gifts that enable one to sing it well; rather, the value lies in that it is the *Lord's* song that is sung, and its singing is offered as service by the musically gifted to the community that assembles to join in the *Lord's* singing. Similarly: a spirituality of music ministry is rooted primarily in the pastoral musician's being fully *present* to the Sacred as it is revealed in the musician's heart, in the self-giving of the musician's offering, and in the community through which the musician offers back to God, with thanksgiving, the gifts received.

A spirituality for pastoral musicians (and all liturgical ministries) involves the "emptying out" of self-interest and self-esteem (dying to oneself) so that one may offer to the community what belongs to it. My gifts are not mine to give; they belong to the community that calls them forth for the service of God's people. This deeply are we enmeshed, by baptism, in the lives of our brothers and sisters. We are called to live as the community described in the Acts of the Apostles: to be of one heart and one mind. None of us claims anything as our own; rather, we let everything be held in common (see Acts 4:32).

MINISTRY: TERRITORY AND OWNERSHIP

The danger in the spirituality that devolves from the particular expression of Christian ministry is its tendency to focus and even isolate the minister in that expression. When we name the gifts and the gifted, we must always take care to name the Giver and to be explicit *for* whom the gifts are given. *My gifts are not mine to give!* An otherwise wonderful experience of celebration and learning, the 1981 Detroit convention of the National Association of Pastoral Musicians (NPM) was curiously titled, "Claim Your Art!" One wonders who was to do the claiming, for whom was the claiming, and for what purpose would liturgical arts be claimed? Ministers who "stake a claim" on their ministry need to remember that the territory has already been deeded to God's people at prayer.

Finally, ministry and spirituality of origin later than that of the baptismal font risk segregation from the broader Gospel mission of the community served. This kind of segregation is revealed when parish musicians are unfamiliar with or not interested in the work of the parish justice and peace committee. A few observations:

— It is not expected that everyone be part of every ministerial effort in a parish community.

— There are, however, elements of parish life and ministry deserving of the attention, interest and support of all the baptized.

— The words of justice, reconciling, care for the poor, hospitality, and prayer are the mission of the whole community and of its individual members.

— Some in the community are called to leadership in these Gospel-missioned works, but the work of the Gospel cannot be confined or consigned to the community's leadership. A working committee does not free the community at large from the work of that committee.

— A community of persons enmeshed in the mystery of Jesus will discover that its several ministries offer the fullest service when they are understood to be complementary and interdependent.

This interdependent complementarity is not simply a coincidence; it is so because the work of all parish ministries (including those who serve the coffee and doughnuts) is *one* work, and it is one because it is the *Lord's!*

LITURGY AND THE WORK OF JUSTICE

At the beginning of this chapter it was noted that the ranks of the liturgical ministries fill up much more quickly than do the ranks of the peace and justice ministries. This imbalance is one that should cause us to be concerned. We have much work to do in reminding ourselves that the Sunday assembly for Eucharist is validated or falsified by how the community's ritual translates itself into the work of the reign of God through the week. The community that roots itself in a baptismal ministry and spirituality can never dispense itself from the work of justice, peace, and reconciliation.

Each Sunday we pray in the Preface, "It is right to give him thanks and praise... we do well always and everywhere to give you thanks..." This is how the International Committee on English in the Liturgy (ICEL) has chosen to translate: Dignum et justum est... vere dignum et justum est, aequum at salutare, nos tibi semper at unique gratias agere.... A fuller translation would read: "It is right and *just*... It is truly right and *just*, proper and helpful toward salvation, that we always and everywhere give you thanks...." It is unfortunate that the Latin justum (just) was "lost in the translation." The members of the liturgy and the justice and peace committees, *and the whole assembly of the baptized*, would be well served in hearing and praying each week this intimate connection between the work of worship and the work of justice. The "connection" is, in reality, a *unity* because the work of liturgy and the work of justice are the work of the *Lord*; this work is ours too; we have been invited to "do this in memory" of the Lord.

ONE BREAD, ONE CUP, ONE MINISTRY

There is much overlapping in the reflections we have offered. This is to be expected when we are speaking of *one* ministry (the Lord's) and of one spirituality (rooted in our baptism). Our reflections also all reveal some specificity precisely because the gifts and ministries are *many*. This is not to say that they compete with one another, rather they complement and serve one another as they serve God's people at prayer. In a kitchen, the one who washes the dishes receives less public attention than does the one who prepares the meal. Still, without the scullery help, the chef's creations will never make it to the table. The service of both contributes to the nourishment of the diners and when either is absent, the people go hungry. It is much the same at the Lord's table and among those who serve that table. Value, esteem, and importance are determined not by the particular service rendered but by the Lord's service in which we have shared and through which God's people are served and saved.

Earlier we noted the anomalous situation in which the servants at the Lord's table receive top billing and front row seats. Although such attention may lead to misunderstanding, it is also appropriate. This is so, not because those who serve merit attention to themselves, but because the service they render is revealing of Christ's service in our midst. It is beneficial to the assembly to know that the baptismal impulse to imitate and incarnate the Lord's work is alive and flourishing in their midst. This notion will be clearly understood in the community whose ministers first recognize it themselves. As the community begins to name the ministry of lectors, presiders, and musicians as the *Lord's* ministry, it will begin to name its own assembled self as the body of Christ. The Church, Christ's body, *is* the Lord's ministry in the building up of the city of God. The new Jerusalem is as near or far away as how the local church community enfleshes the dying and rising of Jesus who is its Sovereign.

The liturgy is not some theatre where actors on stage take bows and applause at curtain call. It is, however, that arena of holy ground where God's people stand naked and empty-handed in the Creator's presence. Our time and prayer in this holy place are served by sinners like ourselves whose only vesture is ours, too: we are all clothed in Christ as the new creation. These servants point the way for all who assemble. Their proximity to table and ambo is one of service, not priority. These servants are seen and heard so that all might see and hear the Lord among us. If they are the first to be served from the table, it is so they might be nourished for the serving of others. They are distinguished not so much by what they do but by whose work they have become in its doing.

As we began, we shall conclude these reflections with the words of St. Paul:

> I plead with you, then, as a prisoner for the Lord,
> to live a life worthy of the calling you have received,
> with perfect humility, meekness, and patience,
> bearing with one another lovingly.
> Make every effort to preserve the unity
> which has the Spirit as its origin
> and peace as its binding force...

There is but one body and one Spirit,
just as there is but one hope given all of you by your call.
There is one Lord, one faith, one baptism,
one God and Father of all,
who is over all, works through all, and is in all.
...and you must lay aside your former way of
    life and the old self
which deteriorates through illusion and desire,
and acquire a fresh, spiritual way of thinking.
You must put on that new person created in God's image,
whose justice and holiness are born of truth. (Ep 4:1-6,22-24)

ENDNOTES

[1] *Rite of Christian Initiation of Adults*, no. 268, Provisional text, (Washington DC: United States Catholic Conference, 1974).

SUGGESTIONS FOR IMPROVING WORSHIP FOR YOUTH

Thomas N. Tomaszek

I have organized some specific suggestions for improving worship for youth into four categories: the Need for Experiences of Community, the Need for Peer Group Liturgies, the Need for Advocacy, and the Need for Liturgical Formation.

SUGGESTIONS FOR PROVIDING EXPERIENCES OF COMMUNITY

1. Encourage youth to attend weekend liturgy together. (They may have to agree to an every other week rotation to allow for family time.) Announce which service you will be attending and ask youth to join you for breakfast (or supper) afterwards. If this is not possible, meet in the lobby or church hall before or after a weekend liturgy for casual talk.

2. Offer to convene a special liturgy planning committee of youth who will prepare a parish Back-to-School liturgy in the fall, a liturgy for the Feast of Holy Family in winter, a Graduation liturgy in the spring, and a Vacation Blessing liturgy in summer. That's at least four times a year that youth will have contact with the parish.

3. Have the young people sponsor a coffee/juice and donut Sunday once a month or once a season (maybe after those special liturgies as above). Use it as a publicity event for announcing other projects or youth events. Have each youth invite another friend who doesn't regularly attend weekend liturgy.

4. Above all, begin to understand that all community building opportunities for youth will help them to feel more a part of the worshipping assembly. This means regularly scheduling activities and events which counterprogram the variety of opportunities available to youth through school activities, and other organizations, etc.

SUGGESTIONS FOR PEER GROUP LITURGIES

5. Schedule special youth Eucharistic liturgies, prayer services, or communal reconciliations periodically. Involve youth in the planning of these times so that the liturgies reflect their preferences in music, prayer

styles, storytelling, and environment. One suggested pattern is mentioned in #2 above. Another effective approach is to collaborate with other area parishes or the Catholic high school. High school and campus ministers would most likely have a good sense of youth liturgy and homiletics. (These events are most effective if they happen on a regular basis.)

6. Schedule a Word service for youth a half hour before the most attended Sunday liturgy. (Perhaps a young adult would take responsibility for this session or would coordinate youth in rotating the preparation.) Include time for listening to contemporary Christian music or other reflection music, storytelling, and for sharing about the week's events. (The idea is that you may not be able to change the parish liturgy, but you can provide a meaningful worship time for youth each week which leads them to participate in the community prayer.)

SUGGESTIONS FOR ADVOCACY

7. Appoint or designate one adult (more if needed) to act as a lobbyist for the needs of youth within your worship community. This person should maintain a close working relationship with two or more youth from your community, thereby enabling the young people to speak on their own behalf, and to ensure a realistic perspective of youth needs, not just adult expectations.

8. Lobby for two youth to be chosen as voting/active members of any liturgy planning committees especially those for special feasts such as Christmas and the Easter Triduum. Have these youth give regular reports back to the other youth for comments and suggestions.

9. Lobby the presiders and homilists to use at least one example in the homily or prayers each week which will relate directly to the lives of young people. Propose your willingness to supply such examples from a group of youth if they would be used regularly.

10. Survey youth to find out which songs from the hymnal or missalette they particularly like and which songs they consider boring. Involve the liturgist or choir director in your plan, or if this is not possible, diplomatically present the results later. Make sure two or three articulate youth are present at that meeting to help explain some of the choices. The purpose here is to show that certain songs are more likely to gain a response, rather than to only highlight the negatively received songs. (Note: this meeting may require some pre-lobbying on your part.)

11. Be a talent scout for youth who are good singers, instrumentalists, or artists. Link them with those who are responsible for planning liturgies and environment or music in your community. (A good source of information might be high school art or music teachers.)

12. Seek youth who can assist in planning the church environment for the seasons. Artists and other artisans-in-training should be encouraged to use their gifts.

SUGGESTIONS FOR LITURGICAL FORMATION

13. Establish an apprenticeship program for youth involvement in the liturgical ministries (greeters, lectors, Eucharistic ministers). In this model, a youth advocate pairs adolescents with adults who agree to act as "mentors." For example, an established lector might work with a young person on technique, then split the readings at her next scheduled responsibility.

14. Integrate a capsule curriculum on liturgy and the sacraments into the regular youth discussion time. Smaller doses of theory can be combined with experiences of various prayer forms. Focus on relationships and communication.

15. Offer specific liturgical and skill training for young singers, cantors, instrumentalists, and liturgy planners. (The content could include music reading sessions, skills building, input on the liturgical ministries, and opportunities to prepare liturgies for their peers.)

16. Spend time discussing the current season of the Church year. Share stories about family customs and rituals which are observed. This is also a good way to reflect on rich cultural traditions which can be included in worship.

17. Schedule opportunities to experience the worship of other cultural groups. Experiences of North American Indian, Hispanic, Asian or African-American spiritualities can open understandings of the diversity of our faith tradition and prayer styles.

18. Form Bible study or informal discussion groups to read the upcoming readings from the Lectionary. (This should be done on a regular basis to be effective.) Have group members take turns summarizing the discussions and offer the results to the regular homilists. Ask them to include parts of the discussions in their homilies.

19. Use the same procedure of reflection, discussion, and presentation for sets of general intercessions or prayers of thanksgiving. (Make sure the homilists or liturgists are aware of the process you use so that results will be taken credibly.)

Chapter 13

Prayer and Spirituality

Kathleen Fischer

When I teach courses on prayer, I find that people often believe that prayer leads them to God but that it at least temporarily pulls them away from any concern for action and other people. No matter what else we might have learned about prayer, we somehow retain an image of it as a kind of private experience that has to be consciously reintegrated with the rest of life, much the way a hiker in the wilderness has to find her way back to civilization again. The sense of prayer as intrinsically isolated from life stems in part from the split we have established between God and the world; seeking the face of God then means turning from the world. It also arises from the fact that the form of prayer that makes our bonds with others most explicit, intercessory prayer, has been relegated to lowest rank. Although it is perhaps the most universal and spontaneous of human prayers, and one of the prominent forms of biblical prayer, we are slightly apologetic about our intercessions, convinced that they are evidence of the elementary state of our prayer life.

Prayer, no matter what its mode, is in fact the path to increased awareness of our oneness with God, with one another, and with the world. Prayer does not take us away from action and other people; it takes us to them by uniting us with the ground and center. As the Psalmist says,

I shall walk in the presence of God
in the land of the living. (Ps116:9)

When we pray, we no longer see things as cut off from their deeper reality but as an organic whole. Our ordinary consciousness constantly separates and isolates things. Preoccupation with immediate worries or past problems as well as the scattered nature of our busy lives dulls our awareness of God's presence. Prayer opens us to the ground of love through which all things find their identity and uniqueness.

Even in the most solitary prayer, we remain linked with the whole world. St. Basil expressed this bond between prayer and other people succinctly when, after a trip to the eremitical settlements of the Egyptian desert, he remarked, "That is all very well, but whose feet will they wash?" Rather than isolating us from others, prayer can deepen our sense of relatedness to all creation.

CONTEMPLATION AS A PATH TO RECONCILIATION

A technological society such as ours is built on the manipulation of the environment. Technology drives us to use things to make other things. So we chop down trees to develop paper and wood products. We learn to create artificial organs and do transplants. Genetic engineering gives us the ability to control life processes. All such activity presupposes a certain kind of stance before reality. We look at a field in terms of what it will produce for human consumption. We approach land as a means of providing human sustenance. As a people we are productive, active, striving for speed and efficiency.

Technology has been able to bring many improvements to human life; it has eliminated diseases and freed us to create works of beauty. These are blessings and true human achievements. But we must be aware of what it does to our attitude toward creation and others. This blindness is apparent, for example, in the actions of multinational corporations in underdeveloped countries. With a focus on profit rather than people, they often introduce technology which dislocates populations, destroys land and forests, and increases the country's poverty. Without a glimpse of a purpose and presence that transcends our own and to whose service we are bound, technology can become simply self-indulgent. We fail to see it as a power integrated with nature and instead view it as a power over nature.

Technology promises a kind of contentment and happiness that it simply cannot deliver. It is a truism to say that affluence has left us with deep unfulfilled longings. In *Morning Light*, his spiritual journal, Jean Sulivan states this truth convincingly.

> Human beings are not looking for just anything but for the absolute, even when they believe they are turning away from it, or when they unknowingly repress it in a search for material things. Every passion is an arrow aimed at the other shore. (Sulivan 27)

Material prosperity and consumption have spawned societies of violence and neurosis, what Jane Wagner, in *A Search for Signs of Intelligent Life in the Universe*, terms the disease of "affluenza."

There is another stance toward life, frequently thought of as the preserve of monks and mystics but really essential to all human living. It is the contemplative or receptive mode of encountering the world. Contemplation allows us to take in the world and receive its gifts. We then retain the sense of wonder and awe that belong to true human living. Not all of us will be contemplatives in the sense of withdrawing to monasteries or retreats, but we all need the contemplative dimension in our lives. Jesus was a contemplative in the midst; he was aware of the divine presence in the smell and texture of the fields of ripening wheat, the gathering clouds of a coming storm, the faces of the hemorrhaging woman and the blind man, uplifted in the pleas for healing. Contemplation fosters a sense of oneness with all of life. In a talk which he gave in Calcutta a few weeks before he died, Thomas Merton speaks of this communion:

> Not that we discover a new unity. We discover an older unity… we are already one. But we imagine that we are not. And what we have to recover is our original unity. What we have to be is what we are. (Merton 308)

Contemplation is the foundation of ecological sensitivity and the concern for a communal life.

Many spiritual traditions speak of contemplation as an experience of being aware and awake, mindful and attentive. What this language presupposes is that we are in fact always in the presence of God. We are always one with other people and all that is. Contemplation enables us to become *aware* of what is always there. This awareness revolutionizes our existence; it makes us live in the world in a different way, alert to the inner connections of God and creation. We open ourselves to an experience of oneness with God in order to experience more fully the divine in all of life. This is the basis of love of the earth and of others. Such a sense of unity undergirds our efforts to treat all of creation with care.

The root meaning of the word "contemplation" is to gaze attentively at something. The Carmelite William McNamara describes it as a long, loving look at the real. Contemplation allows us time to see things in their essence, to capture their uniqueness and their gifts. It is a natural next step to treat all creatures with regard and reverence, evidencing respect for that essence we have now seen.

We prepare for the gift of contemplation by cultivating the power of attention. It is this attentive caring that allows us to see each person and the world anew. It rewards us with the gift of wonder. People who seem alien or dangerous change when we take them in attentively. Only then do we see them as individuals and not as strangers. The same is true of nature. Sometimes when we are walking near a lake or stream, we may pause to take in the qualities of water. We let it teach us what it can. Moments like these make it easier to treat water with care, harder to pollute it thoughtlessly.

Contemplation is the attitude of heart required by an interrelated world view. What the contemplative sees is that center of love in which all things find their uniqueness. Out of such an experience we learn to see the face of God in the face of every other human being and all of creation. Even when convinced of its importance, however, we may wonder how we are to keep alive this contemplative attitude.

HOW DO WE NURTURE OUR CONTEMPLATIVE LIVES?

Sometimes we are afraid even of the word contemplation. It seems beyond our powers. Life is busy and complicated enough for most of us, and practical worries about job and family take top priority. Contemplation would be nice, perhaps, but who has time or energy to pursue it? Nurturing the contemplative within each of us requires first of all that we believe we are all contemplatives by nature, that it is not something reserved to the privileged few. Next we must believe that it is the only way to heal the alienation and longing our hearts experience.

Once we are convinced of this, there are many paths to contemplation. Formulas and methods are less important than the goal of becoming aware of God's presence in our lives and finding ourselves and all of reality in God. The various exercises are meant to lead us to a point where this awareness of God's presence becomes a dimension of all of life.

It is helpful to think of prayer as listening to God. Since God's Word to us is found in many different places, we can pray in many ways: not just by reading the Scriptures, but by walking or sitting in the presence of the beauty and power of nature — the pounding of the ocean against the shore, the abundance of wildflowers as the desert blooms in the spring, the variety of colorful birds we find in our homeland. We contemplate as we lift up the events of our lives — our longing for friendship and healing, the conflicts we experience with family or co-workers, the headlines in the newspaper that trouble or comfort us. We contemplate by reflecting that God is present here with us as we change a baby's diaper, make our way in heavy commuter traffic, or root for our daughter's team at a volleyball game. All of these are ways of being attentive and alert to God's presence, letting it transform our consciousness. From such prayer comes a renewed sense of our dependence on God and our interdependence with one another. It opens out into praise, gratitude, and a quiet movement towards repentance.

God's presence may also be experienced as a kind of absence or darkness, a desert in which we must trust that God is with us even when we have no tangible sense of the divine Presence. We listen for God's voice and hear only silence. One young man told me that he believed he had no prayer life because he did not find God in sunsets, trees, and flowers, as others did. He knew only a void within, what he called a deep and dark cave. A breakthrough came in this man's spiritual life when he realized that such emptiness can paradoxically be a kind of fullness, that absence can be a form of God's presence. This path has been called the *via negativa* or apophatic way to God. We all walk it at times, and it is the primary path of prayer for many people. It serves as a constant corrective to a too simple identification of human feeling with the reality of God's presence.

Spiritual writers recommend a form of prayer especially suited to this path, the prayer of awareness or centering prayer. Based in the writings of such spiritual classics as *The Cloud of Unknowing* and the works of Thomas Merton, this prayer is a way of simply resting in the presence of God beyond all words, images, or concrete experience. It is an exercise in prayer which has as its goal the contemplative attitude toward all things we have been describing. It attains it by a kind of inner conversion, a transformation of consciousness, where our way of seeing God and all else changes.

The author of the spiritual classic, *The Cloud of Unknowing*, suggests an approach to help us simply be, one which puts all things except God under a "cloud of forgetting." Choose a word, preferably one of a single syllable, like "God" or "love."

> But choose one that is meaningful to you. Then fix it in your mind so that it will stay there come what may. This word will be your defense in conflict and in peace. Use it to beat upon the cloud of darkness above you and to subdue all distractions, consigning them to the *cloud of forgetting* beneath you. (Johnston 56)

Such prayer asks that we simply *be*, letting go of our thoughts, plans, concerns, and anxieties. We let ourselves be in faith and love with the Presence within, returning gently to our word whenever other concerns enter our awareness. Some manuals on prayer suggests that we spend 20 minutes in the morning and 20 minutes in the afternoon or evening in this exercise of contemplation. They also offer help in answering specific questions which arise as we try this kind of prayer. [1]

Many people today are discovering the support that small groups can provide for their attempts to pray. Some meet weekly or monthly to do centering prayer together. Others have formed small intentional Christian communities where prayer and action are joined to biblical reflection. This is another way of teaching us that while prayer may sometimes be private, it is not isolated.

INTERCESSION AND INTERDEPENDENCE

Intercessory prayer has always been a prominent part of the human search for God. That is because it is instinctive. It is the type of prayer Jesus talks most about and engages in himself in the Gospels. Christians have been convinced that prayer, as well as action, makes a difference in the continuation and completion of God's work of creation. However, many Christians have a somewhat schizoid view of petitionary prayer. On the one hand, Scripture exhorts us to pray for our own and others' needs and offers numerous examples. On the other hand, theological emphasis on the fact that God knows the future and is unchangeable has undermined the meaningfulness of such prayer. According to much traditional theology, prayer does not really change or influence God's interaction with the world; rather, it brings about a change in the persons who pray, enabling them to view life from the divine perspective.

Individual Christians have responded in various ways to this split between theology and experience. Some have ignored the theology and continued to petition God; others have heeded the theology and have given up petitionary prayer altogether. The questions remain: What does it mean to say that God hears our prayers? Can the prayer of one person really bring about a change in the life of another?

A solution to this dilemma can be found in the contemporary movement of process theology. This is a theological approach that takes seriously our experience of the world as dynamic and relational. [2] A process world view enables us to pray with the intellectual conviction that prayer does, in fact, matter to God as well as to the person praying and the persons for whom prayer is offered. It is possible to find meaning in such a world for both the belief that God is all-knowing and the deep conviction at the root of Christian prayer, whether of thanksgiving, praise, or petition, that it really makes a difference somehow even to God that we pray.

In a process world we affect God by what we are, feel, and do. This flows from an emphasis on interdependence. God's love is compassionate, taking the world's experience into the divine experience, suffering with its sufferings and rejoicing with its joys. God receives from the world, as a free subject, the effects of the world's action. God is affected by our sufferings, triumphs, failures, and joys. These events are transformed in the divine freedom and according to the pattern of the divine wisdom are then influential in God's ongoing guidance of the world.

God takes account of human prayers, although in their initial form they may not be compatible with the breadth of divine purpose and must be transformed in God's love. They open up new possibilities for God's dialogue with creation in its next moment of existence.

An example may help make clear how this is so. I work with an 80-year old woman, whom I will call Martha, who is confined to a wheelchair and lives in a nursing home in Seattle. Her granddaughter, who is very dear to her, is involved in the peace movement and sometimes takes part in non-violent actions opposing nuclear arms. Martha believes in peace as much as her granddaughter does but feels helpless to do much about it. She can pray, however. In prayer she unites herself with her granddaughter and others in the peace movement and prays for their strength, safety, and success. In doing so, she brings to conscious awareness our unity in the one body of Christ. As Martha directs herself to her granddaughter's concerns, she becomes part of her granddaughter's particular situation which is now different than it would be had she not prayed. God responds to her praying, for her prayer changes the world by adding new redemptive possibilities to the current situation. This does not mean that God does not already desire peace. However, in a process world God works with what is, in order to lead the world toward what it can be. Prayer changes the world by adding a new reality to that world; it enriches the total situation with which God can work. Martha's granddaughter and others in the peace movement can receive new and stronger aims or possibilities from God because of her prayers. And so, the world is different because of Martha's prayers. [3]

Let us look at another example of a common experience of intercessory prayer. We love someone who is ill or in a troubling situation — it may be a friend who is dying of cancer, a husband who is out of work, a daughter who is struggling with a major decision. We tell this friend, husband, or daughter, "I'll pray for you." Then we remember them in our personal prayer or we include them in the petitions of a Eucharistic celebration. What is happening here? Are we merely comforting them? Or does our praying affect God? Process theology helps us see that such prayer does, in fact, make a difference to God. While it does not necessarily mean that the person will be cured of cancer, get a job, or be freed from the struggle with problems, it adds a new dimension to the situation. In the ongoing divine relationship to the world, God takes account of and receives our prayers. They are of course transformed in God's life, but they insert new love and strength into the situation of the person for whom we are praying, and they are received by God and become a real factor in God's ongoing guidance of the world. We have made a difference. Prayer not only changes us; it affects God and those for whom we pray.

What does process theology say regarding God's knowledge of the future? God knows completely all possibility, and in this sense is all-knowing; but God does not know what any one individual will do. God knows what would be most enriching for an individual if it were chosen, but the individual's free choices cannot be determined or known until they are made. Once made by the individual, they are taken up into God's life and included in the ongoing divine concern for the world. It is therefore possible to say both that God knows human needs and that one should express these needs to God. God knows all of the relevant possibilities and is able to deal with any situation which might arise. But God's knowing in advance what concrete possibilities will actually be chosen are impossible because this would negate the meaning of human freedom.

The process understanding of prayer also preserves God's freedom. Prayer, including prayer of intercession, plays a real role in the history which we are called to create with God. But this does not mean that God fulfills every request in its form of presentation. Faith in prayer has always meant that if God is God, then the divine response will be free and based in God's total view; prayer must undergo transformation and refinement. Belief in prayer does not necessarily mean that our expectations will be met. They will often be denied, challenged, altered, or negated. God's judgment or evaluation of the world takes place at every moment of the experience of the world. Our prayers are received by God with freedom and in freedom are poured back into the world as expressions of God's and in the world's love.

In addition to making a difference to God, intercessory prayer is a means of strengthening human community. Our decisions create a different world in which others can interact. Since in a process view every entity is affected by every other entity in spacetime, sin poisons the whole cosmos, while love enriches that cosmos. Prayers of intercession are expressions of love in a faith context. The profound experience of prayer lives not only in the separate self; intercession is one of the ways of deepening communion with others as well as with God, thus bringing about the reign of God.

Prayer and action are tightly united in this notion of intercessory prayer. Sallie McFague describes such intercession in *Models of God.*

We ask God, as one would a friend, to be present in the joy of our shared meals and in the sufferings of the strangers; to give us courage and stamina for the work we do together, to forgive us for the lack of fidelity to the common vision and lack of trust in divine trustfulness. Finally, we ask God the friend to support, forgive, and comfort us as we struggle together to save our beleaguered planet, our beautiful earth, our blue and green marble in a universe of silent rock and fire. Just as betrayal is the sin of friendship in which one hands over the friend to the enemy, so intercessory prayer is the rite of friendship in which one hands over the friend to God. (McFague 179)

A prayer of intercession, our expression before God of concern for the well-being of others, may take the form of work with abused women or volunteering to help build housing for the homeless. In faith, we give bodily form to our concern for all others in the world.

God is not only the source of order in our world but also the source of newness. God knows all possibilities. One role of prayer is to open us to these new ways of looking at things. Judged from this viewpoint, prayer should enable us to view the world in a fresh way, to see opportunities where we had not noticed them before. Many biblical characters portray this kind of prayer. There is first of all Mary of Nazareth. One thing that characterizes her is the openness to possibility that flows from her readiness to do God's will. As portrayed in the Gospel of Luke, for example, she speaks of a God who can make new things happen even in the midst of established customs. Like her ancestress Hannah, Mary prays a prayer of hope in the midst of shadows. Mary's prayer also binds together many of the themes we have explored. It rises up out of her own spirit, but a spirit rooted in the past and present experiences of her people, and it expresses her conviction that God cares, as she does, for the future of the community.

ENDNOTES

[1] Two helpful books are M. Basil Pennington, *Centering Prayer. Renewing An Ancient Christian Prayer Form* (New York: Doubleday & Co., 1980); and Thomas Keating, *Open Mind, Open Heart. The Contemplative Dimension of the Gospel* (New York: Amity House, 1986).

[2] A helpful introduction to this theological perspective is John B. Cobb, Jr. and David Ray Griffin, *Process Theology. An Introductory Exposition* (Philadelphia: The Westminster Press, 1976).

[3] For further discussion of this, see Marjorie Suchocki, *God, Christ, Church. A Practical Guide to Process Theology* (New York: Crossroad Publishing Co., 1982), pp. 203-210.

WORKS CITED

Johnston. William, ed. *The Cloud of Unknowing and the Book of Privy Counselling.* New York: Doubleday & Co., 1973.

McFague, Sallie. *Models of God.* Philadelphia: Fortress Press, 1987

Merton, Thomas. *The Asian Journey of Thomas Merton.* Editors Naomi Burton, Brother Patrick Hart, and James Laughlin. New York: New Directions Publishers, 1973.

Sulivan, Jean. *Morning Light.* Trans. Joseph Cunneen and Patrick Gormally. New York: Paulist Press, 1988.

Wagner, Jane. *A Search for Signs of Intelligent Life in the Universe.* New York: Harper and Row, 1986.

APPROACHES TO PRAYER

Jacquelin Bergan and S. Marie Schwan

Prayer is our personal response to God's presence. We approach God reverently with a listening heart. God speaks first. In prayer, we acknowledge God's presence and in gratitude respond with love. The focus is always on God and what God does.

The following suggestions are offered as ways of supporting and enabling attentiveness to God's word and our unique response:

A. DAILY PATTERN OF PRAYER

For each period of prayer, use the following pattern:

1. PREPARATION

Plan to spend at least 20 minutes to one hour in prayer daily. Although there is nothing "sacred" about 60 minutes, most people find that an hour better provides for their quieting of self, the entrance into the passage, etc.

During the previous evening, take time to read the commentary as well as the Scripture passage for the following day. Just before falling asleep, recall the Scripture passage.

2. STRUCTURE OF THE PRAYER PERIOD

Quiet yourself; be still inside and out. Relax. Breath in deeply, hold your breath to the count of four, then exhale slowly through your mouth. Repeat several times.

Realize you are nothing without God; declare your dependency on God.

Ask God for the grace you want and need.

Read and reflect on your chosen Scripture passage, using the appropriate form. (See: Forms of Solitary Prayer)

Close the prayer period with a time of conversation with Jesus and his Father. Speak and listen. Conclude with an Our Father.

3. REVIEW OF PRAYER

The review of prayer is a reflection at the conclusion of the prayer period. The purpose of the review is to heighten our awareness of how God has been present to us during the prayer period. Writing the review provides for personal accountability, and is a precious record of our spiritual journey. To write the review is a step toward self integration.

In a notebook or journal, after each prayer period, indicate the date and the passage. Answer each of the following questions:

1. Was there any word or phrase that particularly struck you?

2. What were your feelings? Were you peaceful?… loving?… trusting?… sad?… discouraged? ... What do these feelings say to you?

3. How are you more aware of God's presence?

4. Is there some point to which it would be helpful to return in your next prayer period?

B. VARIOUS FORMS OF SOLITARY PRAYER

MEDITATION

In meditation one approaches the Scripture passage like a love letter; this approach is especially helpful in praying poetic passages.

1. Read the passage slowly, aloud or in a whisper, letting the words wash over you, savoring them.

2. Stay with the words that especially catch your attention; absorb them the way the thirsty earth receives the rain.

3. Keep repeating a word or phrase, aware of the feelings that are awakened.

4. Read, and reread the passage lovingly as you would a letter from a dear friend or as you would softly sing the chorus of a song.

CONTEMPLATION

In contemplation, we enter into a life event or story passage of scripture. We enter into the passage by way of imagination, making use of all our senses.

In contemplation, one enters the story as if one were there:

1. Watch what happens; listen to what is being said.

2. Become part of the mystery; assume the role of one of the persons.

3. Look at each of the individuals; what does he/she experience? To whom does each one speak?

4. What differences does it make for my life, my family, for society, if I hear the message?

3. CENTERING PRAYER

In centering prayer we go beyond thought and image, beyond the senses and the rational mind to that center of our being where God is working a wonderful work (Pennington 18).

In centering prayer, we spiral down into the deepest center of ourselves. It is the point of stillness within us where we most experience being created by a loving God who is breathing us into life.

1. Sit quietly, comfortable and relaxed.

2. Rest within your longing and desire for God.

3. Move to the center within your deepest self. This movement can be facilitated by imaging yourself slowly descending in an elevator, or walking down flights of stairs, or descending a mountain, or going down into the water, as in a deep pool.

4. In the stillness, become aware of God's presence: peacefully absorb his love.

MANTRA

One means of centering prayer is the use of the "mantra" or "prayer word." The mantra can be a single word or a phrase. It may be a word from Scripture or one that arises spontaneously from within your heart. The word or phrase represents, for you, the fullness of God. The word or phrase is repeated slowly within oneself in harmony with one's breathing. For example, the first part of the Jesus prayer is said while inhaling and the second half while exhaling.

MEDITATIVE READING

One of the approaches to prayer is a reflective reading of Scripture or other spiritual writings. The reading is done slowly, pausing periodically to allow the words and phrases to enter within you. When a thought resonates deeply, stay with it, allowing the fullness of it to penetrate your being. Relish the word received. Respond authentically and spontaneously as in a dialogue.

JOURNALING

Journaling is meditative writing. When we place pen on paper, spirit and body cooperate to release our true selves. To journal is to experience ourselves in a new light as expression is given to the fresh images which emerge from our subconscious. Journaling requires putting aside preconceived ideas and control. Meditative writing is like writing a letter to one we love. Memories are recalled, convictions are clarified, and affections well up within us. In writing we may discover that emotions are intensified and prolonged.

There are many variations for the use of journaling in prayer. Among them are the following:
* writing a letter addressed to God;
* writing a conversation between oneself and another; the other may be Jesus or another significant person. The dialogue can also be with an event, an experience, or a value. For example, death, separation, or wisdom receive personal attributes and are imaged as persons with whom one enters into conversation;
* writing an answer to a question, e.g., *"What do you want me to do for you?"* (Mk 10:51 or *"Why are you weeping?"* (Jn 20:15);
* allowing Jesus or another Scripture person to "speak" to us through the pen.

REPETITION

Repetition is the return to a previous period of prayer for the purpose of allowing the movements of God to deepen within one's heart. Through repetitions, we fine-tune our sensitivities to God and to how he speaks in our prayer and within our life circumstances. The prayer of repetition allows for the experience of integrating who we are with who God is, revealing God's self to be for us.

Repetitions are a way of honoring God's word to us in the earlier prayer period. It is recalling and pondering an earlier conversation with one we love. It is as if we say to God, "Tell me that again; what did I hear you saying?"

The period of prayer that we select to repeat is one in which we have experienced a significant movement of joy or sadness or confusion. It may also be a period in which nothing seemed to happen, due, perhaps, to our own lack of readiness at the time.

1. Recall the feelings of the first period of prayer.

2. Use, as a point of entry, the scene, word, or feelings that was previously most significant.

3. Allow the Spirit to direct the inner movements of your heart during this time of prayer.

C. SPIRITUAL PRACTICES AND HELPS

EXAMEN OF CONSCIOUSNESS

The examen of consciousness is the instrument by which we discover how God has been present to us and how we have responded to his presence through the day. St. Ignatius believed this practice was so important that, in the event it was impossible to have a formal prayer period, he insisted that the examen would sustain one's vital link with God. The examen of consciousness is not to be confused with an examination of conscience in which penitents are concerned with their failures. It is, rather, an exploration of how God is present within the events, circumstances, feelings of our daily lives.

The following prayer is a suggested approach to examen. The written response can be incorporated into the prayer journal.

1. God, my Father, I am totally dependent on you. Everything is gift from you. *All is gift.* I give you thanks and praise for the gifts of this day...

2. Lord, I believe you work through and in time to reveal me to myself. Please give me an increased awareness of how you are guiding and shaping my life, as well as a more sensitive awareness of the obstacles I put in your way.

3. You have been present in my life today. Be near, now, as I reflect on:

> your presence in the *events* of today...
> your presence in the *feelings* I experience today...
> your *call* to me...
> my *response* to you...

4. Father, I ask your loving forgiveness and healing. The particular event of this day that I most want healed is...

5. Filled with hope and a firm belief in your love and power, I entrust myself to your care, and strongly affirm... (Claim the gift you most desire, most need; believe that God desire to give you that gift.)

FAITH SHARING

A faith sharing group is not a discussion group, nor a sensitivity session, nor a social gathering. Members do not come together to share and receive intellectual or theological insights. Nor is the purpose of faith sharing the accomplishment of some predetermined task.

The approach to faith sharing is one of reading and reflecting together on the Word of God. Faith sharing calls us to share with each other, out of our deepest center, what it means to be a follower of Christ in our world today. To authentically enter into faith sharing is to come to know and love each other in Christ whose Spirit is the bonding force of community.

A group of seven to ten members gathers at the prearranged time and place.

1. The leader calls the group to prayer and invites them to some moments of silent centering, during which they pray for the presence of the Holy Spirit.

2. The leader gathers their silent prayer in an opening prayer, spontaneous or prepared.

3. One of the members reads a previously chosen Scripture passage on which participants have spent some time in solitary prayer.

4. A period of silence follows each reading of the Scripture.

5. The leader invites each one to share a word or phrase from the reading.

6. Another member rereads the passage; this is followed by a time of silence.

7. The leader invites those who wish, to share simply how this passage personally addresses them, e.g., challenging, comforting, inviting, etc.

8. Again the passage is read.

9. Members are invited to offer their spontaneous prayer to the Lord.

10. The leader draws the time of faith sharing to closure with a prayer, a blessing, an Our Father, or a hymn.

WORKS CITED

Pennington, M. Basil. *Centering Prayer*. Garden City NY: Doubleday & Co., 1982.

Chapter 14

Justice, Solidarity, and Spirituality

James McGinnis

Solidarity with God, with the human family, and with the whole of creation is very difficult if not impossible, if we live immersed in material comforts. Reducing the amount of material goods on which we depend, as well as our attachment to them, can help us become more single-minded in living our faith and responding to the call of discipleship. We need to root out the obstacles in our lives that keep us from risking and from loving more deeply. Being too comfortable can also dull our sense of urgency and passion for justice. We are called to "hunger and thirst for justice," not just dabble at it in our spare time. Further, learning to live on less can help us identify more fully with the majority of the human family who have little in the way of material goods. Finally, the self-discipline involved in simplifying our lives can help us become more fit instruments of solidarity. Committing ourselves to discipleship demands a willingness to take risks and to persevere for a lifetime. Spiritual, mental, and physical stamina are essential.

The Gospels are emphatic:

* "Do not store up treasures for yourselves on earth, where moths and woodworms destroy them and thieves can break in and steal. But store up treasures for yourselves in heaven, where neither moth nor woodworms destroy them and thieves cannot break in and steal. For where your treasure is, there will your heart be also" (Mt 6:19-21).

* "No one can be the slave of two masters; they will either hate the first and love the second, or treat the first with respect and the second with scorn. You cannot be the slave of both God and money" (Mt 6:24).

* "Look at the birds in the sky. They do not sow or reap or gather into barns; yet your heavenly Father feeds them. Are you not worth much more than they are?... Think of the lilies of the field... So do not worry; do not say, 'what are we to eat? what are we to drink? how are

we to be clothed?' It is pagans who set their hearts on all these things. Your heavenly Father knows you need them all. Set your heart on God's kingdom first, and on God's righteousness, and all these other things will be given you as well" (Mt 6:25-33).

How often have we heard these words! How often have we dismissed them as unrealistic. "Lilies of the field" — is Jesus serious? "Birds in the sky" — isn't that a little irresponsible? Maybe birds can fly around and pick up the food they need, but that is no model for responsible parenthood, for fidelity on the job, for developing our talents.

Do you find yourself raising objections: "We have to be more practical and plan for the future. How will my children get the education they deserve? Who will provide for our retirement?" What does Jesus want of us? We live in a society that does not provide quality health care and education unless you can pay for it. There is no guarantee of a job in the U.S. People have to make it on their own. Adequate housing is not regarded as a right. Neither is an adequate diet, despite food stamp programs. The U.S. may have "social security," but there is no real social and economic security for the poor, the elderly, for anyone who is not wealthy. The "safety net" is anything but safe. We have many reasons for worrying about the future.

I can easily apply these scriptural passages to people whose major concern in life is to "get ahead," perhaps at any cost; to people for whom consumption is their god. They often burn themselves out at work, pay little attention to their families, buy an endless string of unnecessary things. But that's not most of us. And yet we *are* tempted to get ahead, to buy nice things, to live in nice neighborhoods, with nice houses and nice furnishings. We like comfort when we can get it. And some of us get it often. When I take time to think about Jesus' words, I am often troubled, and my guess is that you are too.

Is this what Jesus want of us — "to sell all we have and give it to the poor and come follow him"? Maybe we could sell a few things, but is Jesus serious about selling everything? What does he want of us? To do whatever it takes to follow him all the way? To set our hearts first on God's Kingdom of Shalom? To lay down our lives for our friends? What does it mean to follow Jesus, to give the Kingdom of God our whole heart, to lay down our lives for our friends, to "sell all" that would compromise such a commitment? And how do we do this in a society that does not provide security for its lilies or birds or people?

You are probably like me, unwilling to take drastic measures like St. Francis of Assisi. You probably do not anticipate being knocked to the ground as Paul was. You are probably comfortable moving one step at a time. Here we'll look at ways to take a few steps in the direction of living more on Gospel terms than on society's or the bank's. I have discovered these through a combination of three "Ps — prayer, principles, and practice. I start with prayer, understood as listening to God with silent and open hearts, letting the Word of God penetrate our hearts. But I see it including joining with others in struggling with Jesus' challenging call. In prayer we learn more about God's Kingdom of Shalom and find the courage to embrace God's will and follow Jesus more fully. Our prayer will be enlightened as we take practical steps to get rid of the baggage that keeps us from following Jesus. In prayer, both private and communal, we discover the principles that guide our practical steps. Here we'll look at four: a preferential option for the poor; connecting with the earth; simplifying our lives; and finding support.

PREFERENTIAL OPTION FOR THE POOR

Listen to our contemporary prophets:
* "In the face of each poor person, I see the face of Jesus" (Mother Teresa).

* "Several times I have decided to leave El Salvador. I almost could except for the children, the poor, bruised victims of this insanity. Who would care for them? Whose heart could be so staunch as to favor the reasonable thing in the sea of their tears and loneliness? Not mine, dear friend, not mine" (Jean Donovan 212).

* "God's love encompasses all people; but God has demonstrated a special concern for poor people, the needy, the helpless, and the oppressed and acted on their behalf to bring justice. God calls the Church to commit itself to be an advocate with and on behalf of the poor, the powerless, the victims of injustice" (*Christian Faith and Economic Justice* no. 29.324).

* "The example of Jesus poses a number of challenges to the contemporary Church. It imposes a prophetic mandate to speak for those who have no one to speak for them, to be a defender of the defenseless, who in biblical terms are the poor. It also demands a compassionate vision that enables the Church to see things from the side of the poor and powerless, and to assess lifestyle, policies and social institutions in terms of their impact on the poor....Finally, and most radically, it calls for emptying of self, both individually and corporately, that allows the Church to experience the power of God in the midst of poverty and powerlessness" (*Economic Justice for All* no. 52).

Both these church reflections provide contemporary comment on what the Hebrew prophets proclaimed in unambiguous terms. To cite but one passage from Jeremiah, where he compares the current king of Israel with the king's father: "Your father ate and drank, like you, but he practiced honesty and integrity, so all went well for him. He used to examine the cases of the poor and needy, then all went well. Is not that what it means to know me? — it is Adonai who speaks" (Jer 22:15-16). Taking up the cause of the poor is what it means to *know* God. *God cannot be known apart from active solidarity with the poor.*

On what terms are we to make decisions about economic matters? We are to do so "in terms of their impact on the poor." Mother Teresa and Jean Donovan have both given their lives for their friends, God's special ("preferential option") friends, the poor. So must we, somehow. Compassionate service is the first way — devoting some part of our heart and treasure to one-to-one time with the poor. This can be done in a nursing home, a shelter for the homeless, a food pantry. Hospitality — opening our hearts and home to others — can involve our whole family, especially if our home is involved. Hospitality is a whole orientation of our person — being available to others. Making space in our heart and home for a troubled teen, an overnight visitor, a lonely neighbor, a refugee, or one of our children's friends is an appropriate and important response to Jesus' call to the spiritual as well as the corporal works of mercy (see Mt 25:31-46).

But we can connect with the poor in other ways and live and work sacrificially in a way that alleviates their poverty. Lifestyle connections are as unlimited as our imaginations:

* A *"world bank"* on our dinner table can remind us to eat sacrificially and to share the savings with those who are hungry. The "Operation Rice Bowl" box (from Catholic Relief Services) and similar campaigns from Church World Service and other Protestant outreach programs provide similar reminds, especially appropriate during Lent. [1]

* *Public transportation* in some areas provides an experience of solidarity with the poor, for that is generally their only form of transportation. It can be an experience of inconvenience that the poor live with daily and that most of us convenience-oriented persons do anything to avoid. Public transportation is the North American urban counterpart of Gandhi's spinning wheel. Gandhi spent an hour a day at his spinning wheel so that his body as well as his mind and heart would experience the life of the economically poor. He also wanted to show them how they could provide for their own clothing needs, rather than rely on the British. Gandhi felt it essential to take on the life of the poor if he we going to be "one" with them. "Urban plunges," living on a welfare budget for a month, spending a weekend in a shelter for the homeless provide important momentary experiences that can touch our hearts and minds.

But perhaps there needs to be something more regular in our lives that connects us with the poor in ways that nurture our sense of solidarity.

Besides public transportation, what are some other possibilities? Clinics rather than private doctors? Public rather than private education? Public vs. private recreational activities and facilities? Are there others that make more sense for your circumstances? One friend of mine related how she felt the need for what she called a "zone of discomfort" as a way of identifying with the poor. She and her daughters chose to replace the portable air conditioner in their trailer home with a fan. Later they decided to share the dollar savings with the poor.

   * By *eating "connectedly"* we can make explicit our food connections with the poor and turn these external links into bonds of internal solidarity. The decision to boycott grapes, for example, can be an opportunity for solidarity with U.S. farm workers and their families suffering from poisonous pesticides. A picture of a farm worker on the dinner table, perhaps as part of a "Shalom Box," can remind our household of our connection with these providers of our food. Buying directly from local farmers at a farmers' market, rather than always from giant supermarkets, provides another opportunity for solidarity.

   If your economic situation is like mine — middle class — or if you are better off financially, you will probably find the following reflection on voluntary poverty quite challenging. I do, every time I go back to it. It is from Gustavo Gutierrez, a deeply prayerful Peruvian theologian most famous for his book, *A Theology of Liberation*, in which he writes about the redemptive character of voluntary poverty, the ways poverty helps create a oneness with the human family, especially with those members who are suffering. It is not that Gutierrez sees poverty as ideal or even as good. On the contrary, he is reminding us to work *against poverty*. Nor is he suggesting that those of us who are not poor "play at" being poor. Rather, he challenges us to let go of the privileges we have *at the expense of the poor*. Poverty, he says,

> has a redemptive value. If the ultimate cause of human exploitation and alienation is selfishness, the deepest reason for voluntary poverty is love of neighbor.... It is not a question of idealizing poverty, but rather of taking it on as it is — an evil — to protest against it and to struggle to abolish it. As Ricoeur says, you cannot really be with the poor unless you are struggling against poverty. Because of this solidarity — which must manifest itself in action, a style of life, a break with one's social class — one can also help the poor and exploited to become aware of their exploitation and seek liberation from it. Christian poverty, an expression of love, is solidarity with the poor and is a protest against poverty.... It is a poverty which means taking on the sinful condition of people to liberate them from sin and all its consequences. (Gutierrez 300-301)

When we find the courage to relinquish some of our privileges and to join with the poor in concrete action to challenge economic, political, and church institutions to change unjust practices and policies, we experience a special solidarity. We are taking another step in embracing Jesus' special love for the poor (see Lk 4:16-18) and that radical "emptying of self" that the Catholic bishops identified as essential.

Gandhi was clear in the explanation of his half-nakedness while in jail: "If I want to be one with the people of India, I must live like them." How can we apply this to our lives? I think immediately of my clothes closet and how many of the items I really need or have even worn in the last year. Such questioning always leads me to pull a few more items to share with those who have so much less. I read vividly the statement of St. Ambrose that "you are not making a gift of your possessions to the poor. You are handing over to them what is theirs. For what has been given in common for the use of all, you have arrogated to yourself. The world is given to all, and not only to the rich." [2] Even more graphic are similar statements attributed to St. Basil, another early Father of the Church: "The bread which you do not use is the bread of the hungry. The garment hanging in your wardrobe is the garment of the one who is naked. The shoes you do not wear are the shoes of the one who is barefoot."

Friends of ours have an "exchange system" for their purchases. Whenever possible, they circulate out of their house to someone in need an item comparable to each new item they bring into their house. This works especially well with clothing, with reading material, with toys, sometimes with appliances and other larger household items. It doesn't reduce our standard of living, but it keeps something of a lid on it.

Relinquishing privileges, especially those we have at the expense of the poor, means downward mobility, something quite counter to the prevailing culture and thus difficult for many of us caught in that culture. The "good life" does look and taste good. It is hard to let go of it. Other "experiments with truth," to put it in Gandhian terms, are to let go of luxury foods and drink, buy more second-hand clothing, get used furniture, learn to repair more things, participate in exchanges in our neighborhood or church. Can we occasionally use our own labor, as in baking bread or washing dishes by hand, rather than always choosing labor-saving and time-saving appliances and foods?

Henri Nouwen, Richard Rohr, and Jim Douglass suggest that relinquishing privileges and downward mobility can move us to deeper levels inside ourselves. [3] Besides letting go of things, are we willing to let go of the need to be productive (or "relevant), the need to be recognized and acclaimed (or "spectacular"), and the need to be in control (or "powerful")? Nouwen sees these as the three temptations of Jesus confronting us in 20th century affluent North America. Are we willing to identify with the humble Jesus of Philippians 2:6-8 and to become downwardly mobile in terms of productivity, recognition, and power?

The example of St. Francis of Assisi is even more challenging. I am moved by Francis's radical emptying of himself, letting go totally of his privileged youth in dramatic gestures, like completely stripping himself in front of his father, bishop, and much of the town of Assisi and declaring that from then, God would be his only "father." Tattered robes, a cave for a home, begging for food, working with lepers, trusting totally in God to provide what he needed — this was the "fare" Francis foresaw for any true follower of Jesus' Gospel. There is no way to imitate all the specifics of Francis's experiment with poverty, but we can experiment. And we can, and should, take on the spirit of Francis's poverty, even if its external manifestations are not entirely appropriate. I'll try to explain this in terms of love, humility, and joy, poverty's three special companions for Francis.

Francis's description of poverty was *vivere sine proprio* — "to live without possessions." Why? For love of God. To become one with God, to realize the Kingdom of God in ourselves, to experience that oneness that embraces all of reality, we must let go of everything else. In Gandhian terms, we must "reduce ourselves to zero" in order to realize All. Jesus' advice to the rich young man was "to sell all, give it to the poor, and come, follow me." In other words, get rid of everything that would hinder your commitment to me and follow me, love me, totally. I will lead you to everything. Love is the goal. Poverty is the way. It is "the gateway through which we pass into freedom *from* our egos, into the freedom *for* God," as two contemporary Franciscans put it. The original and truest Franciscan with Francis, his "soul sister" Clare, put it similarly: "This poverty, my beloved brothers and sisters, cling to with all your being, and *for the love of our Lord Jesus Christ* do not under any circumstances, want to possess anything" (italics mine). [4]

Vivere sine proprio — but, how do we live without possessions, especially in the interior senses of this injunction? In summary, the Gospel, as Francis understood it, asks us to renounce all earthly possessions, *everything that would give us security. We are to renounce all claims.* Yes, this does mean letting go of all earthly possessions. It does mean not using more than what I need to live a full human life. Perhaps I don't need to *own* everything, even anything. For example, we can use the public library for our reading needs. Even if we do own things, we can move in the direction of St. Paul's injunction, "whether I feast or fast, I do all for the love of Christ Jesus." Whether I have a car that works well or not, I'll use what I have for the love of God. I'll enjoy it, use it well while I have it, but should I lose it tomorrow, I don't fret, get bitter, stop my work. I don't let it affect my love of God and the ministry to which I am called. I'll simply take the bus or ask a friend for a ride. Francis probably had that kind of detachment or indifference in mind.

Beulah Caldwell, a Cherokee friend of our family, has shown us a similar attitude toward possessions characteristic of Native American peoples. Things are gifts in two senses. Besides being gifts of God to us, our things can become gifts of ourselves to others. Several times Beulah has gifted us with her best pottery. Admire a work of art in the home of many Native Americans and you may find yourself the recipient of that art. I recently had a brief debate with myself about how to distribute pictures from a special trip. Immediately I set aside the best ones for myself, parcelling out the left overs for my friends. That act of possessiveness haunted me. Soon afterward I wanted to give two friends a thank-you gift. When I gave them the crucifix I brought back from Nicaragua, the crucifix became even more special to me, especially when I see it hanging in their home. Why do we keep the best for ourselves and give others our left-overs?

If I care too much about my possessions, I spend time worrying about them, protecting them from others. I try to serve two masters. Francis's insight into the relationship between property and violence, materialism and militarism, is amazingly contemporary. Speaking to the Bishop of Assisi, who had told Francis that his ideal of poverty was too difficult, Francis stated: "My Lord, if we had possessions, we should also need weapons for their protection. From that proceeds the contentions and quarrels that obstruct the love of God and humankind. For that reason we want to possess naught of the things of this world."

Raymond Hunthausen, recently retired Catholic archbishop of Seattle and a Franciscan in spirit, echoes Francis's words: "Nuclear arms protect privilege and exploitation. Giving them up would mean our having to give up economic power over other peoples. Peace and justice go together. On the path we now follow, our economic policies toward other countries require nuclear weapons. Giving up the weapons would mean giving up more than our means of global terror. It would mean giving up the reason for such terror — our privileged place in the world."

We are to let go of all security other than God — which Francis described as "renouncing all claims." And not just claims of property and money, but all claims — gender, position, age, experience, effort. I should not reject any persons, any tasks, because they are "beneath me." Each time I hear myself about to say, "men don't," "directors don't," or "your father doesn't," I need to resist this temptation to place myself above others rather than at their service. Any time I am about to say "you owe me" (money, a favor, a wage, "consideration"), I should reflect first. Not that I cannot ask for and hope for a favor in return for all the favors I've done for that person, but I need to let go of any hint of demand that would hinder the other's free response. Francis says this is especially true in our relationship to God. God owes us nothing. All my good deeds do not merit me anything. "Salvation" — God's Kingdom of Shalom — is an entirely free gift. And that, says Francis, should be our stance toward everyone we encounter.

To renounce all claims — even to my time. It's not mine in the first place. How hard it is for me to face this! God gives me this day in order to love. I have an agenda of what I think this means in terms of all the responsibilities and people in my life. But should God see my day a little differently and send unexpected people and situations my way, I hope I'm "available." All this requires humility, poverty's second friend. Just as nothing is "beneath me," so too God's agenda for me may not be my original agenda. If it's not, then I had better make it mine. I am not the one in control. Jesus the Lord, not just of history, but of *my life and my "today."*

Poverty's third friend is joy. The haunting song from the movie *Brother Sun, Sister Moon* has this refrain: "If you want to live life free, take your time, go slowly. Do few things but do them well...." This is another hard saying for someone like me who is so task-oriented. If I can make four calls in 30 minutes instead of just two or three, all the better. If I can plan a workshop at the same time as I am doing the dishes or even listening to one of my children describe a movie, why not? I eat quickly, write quickly, move quickly through almost every task I do. Have you ever found yourself saying "I'm eating on the run" or "I'll just grab a bite"? I know I don't slow down enough to savor or relish people, experiences, the goodness of creation. Even the words "savor" and "relish" have a wonderful sound to them. I need to savor many more moments in my day, even if only for a few seconds. I think Francis was such a joyful person, even in his poverty, because he savored the simple things of creation. He savored his moments with people, with God. He savored each morsel of food. He took nothing for granted. He wasn't "satiated" in our materialistic sense. How many people caught up in affluence are never satisfied — always more, newer, bigger, better. And always the next project, all the items on my agenda that keep me from enjoying what I am about at this moment. Presence, simplicity, joy — they seem to go together.

Francis renounced all possessions, all earthly security, all claims because he belonged totally to God. He saw himself as a visitor and pilgrim on earth and put this in his rule for Franciscans: "The brothers should acquire nothing as owners, neither a house nor a foundation, nor any other thing. And just as 'pilgrims and strangers' (1 P 2:11) who in this world serve the Lord in poverty and humility, they should with confidence ask alms...." In the end we will have to let go of everything anyway if we want to embrace God at the moment of death, so why not prepare for that surrender in the present? And not just prepare for it, but begin to live it in the present.

God's Kingdom of Shalom is to be lived in the present as much as we can. In so doing, we offer ourselves as witnesses of that Kingdom, as Francis and Franciscans have been doing for eight centuries. Whether we like it or not, we are called to be witnesses that God's Kingdom of Shalom is breaking out in the world. It is possible to live it. The world needs desperately to see it. Our journey is not a private affair. That doesn't make it any easier, but it gives it more significance. I will struggle to be faithful to what I think is my calling, so that your faith and hope are increased. Isn't that what it means to be followers of Jesus? Isn't that the "oneness of life" we are trying to embody?

CONNECTING WITH THE EARTH

In the beautiful hymn of Chief Seattle, he instructs us non-Native American people: "Teach your children what we have taught our children — that the earth is our mother. Whatever befalls the earth befalls the children of the earth....This we know. The earth does not belong to us; we belong to the earth."

Rural families as well as Native American communities have much to teach us "city folks" about the message of the Scriptures embodied in passages such as: "The earth is the Lord's and the fullness thereof" (Ps 24); "the land belongs to me, and to me you are only strangers and guests" (Lv 25:23). We do not really own anything. We are *stewards* of the earth and of its rich variety of resources.

SIMPLIFYING OUR LIVES

In our experiments with truth to simply our lives, the process is more important than the product. There is no "right answer" that satisfies all households, congregations, situations. There are no quantitative measures of what constitutes a "simple lifestyle" or "Gospel living." There are some qualitative measures that are helpful, for example: "will this particular service, product, or location I am considering made more compassionate or less compassionate, bring me closer to the poor or separate me further from the poor?" Gandhi's way of putting this question is dramatic: "Whenever you are in doubt or when the self becomes too much with you, try the following expedient: Recall the face of the poorest and most helpless person you have ever seen and ask yourself if the step you contemplate is going to be of any use to him....Then you will find your doubts and your self melting away."

"Right answers" or "good answers" will *emerge* from a process that involves prayer, study, discussion, and action. Prayer, especially the voice of God in Scripture, readies our hearts to hear voices different from the prevailing societal voices and values. God speaks to us through other prophets as well and their voices can help us on our journey.

The discernment necessary for raising the right questions and facing challenging answers involves other people. We need to place ourselves in relationship to people who challenge us by their fidelity and courage, who help us understand ourselves, and who can support us in difficult choices and actions. Whether from a spiritual director, a support group, or a trusted friend, outside feedback, challenge, and support are essential.

Third, the process involves mutuality, especially when a family or community is involved. Decisions that affect the whole household should involve all members of the household. Family actions on behalf of the poor or in defense of creation should be the result of family decisions. Regular family or community meetings that include "family service" or "community service" discussions and decisions regarding household purchases and other lifestyle issues are an important tool. They should involve all household members and make sure that the needs of everyone, children included, are taken seriously.

One family who convinced us early about the importance of family meetings described their negative experience this way: "Our teenage daughters because very upset with us one Saturday morning when we announced that we were going to buy a used sofa at a Goodwill store that day. They screamed, 'Mother, you are keeping us poor, we don't have to be poor, and we're embarrassed to bring our friends around this house!' My husband and I had made all those lifestyle decisions without the kids' input and continued to do so. Now our daughters are grown with families of their own, and they are pursuing lives of conspicuous consumption. If we could do it over again, we would definitely involve them in decisions."

Our own family experience of including our children (now teens) into most of our lifestyle decisions over the last ten years has strengthened our conviction about the family meeting process. We have made many compromises, but the children do not seem to resent our values and have internalized them to some extent. All of them, for instance, are still quite comfortable buying their clothes at second-hand stores, especially when they realize how this stretches their individual clothing budgets. Kathy and I made a clear distinction between nonnegotiable values and negotiable ways of living out those values. Concern for the poor, family service, recycling, more simple or less materialistic living are all nonnegotiable. But how much, how often, where, with whom are negotiable.

FINDING SUPPORT

Living on Gospel terms depends heavily on the environment we create by our choices. For instance, where we choose to live (for those who have a choice) has a tremendous influence on our values and especially on the formation of our children's values. The choice of a home affects other choices: where we worship, shop, send our children to school, who their peers will be. If our environment is not conducive to the values we want to promote, then we have to take compensatory steps.

For example, if you live in a monocultural environment, you can compensate to some extent by the reading material and pictures you bring into your home. Worshipping, shopping, or enjoying cultural events in places that put you in touch with people of different racial, ethnic, or religious backgrounds promotes a more inclusive lifestyle. Such steps extend our sense of "oneness" across racial lines.

If you live in a relatively affluent environment, you can compensate to some extent by developing friendships with people from different economic backgrounds. Inviting an elderly poor person to dinner is often less threatening to our children or other reluctant members of our household than providing temporary shelter for a homeless person. Regular community service projects — like serving a meal at a soup kitchen, especially if mutual relationships are fostered; nursing home visits; an outing with residents from a shelter for the homeless — all these can put us in situations and with persons who can broaden our horizons, deepen our compassion, and enliven our faith.

Probably the most important way to support our (and our children's) values is through a family support group. When adults and children come together regularly for joint prayer, study, action, support, and fun, good things happen. Because living on Gospel terms ultimately means a conversion in our lives and a life-long commitment to solidarity with the poor that will lead us to experience the cross of Jesus, we all need the challenge and support of others over the long haul. Children especially need to be with children from other families with similar values. It is hard to be different.

Living on Gospel terms is difficult because Jesus asks us to come follow him, not to suburbia but to the cross. Living as lilies of the field — seeking security more and more in God and less in high-yield investments — is as scary as it is unclear. Can we let to and place that much trust in God's providential love for us? Choosing simplicity or even downward mobility is craziness in a society that exalts the beautiful, the rich, and the powerful, and constantly says that "more is better."

Lent is an especially appropriate time to wrestle with these questions and let Jesus take our hand and lead us another step along his journey through Calvary to the Resurrection. Here is the real "fullness of life," the genuinely "good life" that is God's Kingdom of Shalom. Do we dare to believe and to follow? We have God's promises to be with us always: "I will never forget you. See, I have carved you on the palm of My hand..." (Is 49:15); "you did not choose me; no, I chose you..." (Jn 15:16); "and know that I am with you always; yes, to the end of time" (Mt 28:20).

ENDNOTES

[1] *World Bank* available from the Holy Childhood Association, 1720 Massachusetts Ave., N.W., Washington, DC 20036. *Operation Rice Bowl* is a project of Catholic Relief Services, 209 West Fayette Street, Baltimore, MD 21201-3403.

[2] Quoted by Pope Paul VI, *On the Development of Peoples*, no. 23.

[3] Henri Nouwen's two-part series in *Sojourners* magazine, June and July 1981, is entitled "The Selfless Way of Christ" and "Temptation: The Pull Toward Upward Mobility." Richard Rohr presents his challenging vision and guidance through audio cassettes, available through St. Anthony Messenger. Perhaps most helpful on this topic is a series of eight that includes "Making Room for Freedom: Liberating the Affluent," "What Is the Good Life? Breaking Out of the Consumer Trap," "Leaving Security Behind: Finding a New Center," and "Surrendering: Giving Everything We Are." Jim Douglass's treatment of the temptations of Jesus (paralleling Nouwen's treatment) is in the chapter on "The Yin-Yang of Resistance and Contemplation" in *Resistance and Contemplation*.

[4] Based on Cajetan Esser, O.F.M., and Engelbert Grau, O.F.M., "Life without Possessions: The Concept of Poverty According to St. Francis," a privately distributed paper, October 8, 1972.

WORKS CITED

Christian Faith and Economic Justice. The 196th General Assembly of the Presbyterian Church USA. Louisville: Presbyterian Church USA, 1984.

Donovan, Jean. *Salvador Witness.* New York: Ballantine, 1986.

Christian Faith and Economic Justice. The 196th General Assembly of the Presbyterian Church USA. Louisville: Presbyterian Church USA, 1984.

Gutierrez, Gustavo. *A Theology of Liberation.* Maryknoll NY: Orbis Books, 1973.

National Conference of Catholic Bishops. *Economic Justice for All.* Washington DC: USCC Publications, 1986.

ACTIVITIES FOR CONNECTING JUSTICE, SOLIDARITY, AND SPIRITUALITY

Thomas Bright

ACTIVITY ONE: PORTRAITS OF JESUS

This activity is designed to help group members explore their images of Jesus. Personal images are then compared and contrasted with the Gospel image of Jesus as a person concerned for the poor.

1. Do a portrait tour of your church building, looking at the different images of Jesus expressed in stained glass, statuary, and paintings. Explore the images of Jesus found in books, pictures, holy cards, and statues gathered prior to the group session.

2. Discuss these different images of Jesus. What do these different images tell us about the person of Jesus? How are the images similar or dissimilar? Are there any common elements? Which do you think is closest to a visual portrait of Jesus? Why the multiplicity of images? Why?

3. Move from a discussion of visuals to values. What do the different visual images of Jesus say about his vision and values? Ask the group to list 10 values that are central to their understanding of Jesus.

4. Compare and contrast the visual images and the group's values statement with the Gospel image of Jesus—a portrait that speaks more about Jesus' personality and vision than about his physical appearance. Offer the group a selection of passages to choose from. Include the following: Mt 25: 31-46 (the last judgement); Mt 5: 38-48 (love of enemies); Mk 8: 1-9 (Jesus feeds four thousand); Mk 9: 33-37 (who is greatest); Lk 4: 16-30 (Jesus describes his mission); Lk 10: 25-37 (the good Samaritan); Jn 13: 1-15 (Jesus washes the disciples' feet). What portrait do the Gospels paint of Jesus?

5. Introduce the concept of preferential option for the poor—the responsibility shared by all of God's people to speak out on behalf of those most in need and to work to change the situations that harm them. Refer to the U.S. bishops' economics pastoral, *Economic Justice for All*, specifically the section on "Poverty, Riches and the Challenge of Discipleship" (48-52). Discuss as a group what the world would be like if all people lived like Jesus, sharing his concern for the poor, reaching out in service.

ACTIVITY TWO: PLEDGING ALLEGIANCE TO THE REIGN OF GOD

Use the Pledge of Allegiance as a starting point for exploring what it means to be members of a universal, multicultural Church.

1. Ask a volunteer to stand and recite the Pledge of Allegiance.

2. Discuss: What is the purpose of the Pledge of Allegiance? What are we committing ourselves to as we recite this statement of commitment? What do you think is meant by the phrases: one nation, under God, indivisible, with liberty and justice for all? What image of the United States is presented in the Pledge? What values does the Pledge uphold?

3. Ask: What would it be like to create a new Pledge of Allegiance, not for the flag of the United States, but for the reign of God? What are the images or values of the reign of God that we would want to include? Where would we find these values set forth? What values do we see set forth in Scripture, in Church teaching, in our creeds/statements of belief and in our prayers?

4. Working in teams of three or four, have the group develop Pledges of Allegiance to the reign of God.

5. Share the team Pledges. Compare and contrast the Pledges of Allegiance to the reign of God with the Pledge to the U.S. flag. How do the different pledges complement one another? How are they different? Are there any tensions involved in committing ourselves to both? Why or why not? What would the world be like if all people committed themselves to your Pledge of Allegiance to the reign of God? What's one thing you can do to act on the values and beliefs included in this newest Pledge?

ACTIVITY THREE: DEFINING SUCCESS

Explore the implications of a commitment to sharing resources and service to others within a U.S. culture that often measures worth in terms of independence, security, and accumulated possessions.

1. Prior to your class/meeting: Using tape recorders or camcorders, have the members of your youth group interview a broad spectrum of parish or community members, asking just one simple question: "What does it mean to be a successful person?"

2. Ask members to jot down as they watch/listen to the interviews, the different images and criteria of "success" set forth by those interviewed. List as a group the different images/criteria of success found in the interviews. Group the different images of success together using general values categories developed by the group, for example freedom, caring relationships, security, material comfort. What positive values stand behind each of

these understandings of success? Are there any negatives connected with these same understandings of success?

3. Discuss: Where do our different understandings of success come from? (family, friends, school, church, nation, media) Do you sometimes feel pressured to conform to other people's definitions of success? Could you share an example? Do you ever feel caught between conflicting images of success? Having discussed other people's understandings of what it means to be "successful," how would you respond now to the same question?

4. Reflect together: If Jesus returned to earth now as a 13 to 16 year old person in your community, how do you think he would describe success? What role do you think freedom, caring relationships, security, material comfort would play in Jesus' understanding of success? (Would his definition be different if he came not to your town but to a town in Asia or Africa? Why or why not?) How is Jesus' understanding similar to or different from yours? Even a quick reading of the Gospels would indicate that an essential element of Jesus' understanding of success would be generous sharing of our resources (time, talent, and treasure) with others. What do you have by way of time, talent, or treasure that could be shared with others? Is Jesus' call to live for and share with others realistic in our culture and world? Why or why not? If you wanted to live more like Jesus, what impact would it have on your life? What practical steps would you take? What would it mean for your family and parish community to live more like Jesus?

ACTIVITY FOUR: PRAYING WITH THE EARTH

Celebrate our connectedness with the earth in prayer; grow in our understanding of native American people and their way of prayer.

1. Research and share the history of Native American peoples in your city, state, part of the country. What peoples or tribes are part of the living history of your region? What happened to them and why?

2. Reflect together on the great respect expressed in the Native American tradition for the earth. The earth is often referred to as Mother by Native Americans, stressing the connectedness between all of the earth's people and the responsibility shared by all for protecting the earth's living environment.

3. Share together in a Native American prayer ritual honoring Mother Earth.

NATIVE AMERICAN PRAYER SERVICE
IN HONOR OF MOTHER EARTH

Juan Mancias

Introduction

In the Native American tradition, we are all related through the earth, our mother. As human beings, we come from the same mother and so return at death. The earth has been given to us by the Creator. Further, in Native American understanding, the world's problems lie in the inability to recognize our connectedness to one another and to the earth. To heal ourselves, we must heal our relationships with the earth (environment) and with others. We must remember to take care of the body of Christ, the Church. For we are the people of God, we are sisters and brothers regardless of our appearance. We were all born on this Mother Earth; let us take care of one another.

Through this call to be brothers and sisters, we must take care of our mother; our mother, who nourishes us with food; our mother, who was created by God to sustain life. We walk together and experience each other. As we walk, let us not try to change each other, but let us truly share each other's gifts.

In the Native American tradition, the "Red Road" is the path of humility, respect, and awareness for all creation. So, together, let us walk the straight and narrow road, the "Red Road," which leads to the kingdom of God.

Suggested Setting

The following readings could be done outside, to feel the life of Mother Earth. The group may be in a circle to symbolize the continuity and connectedness of all creation.

Opening Prayer

The leader, using some or all of the above thoughts, gathers all together in prayer.

Scripture Reading

Ecclesiastes 1: 2-11

Responsorial Psalm

Psalm 146: 1-10

Response: Praise God, O my soul.

Reflection

Several young people may wish to reflect on our earth as a gift of God and on our connectedness to the environment and to our fellow humans.

A Prayer of Blessing

A *Prayer in Six Directions* is traditional with these readings. The readings and prayers remember those who have gone before us, our ancestors. This is a special and sacred prayer. The road to respect, humility, and awareness is walked before performing it.

In the Native American tradition, the *Prayer in Six Directions* is a ceremony that takes time to learn—sometimes a lifetime—hence, becoming a sacred way of life. This prayer is done as a blessing and varies among Native American people. Out of respect to the tribes, Mother Earth is given honor so the people may survive.

Begin by quieting yourself and feeling the presence of God. In an unhurried fashion, the directions are greeted. We turn to the East where the sun rises each day. We praise God for the gift of new life, of new days, of our youth. As we turn to the South, we give thanks for those people and things that warm our lives, for growth and development. The West calls us to praise God for sunsets, nights, for the endings in our lives. When we turn to the North, we recall the challenges and difficulties we experience. As we bend and touch Mother Earth, we praise the Creator for the things that sustain our lives. Finally, as we look up into the sky, we thank God for our hopes and dreams. Since we have centered ourselves in the Creator's universe, we remember God's mercy. Now we can enter into prayer.

Suggested Closing Songs

On Eagle's Wings by Michael Joncas (North American Liturgy Resources); *Circles* by Harry Chapin.

(Reprinted with permission from *Building the City of God: Celebrating Our Heritage.* Washington DC: USCC Publishing Services, 1990: 15-16.)

ACTIVITY FIVE: SERVING IN SOLIDARITY WITH THE POOR

People are too easily defined in our society according to economic categories. Direct service opportunities need to be designed in a way that allows people both to work *for* the poor and to work side by side *with* the poor. In this way we meet the poor as "people like us," people with talents and gifts to share, capable of impacting situations and structures that are harmful to the dignity of all.

1. Explore the service opportunities available through your parish, school, diocese, and local community organizations.

2. Select a service opportunity that meets the talents and needs of your group, *and* that allows your group to work alongside those who are poor or otherwise disadvantaged.

3. Before moving to respond to the service need you've selected, learn a bit about why the service is needed. Use the resources of your own community or of the service site to explore questions like: What are the root causes of the problem? How long has it existed and how has it changed through the years? What signs of hope exist that the situation might someday change? Apart from involvement in direct service, what could your group do to help undermine the structures that keep the problem in place? Understanding the history and causes helps us see the people hurt by injustice and inequity in a different light.

4. As you set up your service venture, make sure there's time allotted for people contact. In the case of youth, contact with peers is particularly important. Justice issues are seen much differently by youth when they're viewed through the eyes of their peers. Offer opportunities for continued involvement in the project selected or other ways of staying in contact with the people met.

5. Evaluate the project and bring your new experiences to prayer. Learning with, working with, and praying with the poor are all important elements in solidarity.

ACTIVITY SIX: FOCUS ON PERSONAL REFLECTION

1. What is your image of Jesus and where does it come from? How central to your image of Jesus is his concern for the poor and disadvantaged?

2. What does it mean in your life to have a preferential option for the poor? What is one thing you can be proud of in your response to the poor? What is one area in which you feel called to grow in your response to the poor?

3. How do you balance personal, community, and organizational commitments in your life? How is discipleship realized in each? In which relationships do you find it easiest to live out your faith? In which is it hardest?

4. What does success mean for you? How do you balance Jesus' call to simplicity of lifestyle with the needs for security? How has the balance shifted through your life? What would you like the balance to look like in the future? What's one step you can take now to bring the future close to reality?

5. Who do you consciously pray with and for as church? Does your understanding of Church reach beyond the boundaries of your parish, neighborhood, diocese, and country? Does it consciously include people of other cultural, economic, social, and religious groups? What can you do to expand the content of your praying to include the needs of the wider church and world communities? How can you expand the resources for your praying to include readings, reflections, music and images from other peoples and places?

6. Are you comfortable with how you now steward your time and talents? Where in your life do you meet the poor? Is there a need to increase your personal experience with those who are poor or disadvantaged so that you will be better equipped and motivated to work for justice on their behalf?

Chapter 15

Spiritual Direction With Adolescents

Gregory Rohde

My present challenge takes me beyond my role as a directee and looks at my potential to be a director. Writing this chapter has forced me to look at the dynamics more closely. It has also helped me put spiritual direction in a better context with the Church's larger mission.

Most importantly, working on this chapter has had implications for my own ministry. I'm challenged to develop the skills needed in order to present myself as one who may be qualified to do spiritual direction whether with youth or adults.

After consulting youth ministers, high school campus ministers, professional spiritual directors, formation directors for religious communities, and professors of graduate courses on spiritual direction, I've come to three conclusions:

1) There are many resources on youth ministry.
2) There are even more resources on spiritual direction.
3) There is a dearth of resources which combine these two.

This essay will take a brief look at spiritual direction and its relationship to the world of adolescents. It will explore issues such as: What is spiritual direction? Is it possible for adolescents? If it can happen, what does it look like, how does it happen, and who can do it? By no means do I intend to exhaust the subject, but merely to scratch the surface of these issues, raise awareness about them, and, hopefully, generate more questions about them.

DEFINITIONS AND IMAGES

Spiritual direction has a rich history in our Christian tradition, and there are many styles and approaches. There is an equally large number of definitions and images for this tool in spiritual growth.

William Connolly names spiritual direction as the process in which a person "can focus his (or her) life with an awareness and an honesty in response to God's loving, creative, and saving action" (Connolly 101). Katherine Dyckman and L. Patrick Carroll see it as "an interpersonal relationship in which one person assists others to reflect on their own experience in the light of who they are to become in fidelity to the Gospel" (Carroll and Dyckman 20).

In *Spiritual Friend,* Tilden Edwards uses the imagery of a physician to describe the task of a spiritual director. For him, the "physician of a wounded soul" does nothing more than "cleanse the wound, align the sundered parts, and give it a rest. That's all. The physician does not heal. He or she provides an environment for the natural process of healing to take its course" (Edwards 125). This description is an important reminder that, ultimately, the Holy Spirit is the Spiritual Director, using a human relationship as an instrument for guidance.

Alan Jones reflects:

We are men and women with scattered and fragmented hearts. I have left parts of myself behind with family and friends in places which I scarcely remember. The friend of my soul is the one who guards and honors these bits and pieces which I call 'me.' I have also sent fragments ahead of myself, and God knows where they are. My friend knows of them and walks with me towards them. My heart is on its way home, and I have placed it in the keeping of others, for it is only with them that I can find my way home.… Companionship is for the hatching of our hearts. It is for the bringing home of our scattered and fragmented selves, for the making of a heart at home with itself. When I am truly at home with myself in God, I can then be truly present to my friends and fellow pilgrims. (Jones 129)

Jones' reflection speaks strongly of coming home, reminiscent of Meister Eckhart's insight that "God is at home in us. It is we who have gone out for a walk" (Fox 15). This "coming home" motif is about a journey, a journey which one does not make alone. A scriptural correlative is the Emmaus story: Jesus is a companion to the disciples as they make their journey. He walks with them, and, while their hearts are on fire, explains the Scriptures to them and helps them see their recent experiences in the light of salvation history.

Building on this imagery, the spiritual director can be portrayed as both companion and guide. While the disciples were companions to each other, it took Jesus to be both companion and guide. A spiritual director is called to be a companion, one who will be with the other in his or her growth and struggles. A director is also called to be a guide, though, for a guide is one who is more familiar with the path. It is not a relationship of the blind leading the blind.

Another image for the spiritual director is that of midwife. The midwife is not the one who is giving birth, nor the one who planted the seed in order to create the new life. The midwife's role is to be with the parents and assist in the birthing process through the use of her experience, knowledge, and wisdom. Using similar concepts, the director's role can be seen as a coach, a model which is more familiar to the adolescent's experience. A coach is one who helps instill discipline in his or her students in order that they might develop to their potentials. Part of this process includes a greater respect for one's own gifts, respect for the giftedness of others, an appreciation for teamwork, and a discipline that can carry over into other areas of life. Using the story of Jacob with the angel, perhaps the wrestling coach might be the closest approximation to the director. While the coach can help the athlete get in shape, deny himself certain things in order to become stronger, and learn the best techniques and strategies, he or she is helpless except to encourage, advise, and support once the wrestler steps into the mat. The wrestling itself must be done by the wrestler and no one else.

While all of these examples are rich images which paint the role of the director, the one I'll be drawing upon most heavily will be that of companion and guide.

In reflecting on the term "spiritual direction" itself, Dyckman and Carroll claim that it is neither spiritual nor directive (Carroll and Dyckman 20). It is not spiritual in the sense that it also includes the material. Spiritual direction must engage the whole person. One can not fall into the Platonic trap of severing the soul from the body, thus ignoring the truth that the spiritual can not be seen as separate from the material. One's spiritual life incorporates all aspects of that life, not just one small segment of a truncated self.

It is not directive in the sense that the director does not tell the other what he or she must do. Ultimately, the Holy Spirit is the only one who has the authority to direct someone's spiritual life. The director is not the source of wisdom, guidance, or growth but at best only a means through which God can work in the person's life.

GOALS AND TASKS

The goals or tasks of spiritual direction vary with one's style. Most see the basic task as fostering union with God and build their definitions from there (Barry and Connolly 8).

Dyckman and Carroll pose two tasks for spiritual direction: the objectification and articulation of experiences and the interpretation of these experiences through the eyes of faith (Carroll and Dyckman 22). The former pertains to the human need to get in touch with, name, and express the thoughts and feelings we have within us. This itself can be an empowering and healing experience. Once I can put a handle or a label on a problem, it seems so much easier to face. Also, this process helps me obtain quality information about myself and helps me make healthy choices as I become aware of tendencies and patterns within my ways of relating to the world. As shall be seen later, interpreting these experiences through the eyes of faith is part of what distinguishes spiritual direction from counseling. For me to grow spiritually, it is not enough for me to name my experience. I must also be able to see it in the context of how God has acted, is acting, and may act in my life. I see its relationship to my own story of salvation history. Hopefully, an extension can be made to include how *my* story connects with *THE* story, the larger part of salvation history.

COUNSELING OR SPIRITUAL DIRECTION?

Although they are very similar, spiritual direction is not counseling. In terms of the two tasks of direction, articulation and interpretation, counseling is limited to the former. Like the spiritual director, the counselor helps an individual gain a greater self-understanding through getting in touch with one's thoughts and feelings, thus helping them express whatever it is that is happening within. However, the counselor will not address the issues of how these experiences are connected to one's faith life. The common goal of being faithful to the Gospel and responding to God's call, a necessity for the director to have with an individual, is not necessary for the counselor. Also, the director may choose to use prayer, Scripture, or the sacraments in the context of a session. These means are ones which aren't used in most counseling situations. Lastly, the director is conscious that the relationship in which he or she is engaged is one which involves not two, but three people: the director, the directee, and God. While there is often a lot of gray area between the two, the incorporation of one's faith perspective is the distinguishing mark between counseling and spiritual direction.

IS IT POSSIBLE?

"Is it possible to do spiritual direction with adolescents?" This is an important question which is tough to answer. The crux of the issue is one's definition of spiritual direction. If direction is aimed at helping people articulate their experiences and see them in the light of faith, certain skills are needed on the part of the directee. One prerequisite is critical reflection, the process by which I can step outside of a situation in order to assess it better. I can have a different perspective on life once I can step back from it and perceive it from another vantage point. Without critical reflection, spiritual direction is impossible. Piaget's developmental work shows that there is no one age at which this process develops. Regardless of when it develops, a person is unprepared for direction until he or she can reflect critically.

Developmental stages also need to be considered. While some say that direction is impossible until one has taken personal responsibility for their faith life (Fowler's Individuative-Reflective faith), others assert that direction can start earlier and can assist in the process of claiming one's faith. Charles Shelton, asserting the latter, says:

> Certainly, spiritual direction is needed for young people because, during their adolescent years, they must integrate a growing and maturing faith commitment in preparation for adulthood. (Shelton 174)

Jean LaPlace concurs:

> At this age, spiritual direction is simple and almost rudimentary in its manifestations, but is such as to permit the emergence of grace from within the searches and developments of adolescence. (LaPlace 149)

It's unfair to assume that the models of spiritual direction which cater to adults would also work with adolescents. We need to realize that spiritual direction for youth will be tailored to meet their needs and styles.

Lastly, even if the adolescent is capable of being in a spiritual direction relationship, he or she may not want it. This is particularly true for those who are rebelling against institutions and are seeking personal autonomy. Ironically enough, this could also be the key issue to bring someone to a director for assistance.

Assuming that one does want to engage in spiritual direction, is capable of critical reflection, and can find someone who won't expect them to enter direction as an adult would, spiritual direction is possible for adolescents.

HOW DOES IT HAPPEN?

The format of spiritual direction is one key area in which it differs from an adult's approach. Consistency and commitment are two important factors here. Reflecting on his experiences as a high school campus minister, Jeff Pawlak, S.M. speaks of the tension within consistency:

> For the most part, few kids are mature enough to deal with the spiritual life in ways to compare with the spirituality of an adult. The difference is one of maturity and motivation. I don't think we can fault them for that, though, because they are where they need to be. On the other hand, it's amazing how transparent, how honest, how vulnerable they can be when they decide to take their masks off. Direction is

possible for them when they are at those points, but the problem for many of them is that their behavior is not consistent enough for them to participate in an ongoing relationship of direction. For most adolescents, if direction happens at all, it's sporadic and usually centers on a particular issue they're facing at that time. [1]

Jim Gahan, a campus minister for 20 years, identifies commitment as a key to spiritual direction with adolescents:

> When we started our program for spiritual direction at Rosary, the biggest drawback was not that the students didn't want to learn to pray or to grow in their spirituality. They said they wanted both of these. The biggest drawback was their inability to commit themselves to it on a regular basis. Kids don't know from one day to the next what they'll be doing. They're very busy and over-committed these days. They're hit from all sides. With so many choices before them all the time, they usually wait until the last minute, always hoping that something even better will come along. [2]

Given these factors, the format in which an adolescent will enter into spiritual direction has to be a flexible one. It should be an hospitable environment in which the student feels comfortable enough to bring up the issue which he or she wants to discuss. Spiritual direction for youth, then, is usually sporadic and focuses on a key question with which they are currently dealing. Unlike an adult model in which the directee will usually schedule his or her appointment in advance, a youth will be more inclined to just drop in and ask "Can I talk to you about something?" Once their problem is addressed, they may not need to drop in again for several months. It's imperative, though, that they know they could if they needed to.

The sacrament of reconciliation is a common format through which spiritual direction begins. Most youth, if they experience the sacrament at all, do so on retreats. If they are with an adult who cares for them and with whom they can talk comfortably, they may be inclined to approach this person outside of the sacramental context. This can lead to occasional conversations about how life is going and possibly lead to discussions which deal more specifically with their faith life.

Developmentally, most early adolescents (11/12-14/15) are at a point where the norms of the group dictate their behaviors. When it comes to their basic religious stance, many are belongers first and believers second. For this reason, most attempts at direction for early adolescents are done within a group setting. Guided reflections and meditations are good ways to help them relax. They also help the students use their imaginations as a means with which they can pray. Solitude is threatening enough to many adults, much less junior high students. Doing group exercises in which everyone in the room is silent for a short while is one way in which they can become more comfortable with this discipline.

While "belonging" is the operative word for early adolescents, "ownership" is the key phrase for their older counterparts. As one begins to take more responsibility for his or her faith life, there will always be many questions. The director's role in these instances is to avoid the temptation to play "Shell Answer Man (or Woman)" and hand over quick and easy answers to the inquisitive mind and soul. Instead, our task is to help them formulate better questions so they can focus on the key issues of faith instead of getting stuck on peripherals. The director is not there to give answers but to be a resource person who helps the youth find his or her own answers. As a good wrestling coach, the director points out that faith is more than having the "right" answers; it is having the confidence and the courage to wrestle with the questions.

WHAT ARE THE ISSUES?

Spiritual direction differs for adolescents and adults not only in the formats used, but also in the developmental issues addressed. As noted above, "belonging" and "ownership" are two general issues faced in adolescence.

With respect to getting to know God better, most adolescents focus on Jesus as their friend. As they are gaining limited autonomy from their parents, and as the Holy Spirit seems ethereal, few adolescents gravitate toward the first or third person of the Trinity as their chief way to relate to God. Because friendship is paramount to them, they are more inclined to develop their relationship with Jesus, the one who can accept them just as they are, even if they can't.

In addition to the faith part of the adolescent's life, relational, moral, and vocational issues also need to be addressed. In *Adolescent Spirituality*, Charles Shelton lists four specific goals of spiritual direction with adolescents:

1) The growing awareness and sense of God's presence in the adolescent's life; the nurturing and presence of a deepening prayer life that reflects a deepening faith commitment.

2) The developing sense of the adolescent's relational life reflecting deepening commitments and love for others.

3) The development of everyday values, perceptions, attitudes, and goals consonant with the Gospel; focusing on behaviors in the present life of the adolescent.

4) The development of a future orientation that integrates the Gospel with future relationships, career goals, and vocational aspirations.

Shelton also lists eight dilemmas which adolescents need to address somewhere along their faith journeys: decision making, behaviors, world view, values, understanding others, goal striving, maturity, and past experiences (Shelton 181-193).

WHO CAN DO IT?

Who can do spiritual direction with teenagers? Anyone God picks. It's important for us to not forget that God can use whatever means God wishes to help people respond in faith and help bring about his reign. This does not exonerate us, though. It merely keeps us humble and reminds us that we are nothing more than instruments through which God works. We ourselves are not the source of life or growth but only a means through which life may be communicated.

Having kept our role in perspective, I can now say that it's more common for God to work through people who have certain talents or skills. What characteristics should be possessed by someone who is willing to serve as a spiritual director for adolescents? The first characteristics are the same ones for someone directing adults.

GENERAL CHARACTERISTICS

First and foremost, a director needs to be a person of prayer. If I am not in touch with God's presence in my own life, and if I am not committed to continual growth in my own fidelity to God, then how can I do the same for others? If we try to help teens grow in their own faith without committing ourselves to spiritual disciplines, we're hypocrites at best and Pelagians at worst, exalting our own influence out of proportion and forgetting that it is God who does the converting. We are no more than instruments.

If spiritual direction is about articulating my experiences and seeing them in the light of faith, then a director should be a person who can do both of these for himself or herself. He or she also needs to have good listening skills to help me make the connections I may not make on my own.

A director is called to be a continual student. For me to be a good resource for others, I need to have a solid theological base out of which to speak. I also need to have a strong background in psychology and interpersonal dynamics. So that my academic pursuits don't propel me too far into the theoretical, the most important text with which I should be familiar is the script of my own life. I should become familiar with my own faith story and to be able to tell it in light of the Gospel.

If the quality of my personal relationships is a benchmark by which my spirituality can be "measured," then a director should be familiar with the dynamics of healthy relationships. Falling in love with life and living passionately should be goals for which the director strives. The director should be well-versed in the school of falling in love: the vulnerability, the risk, the creativity, the call beyond myself, the service, the desire for unity, the ability to simultaneously embrace and let go. These same characteristics apply to spiritual growth, and it is the director's role to help the directee along the journey.

The dynamics of spiritual growth should not be foreign to the director if he or she is to be a guide as well as a companion. The common elements of spiritual growth—conversion, struggle, integration, call to deeper reality, and a radicality of love—should be areas in which the director has done much study and reflection (Carroll and Dyckman 9).

A director should be able to support and challenge the directee at appropriate times. Support without challenge leads to complacency. Challenge without support leads to suspicion, frustration, and despair. A qualified director will be able to balance these two.

A spiritual director should be a person of integrity and authenticity. His or her role as director should flow from his or her own identity and not be just a task to be performed.

A spirit of hospitality and availability will characterize a director who has created a welcome space for the pilgrim. A directee will probably not last long if he or she doesn't feel welcome or feels like just another appointment in a busy day's schedule.

A good director is characterized by vulnerability and humility. He or she is able to disclose his or her own journey when necessary. He or she will also fill the role of director in a way which doesn't exalt his or her own ego. He or she is aware of his or her own flaws and even presents these to the Lord to somehow be used as a resource in his or her ministry.

The gifts of wisdom, discipline, and detachment, as well as all the other marks of a person whose life is committed to serving God's people, will be possessed by most good directors. The combination of these gifts should assist the director in responding to the particular needs of the directee.

SPECIFIC CHARACTERISTICS

Within youth ministry itself, what characteristics also need to be present? In addition to the ones mentioned above, the director should have a good grasp of adolescent developmental theory. This will help the director understand the student's situation. It will also help the director show the student that the chaos being faced is in some sense "normal" or expected.

The director needs to have a genuine love for kids. Youth have a way of being able to see through hypocrisy and will be able to spot an insincere director.

A spiritual director for adolescents needs to have a respect for the capacities of his or her youth. He or she will not expect the maturity of an adult from his or her directees. He or she will also be patient if their capacity for critical reflection needs more development. Asking open-ended questions and allowing silent times in the dialogue are two ways in which a director can help youth look at their life more critically.

The director of youth must guard himself or herself from burnout. Keeping up with youth is a full-time job. Those directors who overwork themselves do a disservice to themselves and the people they are supposed to serve. Directors have a responsibility to take care of themselves so they can be totally present when needed.

As Shelton points out, youth ministry "can give rise to the satisfying of inner needs for power. There is always the possibility that, beneath the advice and counsel, there lies the insidious personal need for control..." (Shelton 24). Adults should not be in direction to satisfy their own needs for attention, acceptance, or power.

Lastly, a sense of humor, a spirit of hope, and a capacity to celebrate all of life will characterize a director who can invite and welcome our youth as they take more responsibility for their own faith journeys.

CONCLUSION

These are the issues as I see them. I hope this chapter has helped to shed some light on an area in which there is room for much growth. May the Spirit be the Director of us all as we continue to discern how we can help foster the faith growth of our youth as an expression of and response to our own faith commitment. God be with us on our journeys!

END NOTES

[1] Interview with Rev Jeff Pawlak, S.M., Director of Campus Ministry at Chaminade College Prep, St. Louis, MO, 5 March 1989.

[2] Interview with Rev Jim Gahan, Director of Campus Ministry at Duchesne High School, St. Charles, MO, 5 March 1989.

WORKS CITED

Barry, William and William Connolly. *The Practice of Spiritual Direction*. New York: Seabury, 1982.

Carroll, L. Patrick and Katherine Marie Dyckman. *Inviting the Mystic, Supporting the Prophet*. New York: Paulist Press, 1981.

Connolly, William "Contemporary Spiritual Direction: Scope and Principles — An Introductory Essay." *Studies in the Spirituality of the Jesuits* 7 (June 1975): 101.

Edwards, Tilden. *Spiritual Friend.* New York: Paulist, 1980.

Fox, Matthew. ed., *Meditations With Meister Eckhart.* Santa Fe: Bear, 1983.

Jones, Alan. *Exploring Spiritual Direction.* San Francisco: Harper and Row, 1982.

LaPlace, Jean. *Preparing for Spiritual Direction.* Chicago: Franciscan Herald Press, 1975.

Shelton, Charles. *Adolescent Spirituality.* Chicago: Loyola University Press, 1983.

Appendix

Resources on Adolescent Spirituality

SELECTED FOUNDATIONAL READINGS IN ADOLESCENT FAITH DEVELOPMENT

Fowler, James. *Stages of Faith*. San Francisco: Harper and Row, 1981.

Greeley, Andrew. *The Religious Imagination*. New York: Sadlier, 1981.

Groome, Thomas H. "On Being 'With' Late Adolescents in Ministry." *Readings in Youth Ministry*. Washington DC: NFCYM Publications, 1986.

Nelson, John S. "Research on Adolescent Moral and Faith Development." *Readings in Youth Ministry*. Washington DC: NFCYM Publications, 1986.

Parks, Sharon. *The Critical Years —The Young Adult Search for a Faith to Live By*. San Francisco: Harper and Row, 1986.

Shelton, Charles. *Adolescent Spirituality*. Chicago: Loyola University Press, 1983.

Westerhoff, John H. *Will Our Children Have Faith?* San Francisco: Harper and Row, 1976.

Westerhoff, John H. *Bringing Up Children in the Christian Faith*. San Francisco: Harper and Row, 1980.

SELECTED FOUNDATIONAL READINGS IN CHRISTIAN SPIRITUALITY

Broccolo, Gerard. *Vital Spiritualities*. Notre Dame IN: Ave Maria Press, 1990.

Byrne, Lavinia. *Woman Before God*. Mustic CT: Twenty-Third Publications, 1988.

Chittister, Joan, O.S.B. *WomanStrength: Modern Church, Modern Women*. Kansas City: Sheed & Ward,1990.

Collins, Mary. *Women at Prayer*. New York: Paulist Press, 1987.

Cunningham, Lawrence. *Catholic Prayer*. New York: Crossroads, 1989.

Dorr, Donal. *Integral Spirituality*. Maryknoll NY: Orbis Books, 1990.

Edwards, Tilden. *Living Simply Through the Day*. New York: Paulist Press, 1977.

—————. *Living in the Presence*. San Francisco: Harper and Row, 1987.

Finley, Mitch and Kathy. *Christian Families in the Real World*. Chicago: Thomas More Press, 1984.

Fischer, Kathleen. *The Inner Rainbow*. New York: Paulist Press, 1983.

—————. *Reclaiming the Connections*. Kansas City: Sheed and Ward, 1990.

Fleming, David, ed. *The Fire and the Cloud—An Anthology of Catholic Spirituality*. New York: Paulist Press, 1978.

Foster, Richard. *Celebration of Discipline*. San Francisco: Harper and Row, 1978.

—————. *Freedom of Simplicity*. San Francisco: Harper and Row, 1981.

Fox, Matthew. *Original Blessing*. Santa Fe: Bear & Co., 1983.

—————. *A Spirituality Named Compassion*. Revised Edition. San Francisco: Winston Press, 1990.

Grassi, Joseph A. *Changing the World Within*. New York: Paulist Press, 1986.

Green, S.J., Thomas M. *When the Well Runs Dry*. Notre Dame IN: Ave Maria Press, 1979.

Gutierrez, Gustavo. *We Drink from Our Own Wells*. Maryknoll NY: Orbis Books, 1984.

Hug, James S.J., and Scherschel, Rose Marie. *Social Revelation*. Washington DC: The Center of Concern, 1987.

Irwin, Kevin. *Liturgy, Prayer, and Spirituality*. New York: Paulist Press, 1984.

Kolbenschlag, Madonna, ed. *Women in the Church*. Washington DC: The Pastoral Press, 1987.

Lee, James Michael, editor. *The Spirituality of the Religious Educator*. Birmingham: Religious Education Press, 1985.

Leech, Kenneth. *Experiencing God—Theology as Spirituality*. San Francisco: Harper and Row, 1985.

—————. *True Prayer*. San Francisco: Harper and Row, 1979.

—————. *Soul Friend*. San Francisco: Harper and Row, 1977.

McDonagh, Sean. *The Greening of the Church*. Maryknoll NY: Orbis Books, 1990.

McGaa, Ed, Eagle Man. *Mother Earth Spirituality*. New York: HarperCollins Publishers, 1990.

Maas, Robin. *Crucified Love*. Nashville: Abingdon Press, 1989.

Madigan, Shawn. *Spirituality Rooted in Liturgy*. Washington DC: The Pastoral Press, 1988.

May, Gerald. *Addictions and Grace*. San Francisco: Harper and Row, 1988.

—————. *Care of Mind, Care of Spirit*. San Francisco: Harper and Row, 1982.

————. *Pilgrimage Home.* New York: Paulist, 1979.

————. *Simply Sane.* New York: Crossroad, 1982.

Mische, Patricia. "Toward a Global Spirituality." *Whole Earth Papers No. 16.* New York: Global Education Associates.

Nouwen, Henri. *The Wounded Healer.* New York: Doubleday & Co., 1972.

————.. *Reaching Out.* New York: Doubleday & Co., 1975.

Nouwen, McNeill, and Morrison. *Compassion.* New York: Doubleday & Co., 1982.

Palmer, Parker. *To Know As We Are Known.* San Francisco: Harper and Row, 1983.

Riley, O.P., Maria. *Wisdom Seeks Her Way.* Washington DC: The Center of Concern, 1987.

Sobrino, Jon. *Spirituality of Liberation.* Maryknoll NY: Orbis Books, 1985.

Steltenkamp, Michael. *The Sacred Vision.* New York: Paulist Press, 1982.

Twohy, Patrick J. *Finding A Way Home.* Spokane WA: The University Press, 1983.

Wright, Wendy. *Sacred Dwelling: A Spirituality of Family Life.* New York: Crossroads, 1990.

SELECTED READINGS IN SPIRITUAL DEVELOPMENT

Cully, Iris V. *Education for Spiritual Growth.* San Francisco: Harper and Row, 1984.

Gorsuch, John. An Invitation to the Spiritual Journey. New York: Paulist Press, 1990.

Harris, Maria. *Fashion Me A People — Curriculum in the Church.* Louisville, KY: Westminster/John Knox Press, 1989.

————. Teaching and the Religious Imagination. San Francisco: Harper and Row, 1987.

————. *Portrait of Youth Ministry.* New York: Paulist Press, 1981.

Johnson, Susanne. *Christian Spiritual Formation in the Church and Classroom.* Nashville: Abingdon, 1989.

Kovats, Alexandra. *Prayer—A Discovery of Life.* San Francisco: Winston Press, 1983.

————. "I Want to Live: Youth and Spirituality." *Readings in Youth Ministry— Volume 2.* Washington DC: NFCYM Publications, 1989.

McGinnis, James. *Journey into Compassion — A Spirituality for the Long Haul.* St. Louis: Institute for Peace and Justice, 1989.

Moore, Joseph. "Adolescent Spiritual Development: Stages and Strategies." *Readings in Youth Ministry — Volume 2.* Washington DC: NFCYM

Publications, 1989.

Myers, William. *Theological Themes of Youth Ministry*. New York: Pilgrim Press, 1987.

O'Malley, S.J., William J. *Converting the Baptized*. Allen TX: Tabor Publishing, 1990.

Pennock, Michael. *The Way of Prayer*. Notre Dame IN: Ave Maria Press. 1987.

Shelton, Charles. *Adolescent Spirituality*. New York: Crossroads Books, 1983.

Warren, Michael. *Faith, Culture and the Worshipping Community*. New York: Paulist Press, 1989.

——————. *Youth, Gospel, Liberation*. San Francisco: Harper and Row, 1987.

——————. *Youth and the Future of the Church*. New York: Seabury Press, 1982.

Westerhoff, John. *Learning Through Liturgy*. New York: Seabury Press, 1978.

SELECTED READINGS IN SPIRITUAL DIRECTION

Barry, William and Connolly, William. *The Practice of Spiritual Direction*. New York: Seabury, 1982.

Bourdon, M. "The Spiritual Direction of the Adolescent." *Spiritual Life* Summer 1982.

Caprio, Betsy and Hedberg, S.D.B., Thomas. *Coming Home: A Manual for Spiritual Directors*. New York: Paulist, 1986.

Carroll, L.Patrick and Dyckman, Katherine. *Inviting the Mystic, Supporting the Prophet*. New York: Paulist, 1981.

——————. "Giving Each Other a Hand: The Emergence of Spiritual Direction", *Praying* March/April 1989.

Coll, M. *Adolescence and Spiritual Friendship: A Model for Youth Ministry*. Washington DC: Shalem Institute, 1988.

Edwards, Tilden. *Spiritual Friend: Reclaiming the Gift of Spiritual Direction*. New York: Paulist, 1980.

Fleming, David ed. *The Christian Ministry of Spiritual Direction*. St. Louis: Review for Religious, 1988.

Hart, Thomas. *The Art of Christian Listening*. New York: Paulist, 1980.

Jones, Alan. *Exploring Spiritual Direction*. San Francisco: Harper and Row, 1982.

——————. *Soul Making*. San Francisco: Harper & Row, 1985.

Schneiders, Sandra. *Spiritual Direction*. Chicago: National Sisters Vocation Conference.

Shelton, Charles. *Adolescent Spirituality*. Chicago: Loyola U. Press, 1983.

Simons, George. *Keeping Your Personal Journal*. New York: Paulist, 1978.

"Spiritual Guidance for Adolescents: Three Perspectives". Network Paper No. 30. New Rochelle NY: Don Bosco Multimedia, 1990.

Vanderwall, Francis. *Spiritual Direction: An Invitation to Abundant Life*. New York: Paulist, 1981.

ACCESS GUIDES TO YOUTH MINISTRY

EARLY ADOLESCENT MINISTRY
Edited by John Roberto
A gold mine of theory and practice for educators, youth ministers and all adults working with younger adolescents. Family, education, social-cultural influences, catechesis, community-building and other pertinent topics are presented. Means for developing responsive programming are included in the second part. Contributors include: Brian Reynolds, John Nelson, Joanne Cahoon, Laurence Steinberg.
Paperback 207-2 $14.95

RETREATS
Edited by Reynolds R. Ekstrom
A complete resource for learning how to develop youth retreats: the nature and purposes of youth retreats, principles, guidelines, models and strategies for developing your own retreat. Everything from planning to follow-up.The best theory and practice for
- Confirmation coordinators
- retreat ministers
- DREs, campus ministers
- Search, TEC, COR teams

Paperback 152-1 $14.95

JUSTICE
Edited by Thomas Bright and John Roberto
An overview of the scriptural and theological foundations of justice, and the current global social situation. Part One offers biblical and ecclesial foundations of justice while Part Two develops essential principles for justice education, and action with youth. Part Three offers examples of doing social analysis, education and action programming with youth. Included: A resource guide to education, activities, and organizations.
Paperback 149-1 $14.95